THE **Sun**

GUIDE TO THE 2010 WORLD CUP

First published in 2010 by

HarperSport, in association with News Group Newspapers Limited, a subsidiary of News International Limited

HarperSport is an imprint of HarperCollins Publishers

77-85 Fulham Palace Road,

Hammersmith, London W6 8JB

www.harpercollins.co.uk

This book has not been endorsed by, or is in any way associated with, FIFA

1 3 5 7 9 10 8 6 4 2

Created by Interact Publishing Ltd

Commissioning editor: Terry Pratt

Production editor: Jamie Stamper

Writers: Tom Bennett and Steven Hall

Editorial management: Jeff Fletcher

Assistant production editor: Martin Richardson

Database development: Paul Ward

Database management: Peter Watts

Systems management: Neil Waddy

Design: The Consult - www.theconsult.com

Pictures © Action Images

Additional photography © David Clerihew

Additional writing © News Group Newspapers Limited: Rob Beasley, Shaun Custis and Mike Dunn

Harry Redknapp, Terry Venables and Ian Wright

Ian Wright's copy courtesy of SEM

World Cup Guide concept © Interact Publishing (first published in 2006)

The Sun, The Sun Logo and Dream Team are registered trade marks and the Dream Team Logo is a trade mark of News Group Newspapers Limited.

A catalogue record of this book is available from the British Library

ISBN   978-0-00-735830-4

Printed and bound in Italy by L.E.G.O. SpA

CONTENTS

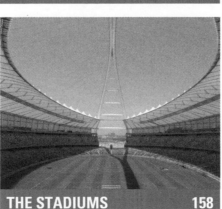

START WORLD CUP DREAMING!

The Sun's World Cup Guide is the best around. Alongside the opinions of The Sun's leading experts, this book contains the most up-to-date guide to the form of the 32 teams and 736 players going to the World Cup.

Our pundits may not agree on everything and some of their words might be controversial but that's the beauty of it – football is all about opinions.

Fabio Capello's England side have a great chance and the depth of quality heading to South Africa suggests this tournament has all the ingredients needed to be the best World Cup ever!

ROB BEASLEY– CHIEF SPORTS CORRESPONDENT

My very first football memory stems from the first match I ever saw and I remember it vividly to this day, even though I was only just seven years old.

The date was July 30th 1966 and I remember sitting at home with my mum and dad watching a small black and white television as England beat West Germany 4-2 at Wembley to become World Champions. I celebrated by running into the back garden and smashing my plastic football into the privet hedge three times imagining I was Geoff Hurst.

And the greatest show on earth has continued to give me so many more unforgettable moments over the years since. That save by Gordon Banks from Pele in 1970, Johann Cruyff and Holland's total football in 1974, Maradona's Hand of God goal in 1986 and David Platt's volley against Belgium in 1990. I was there to see Croatia thrash Germany 3-0 at France 98, was in Sapporo, Japan to witness Beckham's "revenge" penalty against Argentina in 2002, and in Berlin to see Zinedine Zidane's glittering international career come to an inglorious end with that head butt. However, the most pulsating game of all was St Etienne 1998.

Michael Owen's wonder goal, Beckham's red card and Sol Campbell's disallowed effort. Heart-stopping action, heart-breaking outcome. I was shaking from start to finish like every other English fan who packed the stands for that classic encounter.

So am I looking forward to this summer's finals in South Africa? It's a no-brainer isn't it? Roll on June, come on England!

SHAUN CUSTIS– CHIEF FOOTBALL WRITER

Don't you just love a World Cup? In an age where the game has become dominated by balance sheets and talk of clubs going bust, the month long festival of international combat puts the ball at the top of the agenda.

Yes many of the players taking part are multi-millionaires but this is one competition where they are in it for the glory first and not the cash.

For a footballer who truly loves the game it is the ultimate, the true test of greatness. It defines your place in the sport.

England centre-back Rio Ferdinand recalls watching his first World Cup in 1986 sitting on the couch at home marvelling at the grainy pictures and distorted commentary coming from Mexico. He recalls: "I was mesmorised by the whole thing. It was the moment I thought: "God, I'd love to be a footballer.""

Those memories drove him on to become a star with Manchester United and England. He will be going to his fourth, and possibly last, World Cup in South Africa this summer.

Ferdinand sat stunned on the subs bench when David Beckham got sent off in 1998 and England were eliminated by Argentina. He was in tears in 2002 and 2006 as England got knocked out in the quarter-finals.

There is nothing like a World Cup for sheer raw emotion whether you are a player or a fan. And if Fabio Capello's England can win football's greatest prize this summer, expect Rio to be leading the mother of all parties.

TERRY'S
WORLD CUP

The 2010 World Cup finals are almost upon us and what a tournament it promises to be. It will, of course, be the first time the finals have been staged in Africa – proof, if proof was needed, that football is now truly a global game. And that is represented in not only the diversity of the nations taking part, but the quality.

The usual suspects will be there once more. Teams like Brazil, Spain, Italy, Germany, Holland, Argentina and, dare I say, England are once again tipped to do well and reach the latter stages. What makes these finals so intriguing, though, is the improving standard of the teams below them. The saying 'There are no easy games in international football' might have become a cliche, but, by and large, it is true and certainly applies for this World Cup. Emerging football nations, such as Australia, the USA, Ivory Coast and Cameroon will be no pushovers as they try to make their impact on the planet's most eagerly awaited football event. Every single one of the 736 players selected for the finals, along with the millions of fans worldwide, will have dreamt of their country lifting the trophy on July 11...

Can England fulfil that dream? It will be a big ask, but if Fabio Capello's squad can remain injury free and reproduce the quality they showed in qualifying, it could be a summer none of us will ever forget. Let the magic begin...

HARRY'S
WORLD CUP

Not since 1966 have I been as excited and full of expectancy and anticipation about the World Cup.

England have the best chance for more than a generation to make us proud and bring the trophy home. It's no less than they are capable of.

I have long banged the drum that I believe all the ingredients are in place to finally make history with England winning the World Cup away from home for the first time.

The players have been there for a while, the manager is now in place with the right set up to make it happen.

Fabio Capello's decision to curb WAG power is instrumental even though it seems trivial. The players are there to work not play happy families.

I also believe that despite disharmony among certain players the football will be the most important element and that the squad will be totally focused on winning the trophy.

WRIGHTY'S
WORLD CUP

Every time a World Cup comes around I am taken back to that magical time when as a six year old boy I was glued to the television for the entirety of the 1970 finals in Mexico. In an era when the FA Cup Final was virtually the only game to be broadcast live, I had never seen so many matches on the television – and in colour too! What a treat.

And with black players still a rarity in this country and those who were playing over here getting a tough time from the terraces, I watched in awe at all the players who were delighting the world with their skills and ability.

That was the month I decided I wanted to become a professional footballer and those were the players who inspired me to chase my dream.

Some 40 years later and I am still as excited by the greatest footballing event in the world, especially this year in South Africa.

It will be interesting to see the African influence on the tournament that has never before been held on the continent's shores.

And I just know there will be some little boy somewhere watching the games on telly, who will be inspired to become a footballer, just like I was.

INSIDE, THREE OF THE BIGGEST NAMES IN FOOTBALL, HARRY REDKNAPP, TERRY VENABLES AND IAN WRIGHT, HAVE THEIR SAY ON EVERY TEAM IN THE TOURNAMENT

Position	1st	2nd	3rd	4th	5th	6th	7th	8th
Group	E	D	B	H	A	G	C	F
Total FIFA ranking	88	89	98	104	130	147	160	161

SOUTH AFRICA V MEXICO — Johannesburg JSC, Friday 11 June 1500 BST

The world's eyes will be on Johannesburg for the opening game of the 2010 World Cup finals and this is the hosts' chance to show us they can confound the pundits and make an impact on the pitch in front of the fervid support of the Bafana Bafana faithful. Their player of 2009 was undoubtedly Steven Pienaar and if the midfielder is fit, he will be key in this game. So too will Matthew Booth who will have to marshal his defence well to keep out the combined threat of Blanco, Carlos Vela and Giovanni Dos Santos, who was MVP for the tournament when Mexico lifted the CONCACAF Gold Cup.

URUGUAY V FRANCE — Cape Town, Friday 11 June 1930 BST

Hot on the heels of the competition opener, the world will wait to see which France has turned up – the good, the bad or the ugly. France have not been the same since Zinedine Zidane retired and now is the time for someone to stand up and be counted – step forward Franck Ribery. As for Uruguay, they are strong defensively but hopelessly erratic so a lot might depend on how Les Bleus take to their task. Captain Diego Lugano will be one to watch as he tries to marshal his side against the threat of Henry and Anelka – and he is not shy of getting in the box so the French will need to pick him up – especially at set pieces.

SOUTH AFRICA V URUGUAY — Pretoria, Wednesday 16 June 1930 BST

If the opening games go with the odds, this could be a make-or-break game for both sides and a draw will do nothing for either. Both know this is their best chance of three points and with the Praetorian crowd roaring South Africa on, Uruguay will be forced to hold their nerve and rely on their forward line to take their chances when they present themselves. For South Africa, this is a game that will probably define their World Cup. If they lose, they could end up bottom of the group and facing the dreaded null points – but if they can seal a win, it will send the host nation into raptures and set them up nicely for the third match against France.

France's Thierry Henry

FRANCE V MEXICO — Polokwane, Thursday 17 June 1930 BST

This could be the game that decides who tops the group, and for Mexico, the chance to become the first team to make it into the knockout stages of five consecutive World Cup competitions. Regardless of how the two sides fared in the opener, games between the group's leading contenders always tend to be tight and expect nothing less in this encounter. However, France and Mexico do have plenty of attacking options in their current squads.

MEXICO V URUGUAY — Rustenburg, Tuesday 22 June 1500 BST

By this stage, it is likely that Uruguay will have nothing to lose or everything to gain, so expect a feisty encounter between two sides who are not shy and retiring – in the tackle, or in front of goal. Mexico will more than likely be happy with a draw and if they have won both of their games, might even rest a few players.

FRANCE V SOUTH AFRICA — Bloemfontein, Tuesday 22 June 1500 BST

Depending on previous results, this game could be emotional for one of two reasons – either that South Africa are saying goodbye to the tournament, or that they have an actual chance of making it through into the knockout stages. Either way the atmosphere will be electric in Bloemfontein, and for once the focus of all the attention will not be on the heavily criticised French coach Raymond Domenech and his squad. If France need points from this game in order to progress it could be an absolute belter and with so many players – William Gallas and Thierry Henry – both playing in possibly their last World Cup, there could be fireworks. If the 1998 world champions are already through then the hosts may have more of a chance.

VIEW FROM THE EXPERTS

SOUTH AFRICA: The whole continent is praying for a 'home win' but it won't come from the host nation. Portsmouth defender Aaron Mokoena is the skipper and will take Premier League experience to the camp. Bafana Bafana gave Brazil a hard time in the Confederations Cup last year and with home advantage could finish second in Group A but it will be tough.
HARRY'S VERDICT: Last 16.

MEXICO: Under-achievers at the World Cup but this one will be a great stage for young Giovani Dos Santos at my club Tottenham to show what he can do. A gifted attacking player he was a big hit on loan at Ipswich and is technically great.
HARRY'S VERDICT: Group stage only.

URUGUAY: Experienced World Cup campaigners but their best years seem behind them. However, they do have a potent strike partnership in former Manchester United star Diego Forlan and Luis Suarez. A play-off win saw them squeeze into the finals but I still see it being a short-lived stay in South Africa.
HARRY'S VERDICT: Group stage only.

FRANCE: Everyone will be waiting, watching and no doubt wanting them to fail after the way they edged into the finals through the dodgy Thierry Henry handball that led to the decisive goal in the play-off against Ireland. Keep an eye on Lassana Diarra though, what a player.
HARRY'S VERDICT: Quarters.

SOUTH AFRICA: Weakest country in Group A. They put on a fair performance when they hosted last year's Confederations Cup, finishing a creditable fourth out of eight teams, and will be hoping home advantage and their undeniable spirit will see them through this summer. But don't put your money on it.
TEL'S VERDICT: Fall at first hurdle.

MEXICO: Recovered from their disappointing spell under Sven Goran Eriksson to qualify for their 14th finals by finishing one point behind the USA in the CONCACAF group. Skipper Rafael Marquez, the Barcelona defender, has hailed the return of former coach Javier Aguirre for restoring the team's belief and they will once again be difficult to beat.
TEL'S VERDICT: Could just pip Uruguay to qualify.

URUGUAY: Clinched the very last place in South Africa, but they were far from convincing as they had to battle their way through a play-off with Costa Rica to seal their spot at the finals. That was after they won six, drew six and lost six in their qualifying group. Coach Oscar Tabarez needs to get best out of Diego Forlan.

FRANCE: Their passage to the finals received a helping hand from Thierry Henry, but when the 1998 champions arrive in South Africa I fully expect them to make it out of a group, which has to be said is far from challenging. Whether they will progress further? I am not convinced.

TEL'S VERDICT: Poor group is handy for Henry and co.

SOUTH AFRICA: The hosts have a reputation for being a team of individuals, but will need to work as a unit if they are to make this summer even more memorable for their country. They will be hoping Benni McCarthy can repeat the form he has shown in the Premier League.

WRIGHTY'S VERDICT: Must rise to occasion.

MEXICO: Appearing at their 14th finals, they have plenty of World Cup experience. In skipper Rafael Marquez they have a defender who has won plenty of silverware with Barcelona. They are also used to altitude. But despite all this, I still don't fancy them to make much of an impact.

WRIGHTY'S VERDICT: Could struggle to get out of the group stage.

URUGUAY: Another country with a World Cup pedigree, although they made hard work of qualifying, beating Costa Rica 2-1 in the play-offs. They have some talented players, especially Diego Forlan, who regularly hits the net for Atletico Madrid.

WRIGHTY'S VERDICT: Potential to cause an upset.

FRANCE: The 1998 winners have a host of quality players, but the French were far from impressive qualifying. After their controversial play-off win over the Republic of Ireland, I would not be surprised if luck deserted them early on in South Africa.

WRIGHTY'S VERDICT: Shock exit?

"They have some talented players, especially Diego Forlan, who regularly hits the net for Atletico Madrid"

THE LIKELY ROUTES FOR THE TOP TWO TEAMS FROM THE GROUP

For the full draw please see page 80

GROUP STAGE

FIRST GROUP A

> FRANCE

SECOND GROUP A

> SOUTH AFRICA

LAST SIXTEEN

v SECOND GROUP B

> FRANCE v NIGERIA

v FIRST GROUP B

> SOUTH AFRICA v ARGENTINA

QUARTER-FINALS

v FIRST GROUP C or SECOND GROUP D

> FRANCE v ENGLAND

v FIRST GROUP D or SECOND GROUP C

> ARGENTINA v SERBIA

GROUP A
SOUTH AFRICA, MEXICO, URUGUAY, FRANCE

GROUP B
ARGENTINA, NIGERIA, SOUTH KOREA (KOREAN REPUBLIC), GREECE

GROUP C
ENGLAND, USA, ALGERIA, SLOVENIA
GROUP D
GERMANY, AUSTRALIA, SERBIA, GHANA

ROUTE TO THE FINALS

It only took three poor results to leave France scrambling for qualification and facing the play-off lottery and their campaign opener was the worst of the three, as Les Bleus travelled to Austria and suffered a humiliating 3-1 defeat.

They managed to reconcile things partially in their second game by beating eventual group winners Serbia 2-0 but while Raymond Domenech's side went on to draw their third and seventh match of qualification - both against Romania - the Serbs won four straight, leaving Les Bleus playing catch up for the rest of qualifying. When the two sides met again for the return leg and Serbia secured a 1-1 draw, qualification was out of France's hands and a Serbia loss in their last game did not matter.

Cue the play-off against Ireland and, after a poor first leg which France won 1-0, in the return game France were put to the sword by Ireland in Paris. Having taken the lead via Robbie Keane, the visitors missed chance after chance before Thierry Henry used his hand to twice control the ball and cross for William Gallas to fire home from close range.

FINAL QUALIFYING TABLE
EUROPE GROUP 7

	P	W	D	L	F	A	Pts
Serbia	10	7	1	2	22	8	22
France *	10	6	3	1	18	9	21
Austria	10	4	2	4	14	15	14
Lithuania	10	4	0	6	10	11	12
Romania	10	3	3	4	12	18	12
Faroe Islands	10	1	1	8	5	20	4

* France beat the Republic of Ireland in the play-offs.

					Avge FIFA ranking			
1	06 Sep 08	Away	Austria	74	L	**3** 1	Govou 61	
2	10 Sep 08	Home	Serbia	28	W	**2** 1	Henry 54, Anelka 64	
3	11 Oct 08	Away	Romania	21	D	**2** 2	Ribery 36, Gourcuff 69	
4	28 Mar 09	Away	Lithuania	54	W	**0** 1	Ribery 67	
5	01 Apr 09	Home	Lithuania	54	W	**1** 0	Ribery 75	
6	12 Aug 09	Away	Faroe Islands	178	W	**0** 1	Gignac 38	
7	05 Sep 09	Home	Romania	21	D	**1** 1	Henry 48	
8	09 Sep 09	Away	Serbia	28	D	**1** 1	Henry 31	
9	10 Oct 09	Home	Faroe Islands	178	W	**5** 0	Gignac 34, 39, Gallas 53, Anelka 86, Benzema 88	
10	14 Oct 09	Home	Austria	74	W	**3** 1	Benzema 17, Henry 26pen, Gignac 65	
11	14 Nov 09	Away	Rep of Ireland	36	W	**0** 1	Anelka 72	
12	18 Nov 09	Home	Rep of Ireland	36	D	**1** 1	Gallas 103	
	Average FIFA ranking of opposition			65				

MAIN PLAYER PERFORMANCES IN QUALIFICATION

Match: 1 2 3 4 5 6 7 8 9 10 11 12
Venue: A H A A H A H A H H A H
Result: L W D W W W D D W W W D

	Appearances	Started	Subbed on	Subbed off	Mins played	% played	Goals	Yellow	Red
Goalkeepers									
Hugo Lloris	6	6	0	0	488	44.0	0	0	1
Steve Mandanda	7	6	1	0	619	55.8	0	0	0
Defenders									
Eric Abidal	5	5	0	0	450	40.5	0	1	0
Gael Clichy	2	2	0	0	180	16.2	0	0	0
Julien Escude	4	4	0	1	278	25.0	0	0	0
Patrice Evra	10	10	0	0	930	83.8	0	1	0
Rod Fanni	1	1	0	0	90	8.1	0	0	0
William Gallas	10	10	0	0	930	83.8	2	1	0
Philippe Mexes	1	1	0	0	90	8.1	0	0	0
Bacary Sagna	11	11	0	1	999	90.0	0	1	0
Sebastien Squillaci	4	3	1	0	382	34.4	0	1	0
Midfielders									
Alou Diarra	6	4	2	0	405	36.5	0	0	0
Lassana Diarra	10	10	0	0	930	83.8	0	2	0
Yoann Gourcuff	10	9	1	6	756	68.1	1	1	0
Florent Malouda	6	3	3	2	254	22.9	0	1	0
Franck Ribery	6	3	3	1	341	30.7	3	0	0
Moussa Sissoko	2	1	1	0	119	10.7	0	0	0
Jeremy Toulalan	8	8	0	1	691	62.3	0	2	0
Forwards									
Nicolas Anelka	8	6	2	0	626	56.4	3	0	0
Karim Benzema	8	3	5	2	363	32.7	2	0	0
Pierre-Andre Gignac	8	6	2	5	440	39.6	4	0	0
Sidney Govou	5	4	1	2	386	34.8	1	1	0
Thierry Henry	11	11	0	2	965	86.9	4	0	0
Peguy Luyindula	2	2	0	2	130	11.7	0	0	0

FINAL PROSPECTS

It has been a remarkable 12 years of highs and lows for Les Bleus. From the heady days of 1998 World Cup glory in Paris, and the dramatic golden goal victory in Rotterdam that clinched the European Championships in 2000, France have also tasted equally glorious failure.

As reigning World Champions in Japan and Korea 2002, France were stunned by Senegal in the opening game and returned home in humiliation, bottom of their group picking up just one solitary point. Then four years later, France improved throughout the tournament in Germany and reached the final only to be undone by the agony of Zinedine Zidane's moment of madness against Marco Materazzi. The Azzurri went on to clinch the trophy on penalties.

Cue the frustrating qualification campaign for 2010 and the subsequent furore over that Thierry Henry handball in the play-off victory over the Republic of Ireland and you get just over a decade of extreme drama.

How this group of players will fare in South Africa is anyone's guess.

Twelve years have also seen a shift in personnel with France's 'golden generation' all but retired; the likes of Zidane, Patrick Vieira, David Trezeguet, Lillian Thuram, Bixente Lizarazu and Marcel Desailly have all headed into the sunset, leaving Henry as the sole representative of the old guard.

Zidane aside, the departing stalwarts, however, have been replaced by players who are talented in their own right. Defenders William Gallas and Patrice Evra of Arsenal and Manchester United respectively, are both world class players. In midfield they have the proven talent of Lyon's Jeremy Toulalan, who has slipped into the Makelele role; Real Madrid's Lassana Diarra alongside the much coveted play-maker Franck Ribery.

Up front, the indomitable Henry has the experienced Nicolas Anelka for company with able support coming in the shape of Karim Benzema and Andre-Pierre Gignac of Toulouse.

Make no mistake, this side is not as classy as its predecessor but it is – on paper at least – a very talented squad. How this group of players will fare in South Africa is anyone's guess. They are equally capable of imploding and getting on the first plane home as exploding into the knockout phase.

DREAM TEAM TOP 15 RANKING   4

GROUP FIXTURES

URUGUAY	Fri 11 June 1930 BST
MEXICO	Thur 17 June 1930 BST
SOUTH AFRICA	Tue 22 June 1500 BST

KEY PLAYER

THIERRY HENRY BARCELONA

There is not much that hasn't already been said about Barca's Thierry Henry.

The ex-Arsenal striker is a goal machine, one of the strikers of his generation who possesses a grace that makes him a joy to watch in full flight. He knows first-hand the extreme highs and lows of international football and with this likely to be his last World Cup, he will want to bow out in style.

Playing record	12 months lge	wcq
Appearances:	26	11
Minutes played:	1864	965
Percentage played:	54.5%	86.9%
Goals scored:	13	4
Percentage share:	13.8%	20.0%
Cards:	Y2, R0	Y0, R0
Strike rate:	143mins	241mins
Strike rate ranking:	21st	49th

AGE 32 **STRIKER** **DREAM TEAM RANKING** 158

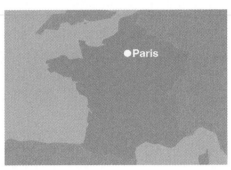

● Paris

Zone	Europe
Population	64m
Language	French
Top league	Ligue 1
Playing season	August - May

Major clubs and capacities
Girondins de Bordeaux (34,371), Lille (18,185), Olympique Lyonnaise (41,044), Paris SG (48,713), Marseille (60,031), AS Monaco (18,500)

Where probable squad players play:

Premier League	7	Ligue 1	8
Serie A	1	Eredivisie	-
La Liga	6	Other Europe	-
Bundesliga	1	Outside Europe	-

Number of French players playing:

Premier League	40	Ligue 1	330
Serie A	14	Bundesliga	11
La Liga	16	Eredivisie	3

World Cup record   * best performance

1930 - Round 1		1974 -	Did not qualify
1934 - Round 1		1978 -	Round 1
1938 - Quarter finals		1982 -	4th place
1950 - Did not qualify		1986 -	3rd place
1954 - Round 1		1990 -	Did not qualify
1958 - 3rd place		1994 -	Did not qualify
1962 - Did not qualify		1998 -	* Champions
1966 - Round 1		2002 -	Round 1
1970 - Did not qualify		2006 -	Final

THE SQUAD

Goalkeepers	Club side	Age	QG
Hugo Lloris	Lyon	23	6
Steve Mandanda	Marseille	25	7
Defenders			
Eric Abidal	Barcelona	30	5
Gael Clichy	Arsenal	24	2
Julien Escude	Sevilla	30	4
Patrice Evra	Man Utd	29	10
Rod Fanni	Rennes	28	1
William Gallas	Arsenal	32	10
Philippe Mexes	Roma	28	1
Bacary Sagna	Arsenal	27	11
Sebastien Squillaci	Sevilla	29	4
Midfielders			
Alou Diarra	Bordeaux	28	6
Lassana Diarra	Real Madrid	24	10
Yoann Gourcuff	Bordeaux	23	10
Florent Malouda	Chelsea	29	6
Samir Nasri	Arsenal	22	2
Franck Ribery	Bayern Munich	27	6
Moussa Sissoko	Toulouse	20	2
Jeremy Toulalan	Lyon	26	8
Forwards			
Nicolas Anelka	Chelsea	31	8
Karim Benzema	Real Madrid	22	8
Pierre-Andre Gignac	Toulouse	24	8
Bafetimbi Gomis	Lyon	24	1
Sidney Govou	Lyon	30	5
Thierry Henry	Barcelona	32	11
Peguy Luyindula	Paris SG	31	2

■ Probable ■ Possible **QG** Qualification Games

KEY GOALKEEPERS

HUGO LLORIS
LYON

Playing record	12 months lge	wcq
Appearances:	36	6
Minutes played:	3240	488
Percentage played:	94.7%	44.2%
Goals conceded:	37	3
Clean sheets:	12	3
Cards:	Y1, R0	Y0, R1
Minutes between goals:	88mins	163mins
Goalkeeper ranking:	13th	11th

AGE 23	DREAM TEAM	RANKING 60

STEVE MANDANDA
MARSEILLE

Playing record	12 months lge	wcq
Appearances:	37	7
Minutes played:	3330	619
Percentage played:	97.4%	55.8%
Goals conceded:	31	7
Clean sheets:	18	3
Cards:	Y0, R0	Y0, R0
Minutes between goals:	107mins	88mins
Goalkeeper ranking:	5th	25th

AGE 25	DREAM TEAM	RANKING 42

KEY DEFENDERS

ERIC ABIDAL
BARCELONA

It was always going to be a tough ask to replace the iconic Lilian Thuram in the French defence and while he might not be in quite the same bracket as the Les Bleus legend, Eric Abidal has successfully taken on the mantle.

Fast and strong, a dangerous crosser of the ball and with a superb positional awareness, he is an established member of Barcelona's World and European conquering squad. He is able to play at left-back or centre-back and his versatility is a bonus for Les Bleus.

Playing record	12 months lge	wcq
Appearances:	24	5
Minutes played:	2022	450
Percentage played:	59.1%	40.5%
Goals conceded:	22	4
Clean sheets:	8	2
Cards:	Y6, R1	Y1, R0
Minutes between goals:	92mins	112mins
Defender ranking:	49th	80th

AGE 30	DREAM TEAM	RANKING 153

BACARY SAGNA
ARSENAL

A player who has stood out since an early age, Bacary Sagna is full of pace, power and technical ability. He is fast maturing into one of the best right-backs in Europe.

Sagna became a first choice at right-back for Raymond Domenech for the World Cup qualifying campaign following their Euro 2008

PATRICE EVRA
MAN UTD

Widely regarded as one of the best left-backs in European football, Patrice Evra has it all - he is fierce in the tackle, lightning fast and superb going forward.

Evra is a Top 12 Defender

AGE 28	DREAM TEAM	RANKING 23

JULIEN ESCUDE
SEVILLA

Playing record	12 months lge	wcq
Appearances:	22	4
Minutes played:	1790	278
Percentage played:	52.3%	25.0%
Goals conceded:	28	2
Clean sheets:	7	2
Cards:	Y7, R0	Y0, R0
Minutes between goals:	64mins	139mins
Defender ranking:	136th	56th

AGE 30	DREAM TEAM	RANKING 874

debacle and played more minutes in qualifying than any other French player.

Playing record	12 months lge	wcq
Appearances:	34	11
Minutes played:	2902	999
Percentage played:	82.7%	90.0%
Goals conceded:	31	8
Clean sheets:	15	5
Cards:	Y3, R0	Y1, R0
Minutes between goals:	94mins	125mins
Defender ranking:	47th	68th

AGE 27	DREAM TEAM	RANKING 91

THE MANAGER

To call Raymond Domenech a 'colourful' character would be something of an understatement.

If being quoted as using star signs in team selection wasn't bad enough, he is widely pilloried by the French media. The confounded French public often tear their hair out at his bizarre selections and tactics.

Yet, he is the longest ever serving French manager – a paradox indeed, yet not one that can be put down to results on the pitch.

Yes, he managed France to a World Cup final but they stuttered and struggled their way through that tournament and since then they have been generally below par – only just making, and hopelessly underperforming in Euro 2008 and getting to South Africa only by virtue of a play-off win against Republic of Ireland, which was based more on Henry's handiwork than any inspiration from the man in charge.

For the French fans he is like an embarrassing uncle they would rather not be seen with in public but this is surely his swansong as the main man and maybe if he can deliver respectability in this tournament he can at least leave on a fond note.

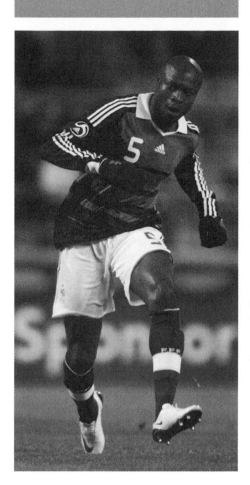

WILLIAM GALLAS
ARSENAL

A commanding centre-half, William Gallas is a stalwart in the heart of defence for club and country and has been for the last five years.

Great in the air and quick over the ground he quietly and consistently provides authority to the whole team.

Gallas is also a genuine goal threat as evidenced when he scored the winner in the second leg of France's controversial play-off game against the Republic of Ireland to take France through to the finals.

He is particularly effective when in the box for set-pieces.

Playing record	12 months lge	wcq
Appearances:	26	10
Minutes played:	2340	930
Percentage played:	66.7%	83.8%
Goals conceded:	23	7
Clean sheets:	11	5
Cards:	Y3, R0	Y1, R0
Minutes between goals:	102mins	133mins
Defender ranking:	27th	64th

AGE 32	DREAM TEAM	RANKING 97

KEY PLAYER

FRANCK RIBERY BAYERN MUNICH

Described by Zinedine Zidane as 'the jewel of French football', Franck Ribery is developing into a talismanic figure.

An impressive all-round footballer, Ribery has pace to burn and skill on the ball to frequently draw comparison with Cristiano Ronaldo. Capable of scoring and creating chances with his direct style he can set the world alight in South Africa.

Playing record	12 months lge	wcq
Appearances:	20	6
Minutes played:	1445	341
Percentage played:	47.2%	30.7%
Goals scored:	4	3
Clean Sheets:	10	5
Cards:	Y4, R1	Y0, R0
Strike rate:	361mins	114mins
Strike rate ranking:	58th	1st

AGE 27	MIDFIELDER	DREAM TEAM	RANKING 534

KEY MIDFIELDERS

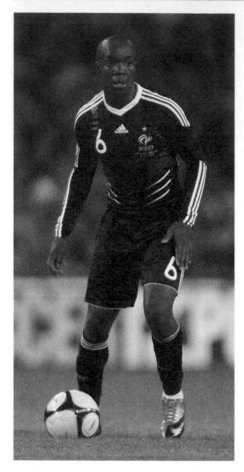

FLORENT MALOUDA
CHELSEA

It is fair to say that it is only in the last 12 months that Chelsea have started to see the best of Florent Malouda.

The midfielder started to show the form that persuaded them to buy him whilst at Lyon, standing out in the Champions League and winning the Ligue 1 Player of the Year 2006/7.

A powerful presence on the left flank, he is equally at home as a forward or tucked in just behind the front men. Malouda is very quick, comfortable in possession and capable of delivering a very dangerous final ball.

Playing record	12 months lge	wcq
Appearances:	29	6
Minutes played:	1755	254
Percentage played:	51.3%	22.9%
Goals scored:	7	0
Clean sheets:	19	4
Cards:	Y1, R1	Y1, R0
Strike rate:	251mins	-
Midfielder ranking:	30th	-

AGE 29	DREAM TEAM	RANKING 230

YOANN GOURCUFF
BORDEAUX

See France's One to Watch.

Playing record	12 months lge	wcq
Appearances:	35	10
Minutes played:	2838	756
Percentage played:	80.9%	68.1%
Goals scored:	14	1
Clean sheets:	20	4
Cards:	Y2, R0	Y1, R0
Strike rate:	203mins	756mins
Midfielder ranking:	19th	70th

AGE 23	DREAM TEAM	RANKING 73

JEREMY TOULALAN
LYON

Playing record	12 months lge	wcq
Appearances:	31	8
Minutes played:	2556	691
Percentage played:	74.7%	62.3%
Goals scored:	0	0
Clean sheets:	12	3
Cards:	Y5, R0	Y2, R0
Strike rate:	-	-
Midfielder ranking:	-	-

AGE 26	DREAM TEAM	RANKING 202

LASSANA DIARRA
REAL MADRID

A highly skilful central midfielder, Lassana Diarra is often referred to as a 'defensive' midfielder but that is an injustice to a player with the skill-set he has at his disposal.

He certainly plays in a deep-lying position but rather than play in the defensive role made famous by Claude Makelele, he links up play with good passing skills, vision and ability to beat the man. This season he has established his place in Madrid's starting line-up - no mean feat with the talent at the Bernabeu - and he will be a vital presence in South Africa.

Playing record	12 months lge	wcq
Appearances:	31	10
Minutes played:	2672	930
Percentage played:	78.1%	83.8%
Goals scored:	1	0
Clean sheets:	17	4
Cards:	Y13, R1	Y2, R0
Strike rate:	672mins	-
Midfielder ranking:	117th	-

AGE 24	DREAM TEAM	RANKING 115

KEY STRIKERS

THIERRY HENRY
BARCELONA

See France's Key Player.

AGE 32	DREAM TEAM	RANKING 158

NICOLAS ANELKA
CHELSEA

After years of wandering aimlessly from club to club, Nicolas Anelka is now proving he is the player we all knew he could be, having established himself a regular for his current club side Chelsea.

In addition to that, he is proving to Raymond Domenech that he is good enough to keep Karim Benzema out of the starting XI and while that might cause controversy in some quarters, with Anelka you know that if your team is creating chances, he will be scoring goals.

Remarkably for such a talented striker the first time he represented his country in World Cup action was just six matches ago in September 2008 as a ten-minute substitute against Austria. Part of the reason for this was his suspect temperament, but his time at Chelsea has seen this diminish as he has matured as a player.

Anelka is a Top 12 Striker.

AGE 31	DREAM TEAM	RANKING 14

KARIM BENZEMA
REAL MADRID

Destined to be one of the finest French strikers of his generation, Karim Benzema is something of a young prodigy in France, having topped the league scorers charts in his breakthrough 2007/8 season, with 20 league goals whilst still only 20.

A roving centre-forward capable of the spectacular, he not only scores goals but also creates them. He faces stiff competition for a starting place from Nicolas Anelka but if he plays he could be just the man to set France's competition performance on fire. He may have to settle for a place on the bench.

Playing record	12 months lge	wcq
Appearances:	33	8
Minutes played:	2391	363
Percentage played:	69.9%	32.7%
Goals scored:	12	2
Percentage share:	13.5%	10.0%
Cards:	Y0, R0	Y0, R0
Strike rate:	199mins	181mins
Strike rate ranking:	53rd	30th

AGE 22	DREAM TEAM RANKING 147

ONE TO WATCH

YOANN GOURCUFF BORDEAUX

An exciting attacking midfielder comfortable orchestrating play from the centre of the pitch, Yoann Gourcuff is one of the young French pretenders threatening to burst onto the world stage in South Africa.

Having risen through the ranks at Rennes, he was bought by AC Milan where he was predominantly an understudy for Brazilian Kaka until - after a frustrating lack of appearances - he returned to France with Bordeaux. With the ability to dictate the pace of the game, score goals and create chances, he has represented France at every level. He was a mainstay of their qualification campaign and could be the man to inspire Les Bleus in South Africa. Gourcuff is a Top 12 Midfielder.

AGE 23	MIDFIELDER	DREAM TEAM RANKING 73

MEXICO

ROUTE TO THE FINALS

Qualifying from the CONCACAF confederation is a long, arduous and complicated process but despite a few setbacks, Mexico navigated all of the hurdles to finish second.

In the second round of qualifying - a one off game - they thrashed Belize 9-0 to reach the third qualifying stage where they edged out Jamaica on goal difference in a tight group, finishing runners up to Honduras to make the fourth round of qualifying. Their stuttering progress led to the dismissal of manager Sven-Goran Eriksson, who was replaced by experienced Mexican Javier Aguirre.

The fourth round pitted them against the USA, Honduras and Costa Rica. Despite losing three times on the road, their strong home form ensured they were only one point behind group winners, the USA.

For final qualification table see Honduras.

				Avge FIFA ranking			
1	15 Jun 08	Away	Belize	175	W	0 2	Vela 65, J. Borgetti 90pen
2	22 Jun 08	Home	Belize	175	W	7 0	Vela 8, J. Borgetti 9, 90pen, Guardado 33, Arce 46, 47, Lennen 90og
3	21 Aug 08	Home	Honduras	43	W	2 1	Pardo 73, 75
4	06 Sep 08	Home	Jamaica	81	W	3 0	Guardado 3, Arce 33, Magallon 63
5	11 Sep 08	Home	Canada	79	W	2 1	Bravo 59, Marquez 73
6	12 Oct 08	Away	Jamaica	81	L	1 0	
7	16 Oct 08	Away	Canada	79	D	2 2	Salcido 35, Vuoso 64
8	20 Nov 08	Away	Honduras	43	L	1 0	
9	12 Feb 09	Away	United States	8	L	2 0	
10	28 Mar 09	Home	Costa Rica	53	W	2 0	Bravo 20, Pardo 53pen
11	02 Apr 09	Away	Honduras	43	L	3 1	Castillo 82pen
12	07 Jun 09	Away	El Salvador	107	L	2 1	Blanco 71pen
13	11 Jun 09	Home	Trinidad & Tobago	79	W	2 1	Franco 2, Rojas 48pen
14	12 Aug 09	Home	United States	8	W	2 1	I.Castro 19, Sabah 82
15	06 Sep 09	Away	Costa Rica	53	W	0 3	Dos Santos 45, Franco 62, Guardado 70
16	10 Sep 09	Home	Honduras	43	W	1 0	Blanco 76pen
17	10 Oct 09	Home	El Salvador	107	W	4 1	Mar.Gonzalez 25og, C. Blanco 71, F. Palencia 84, Vela 90
18	15 Oct 09	Away	Trinidad & Tobago	79	D	2 2	Esqueda 58, Salcido 66
	Average FIFA ranking of opposition			**74**			

MAIN PLAYER PERFORMANCES IN QUALIFICATION

Match	1 2 3 4 5 6 7 8 9 10 11 12 13 14 15 16 17 18	Appearances	Started	Subbed on	Subbed off	Mins played	% played	Goals	Yellow	Red
Venue	A H H H H A A A A H A A H H A H H A									
Result	W W W W W L D L L W L L W W W W W D									
Goalkeepers										
Guillermo Ochoa		7	7	0	0	630	38.9	0	0	0
Oswaldo Sanchez		9	9	0	0	810	50.0	0	0	0
Defenders										
Jose Antonio Castro		3	3	0	1	241	14.9	0	0	0
Israel Castro		7	6	1	0	585	36.1	1	0	0
Aaron Galindo		9	7	2	0	730	45.1	0	0	0
Jonny Magallon		13	12	1	0	1092	67.4	1	1	0
Rafael Marquez		7	7	0	0	604	37.3	1	4	1
Ricardo Osorio		16	15	1	2	1345	83.0	0	1	0
Fausto Pinto		3	3	0	0	270	16.7	0	0	0
Oscar Rojas		4	3	1	0	281	17.3	1	0	0
Carlos Salcido		15	15	0	0	1347	83.1	2	5	1
Midfielders										
Fernando Arce		10	10	0	6	766	47.3	3	2	0
Andres Guardado		16	15	1	6	1237	76.4	3	2	0
Efrain Juarez		4	4	0	0	360	22.2	0	1	0
Matias Vuoso		6	2	4	2	293	18.1	1	1	0
Antonio Naelson		4	2	2	2	226	14.0	0	1	0
Leandro Oldoni		4	4	0	0	360	22.2	0	1	0
Pavel Pardo		7	7	0	2	555	34.3	3	2	0
Luis Perez		7	7	0	3	525	32.4	0	0	0
Gerardo Torrado		12	10	2	1	895	55.2	0	4	1
Forwards										
Cuauhtemoc Blanco		10	5	5	1	538	33.2	3	2	0
Omar Bravo		8	3	5	2	332	20.5	2	0	0
Nery Castillo		7	3	4	2	227	14.0	1	0	0
Giovani Dos Santos		10	9	1	6	695	42.9	1	1	0
Guillermo Franco		6	5	1	4	430	26.5	2	1	0
Carlos Vela		12	10	2	5	868	53.6	3	3	0

FINAL PROSPECTS

An experienced international outfit, Mexico can consider themselves stalwarts of World Cup finals, with this their fifth consecutive appearance at football's elite tournament.

They reached the last 16 in 2006 and their recent tournament history is impressive too. In 2009 they won the CONCACAF Gold Cup, beating the United States in the final on US soil 5-0 in front of 80,000 fans. Despite a challenging group here, they will be expected to reach the knockout stages once again.

They have few players that could be considered household names outside of Mexico but have a wealth of experience in their squad. Striker Cuauhtemoc Blanco and holding midfielder Gerardo Torrado have both been capped more than 100 times.

Add Barcelona defender Rafael Marquez and the precocious talent of Arsenal forward Carlos Vela into the mix and you have a squad to contend with. Providing they manage to ease past South Africa in the opening game of the tournament, they should qualify for the latter stages.

DREAM TEAM | **TOP 15 RANKING** | 20

THE MANAGER

A well respected and experienced coach, Javier Aguirre is in his second spell in charge of Mexico after being re-appointed in 2009 after Sven-Goran Eriksson took the fall for some poor results.

Following on from a successful playing career in which he represented his country 59 times, Aguirre made the move into management in domestic football in his home land. He was called up to manage his country for the first time and took Mexico to the final of the Copa America in 2001 and to the last 16 of the 2002 World Cup.

His achievements brought Spain's Osasuna knocking and after relative success there he moved to Atletico Madrid. He then led Atletico into the Champions League and their most successful season in a decade.

GROUP FIXTURES

SOUTH AFRICA	Thur 11 June 1500 BST
FRANCE	Wed 17 June 1930 BST
URUGUAY	Mon 22 June 1500 BST

Mexico City

Zone	North, Central America & Caribbean
Population	111m
Language	Spanish
Top league	Primera Division
Playing season	August - May

Major clubs and capacities
Cruz Azul (35,000), Pachuca (31,000), Toluca (27,000), Guadalajara (56,750), America (105,000)

Where probable squad players play:

Premier League	2	Ligue 1	-
Serie A	-	Eredivisie	1
La Liga	-	Other Europe	2
Bundesliga	-	Outside Europe	18

Number of Mexican players playing:

Premier League	2	Bundesliga	1
Serie A	1	Ligue 1	-
La Liga	3	Eredivisie	3

World Cup record * best performance

1930 - Round 1	1974 - Did not qualify
1934 - Did not qualify	1978 - Round 1
1938 - Withdrew	1982 - Did not qualify
1950 - Round 1	1986 - * Quarter finals
1954 - Round 1	1990 - Banned from Fifa
1958 - Round 1	1994 - Round 2
1962 - Round 1	1998 - Round 2
1966 - Round 1	2002 - Round 2
1970 - * Quarter finals	2006 - Round 2

THE SQUAD

RAFAEL MARQUEZ BARCELONA

Rafael Marquez is a stylish and gifted defender able to play at centre-back or in defensive midfield.

He is fast, aggressive, a superb tackler but also comfortable on the ball. This combination has seen him become a regular for club and country over the last five years. Injury wrecked much of 2009, but now fit he will be a massive presence.

Playing record	12 months lge	wcq
Appearances:	18	7
Minutes played:	1297	604
Percentage played:	37.0%	37.3%
Goals conceded:	12	6
Clean sheets:	10	1
Cards:	Y3, R1	Y4, R1
Minutes between goals:	108mins	101mins
Defender ranking:	16th	97th

AGE 31 **DEFENDER** **DREAM TEAM** **RANKING** 927

Goalkeepers	Club side	Age	QG
Guillermo Ochoa	America	24	7
Oswaldo Sanchez	Santos Laguna	36	9
Defenders			
Jose Antonio Castro	UANL Tigres	29	3
Israel Castro	Club Universidad	29	7
Aaron Galindo	Guadalajara	28	9
Jonny Magallon	Guadalajara	28	13
Rafael Marquez	Barcelona	31	7
Ricardo Osorio	Stuttgart	30	16
Fausto Pinto	Cruz Azul	26	3
Oscar Rojas	America	28	4
Carlos Salcido	PSV Eindhoven	30	15
Midfielders			
Fernando Arce	Santos Laguna	30	10
Andres Guardado	Deportivo	23	16
Efrain Juarez	Club Universidad	22	4
Matias Vuoso	Santos Laguna	28	6
Antonio Naelson	Deportivo Toluca	34	4
Leandro Oldoni	Club Universidad	32	4
Pavel Pardo	America	33	7
Luis Perez	Monterrey	29	7
Gerardo Torrado	Cruz Azul	31	12
Forwards			
Cuauhtemoc Blanco	Veracruz	37	10
Omar Bravo	Guadalajara	30	8
Nery Castillo	Dnipro	25	7
Giovani Dos Santos	Galatasaray	21	10
Guillermo Franco	West Ham	33	6
Carlos Vela	Arsenal	21	12

■ Probable ■ Possible **QG** Qualification Games

ROUTE TO THE FINALS

As hosts, South Africa were not required to qualify for the tournament, leaving the Confederations Cup as the only real litmus test of their ambitions.

They didn't fare too badly, losing to Spain and beating a woeful New Zealand before securing their place in the latter stages of the tournament with a goalless draw against Iraq. They then faced the mighty Brazil in the semi-final, and in front of 50,000 roaring fans held their own for long periods, losing 1-0 courtesy of a Daniel Alves free-kick in the 88th minute in what was a very open game, with Steven Pienaar the man-of-the-match. In the third places play-off, they were beaten 3-2 by a deflated Spain.

For the remainder of 2009, however, their record was hardly stellar with a solitary win over Madagascar, draws with Japan and Jamaica and losses to Serbia, Germany, Republic of Ireland, Norway and Iceland.

#	Date		Opponent	Avge FIFA ranking	Result			Scorers
1	23 Jan 08	Home	Angola	77	D	1	1	Van Heerden 87
2	27 Jan 08	Away	Tunisia	49	L	3	1	Mphela 87
3	31 Jan 08	Away	Senegal	60	D	1	1	Van Heerden 13
4	01 Jun 08	Away	Nigeria	28	L	2	0	
5	07 Jun 08	Home	Equatorial Guinea	-	W	4	1	Dikgacoi 9, 90, Moriri 33, Fanteni 62
6	06 Sep 08	Home	Nigeria	28	L	0	1	
7	14 Jun 09	Home	Iraq	81	D	0	0	
8	17 Jun 09	Home	New Zealand	87	W	2	0	Parker 21, 52
9	20 Jun 09	Away	Spain	2	L	2	0	
10	25 Jun 09	Away	Brazil	4	L	1	0	
11	28 Jun 09	Away	Spain	2	L	3	2	Mphela 73, 90fk
Average FIFA ranking of opposition				**56**				

MAIN PLAYER PERFORMANCES IN INTERNATIONAL COMPETITIONS

Match	Appearances	Started	Subbed on	Subbed off	Mins played	% played	Goals	Yellow	Red
Venue									
Result									
Goalkeepers									
Rowen Fernandez	1	1	0	0	90	12.0	0	0	0
Itumeleng Khune	7	7	0	0	660	88.0	0	0	0
Defenders									
Matthew Booth	5	5	0	0	480	64.0	0	0	0
Bradley Carnell	1	1	0	0	90	12.0	0	1	0
Bevan Fransman	2	2	0	1	113	15.1	0	0	0
Siboniso Gaxa	6	6	0	0	570	76.0	0	0	0
Bongani Khumalo	1	0	1	0	67	8.9	0	0	0
Mbulelo Mabizela	1	1	0	0	90	12.0	0	0	0
Tsepo Masilela	7	7	0	1	651	86.8	0	1	0
Aaron Mokoena	7	7	0	1	646	86.1	0	1	0
Bryce Moon	2	2	0	0	180	24.0	0	0	0
Nasief Morris	1	1	0	0	90	12.0	0	0	0
Midfielders									
Delron Buckley	2	1	1	1	68	9.1	0	0	0
Lance Davids	2	1	1	0	104	13.9	0	0	0
Kagisho Dikgacoi	8	8	0	0	750	100.0	2	2	0
Innocent Mdledle	1	0	1	0	9	1.2	0	0	0
Benson Mhlongo	4	3	1	0	306	40.8	0	0	0
Teko Modise	7	7	0	2	607	80.9	0	2	0
Surprise Moriri	3	2	1	0	196	26.1	1	0	0
Siyabonga Nkosi	1	1	0	0	90	12.0	0	0	0
Steven Pienaar	7	6	1	4	496	66.1	0	2	0
Ntuthuko Macbeth Sibaya	7	7	0	2	636	84.8	0	3	0
Siphiwe Tshabalala	5	3	2	3	258	34.4	0	0	0
Forwards									
Thembinkosi Fanteni	4	3	1	2	259	34.5	1	1	0
Katlego Mashego	4	0	4	0	51	6.8	0	0	0
Benedict McCarthy	1	1	0	0	90	12.0	0	0	0
Katlego Mphela	2	0	2	0	57	7.6	2	1	0
Bernard Parker	5	5	0	3	463	61.7	2	0	0
Elrio Van Heerden	2	0	2	0	53	7.1	0	0	0
Excellent Walaza	1	0	1	0	14	1.9	0	0	0
Sibusiso Zuma	1	0	1	0	16	2.1	0	0	0

Match header row: 1 2 3 4 5 6 7 8; Venue: A H H H H A A A; Result: L W L D W L L L

FINAL PROSPECTS

The last time a host nation was as little fancied in a World Cup tournament, South Korea stunned the footballing world to make the semi-finals in 2002 – but it would surely take some kind of miracle for 2010 hosts South Africa to do the same.

The bulk of the squad are playing in the South African domestic league and have played no serious competitive games in the last 18 months. It is very difficult to know how they will fare but with just three 'name' players – Fulham's Aaron Mokeona, Steven Pienaar of Everton and West Ham's goal poacher Benni McCarthy – it will be a steep learning curve for this side come June 11th. One thing is for certain, their preparation has hardly been ideal.

The vastly experienced and former World Cup winning Carlos Alberto Parreira was drafted in to lead the team into the tournament in 2007. In April 2008 he quit, citing personal reasons, and was replaced by Parreira's fellow Brazilian Joel Santana.

The Confederations Cup aside, Santana achieved little and when Bafana Bafana lost eight games in nine, the writing was on the wall and he was dismissed in October 2009.

> **One thing is for certain, their preparation has hardly been ideal.**

Parreira then reached an agreement to return but was faced with a team in the doldrums. They lacked confidence and form, with leading striker McCarthy out in the cold following a bust up with Santana.

In terms of personnel, their great hope will be Pienaar. Free of injury for most of the season, he has been in the form of his life for Everton, starring in central midfield or on the left and scoring some crucial goals. If South Africa can get the dynamic playmaker on the ball, he will be a real threat as he can score from anywhere.

McCarthy and Mokoena aside, the other players to keep an eye on are attacking full back, Tsepo Masilela, winger Teko Modise and tireless box-to-box midfielder Kagisho Dikgacoi.

Time will tell if Parreira has been able to turn things around. With two of the teams in Group A South American, Parreira will at least have a good idea of what to expect.

If the hosts were to make it through to the last 16 it would be a major achievement for the manager.

DREAM TEAM TOP 15 RANKING 28

GROUP FIXTURES

MEXICO	Fri 11 June 1930 BST
URUGUAY	Wed 16 June 1930 BST
FRANCE	Tue 22 June 1500 BST

Zone	Africa
Population	49m
Language	Afrikaans, English
Top league	ABSA Premiership
Playing season	August - May

Major clubs and capacities
Mamelodi Sundowns (28,900), Kaizer Chiefs (94,700), Orlando Pirates (40,000), Supersport United (28,900)

Where probable squad players play:

Premier League	4	Ligue 1	-
Serie A	-	Eredivisie	1
La Liga	-	Other Europe	4
Bundesliga	1	Outside Europe	13

Number of South African players playing:

Premier League	5	Bundesliga	-
Serie A	-	Ligue 1	-
La Liga	1	Eredivisie	1

World Cup record ** best performance*

1930 - Did not enter	1974 -Banned from Fifa
1934 - Did not enter	1978 -Banned from Fifa
1938 - Did not enter	1982 -Banned from Fifa
1950 - Did not enter	1986 -Banned from Fifa
1954 - Did not enter	1990 -Banned from Fifa
1958 - Did not enter	1994 -Banned from Fifa
1962 - Did not enter	1998 - *Round 1
1966 - Banned from Fifa	2002 - *Round 1
1970 - Banned from Fifa	2006 - Did not qualify

THE SQUAD

Goalkeepers	Club side	Age	Int
Rowen Fernandez	Arminia B	32	1
Itumeleng Khune	Kaizer Chiefs	22	7
Defenders			
Matthew Booth	Mamelodi Sundowns	33	5
Bradley Carnell	Hansa Rostock	33	1
Bevan Fransman	Maccabi Netanya	26	2
Siboniso Gaxa	Mamelodi Sundowns	26	6
Morgan Gould	Supersport United	27	0
Mbulelo Mabizela	Platinum Stars	29	1
Tsepo Masilela	Maccabi Haifa	25	7
Aaron Mokoena	Portsmouth	29	7
Midfielders			
Delron Buckley	Anorthosis	32	2
Lance Davids	Ajax Cape Town	25	2
Kagisho Dikgacoi	Fulham	25	8
Innocent Mdledle	Mamelodi Sundowns	24	1
Benson Mhlongo	Orlando Pirates	29	4
Teko Modise	Orlando Pirates	27	7
Surprise Moriri	Mamelodi Sundowns	29	3
Steven Pienaar	Everton	28	7
Macbeth Sibaya	Rubin Kazan	32	7
Siphiwe Tshabalala	Kaizer Chiefs	25	5
Forwards			
Thembinkosi Fanteni	Orlando Pirates	26	4
Katlego Mashego	Orlando Pirates	28	4
Benedict McCarthy	West Ham	32	1
Katlego Mphela	Mamelodi Sundowns	25	2
Bernard Parker	Twente	24	5
Elrio Van Heerden	Sivasspor	26	2

■ Probable ■ Possible **QG** Qualification Games

KEY PLAYER

AARON MOKOENA PORTSMOUTH

A tough tackling defender, who can also play in midfield, Aaron Mokoena is South Africa's captain and will be an instrumental player if the hosts are to make it out of the group stages.

Now 29 and at the peak of his powers, he is approaching a century of caps for his country. He remains the youngest ever player to play for South Africa and will be a key figure.

Playing record	12 months lge	Intls
Appearances:	24	7
Minutes played:	1453	646
Percentage played:	40.4%	86.1%
Goals conceded:	30	8
Clean sheets:	8	3
Cards:	Y7, R0	Y1, R0
Minutes between goals:	48	81mins
Defender ranking:	168th	113rd

AGE 29 **DEFENDER** **DREAM TEAM RANKING** 1489

KEY GOALKEEPER

ITUMELENG KHUNE
KAISER CHIEFS

The Kaizer Chiefs goalkeeper broke into the national set-up in 2008, and has since tied down the number one jersey.

A sensational shot-stopper with terrific distribution, Khune can occasionally be suspect when bombarded with crosses. A penalty save off David Villa is the youngster's highlight in international football prior to the World Cup.

| AGE 22 | DREAM TEAM | RANKING - |

KEY DEFENDERS

TSEPO MASILELA
MACCABI HAIFA

A talented attacking full-back, Tsepo Masilela's performances on the left side for Thanda Royal Zulu earned them a place in South Africa's top-flight and him a move to a top Israeli side.

He was a key member of the Maccabi Haifa side that won the Israeli Premier League in 2008-09, and featured in this season's Champions League.

A regular for the national side since 2006, Masilela will expect to play a major part in the host nation's difficult quest to make it into the knock out stages of a World Cup for the first time.

| AGE 25 | DREAM TEAM | RANKING - |

SIBONISO GAXA
MAMELODI SUNDOWNS

South African-based right-back Siboniso Gaxa was discovered by FA Copenhagen's School of Excellence and spent six years at Supersport United – the leading club side in his homeland – before sealing a profitable move to Mamelodi Sundowns.

Decent performances in the 2009 Confederations Cup cemented Gaxa's place in the South Africa first team, but he'll need to be at his best and hope that his defensive team-mates also perform if the Bafana Bafana are to make it out of Group A.

| AGE 26 | DREAM TEAM | RANKING - |

KEY MIDFIELDERS

TEKO MODISE
ORLANDO PIRATES

A pivotal figure for Bafana Bafana going forward, Teko Modise is a skilful winger and one of the most high profile players in the South African Premier League, where he plays for the Orlando Pirates.

With more than 40 caps for South Africa, he is one of the most experienced members of the team and in 2008 became the inaugural PSL footballer of the year.

| AGE 27 | DREAM TEAM | RANKING - |

KAGISHO DIKGACOI
FULHAM

Playing record	12 months lge	Intl
Appearances:	4	8
Minutes played:	66	750
Percentage played:	1.7%	100%
Goals scored:	0	2
Clean sheets:	3	2
Cards:	Y0, R1	Y2, R0
Strike rate:	-	375mins
Midfielder ranking:	-	41st

| AGE 25 | DREAM TEAM | RANKING - |

MACBETH SIBAYA
RUBIN KAZAN

An experienced and composed holding midfielder, Macbeth Sibaya is one of the few South African players to play in Europe.

He has spent the last seven years at Russian side Rubin Kazan, where he picked up Russian league winners' medals twice on the bounce.

| AGE 32 | DREAM TEAM | RANKING - |

THE MANAGER

One of only two men to have led four nations into the World Cup finals Carlos Alberto Parreira is one of the most experienced and successful international managers of all time.

He has had an incredible 11 spells as an international manager, taking Brazil to World Cup triumph in 1994 and marshalling Kuwait, United Arab Emirates and Saudi Arabia in the 1982, 1990 and 1998 tournaments respectively.

This is his second spell in charge of South Africa and his record, especially against European competition, is poor. However, his side did well – admittedly in his absence – in the 2009 Confederations Cup on home soil, making it to the semi-finals where they narrowly lost to Brazil.

Parreira walked out on Bafana Bafana in April 2009 but returned in October and will hope to enhance his reputation further by taking the hosts into the knockout stages of the 2010 tournament.

KEY STRIKER

BENNI McCARTHY
WEST HAM

A predatory goalscorer with a proven track record at the highest level, Benni McCarthy has had a tough 18 months but will hope to put all of the problems behind him as he looks to fire Bafana Bafana to the knockout stages.

Struggling for fitness, form and a place in domestic football, McCarthy was also out in the cold internationally having fallen out with the South African hierarchy. With Carlos Alberto Parreira back at the helm, McCarthy will be given every chance to be the attacking focal point of this team and his move to West Ham should help.

Playing record	12 months lge	Intl
Appearances:	28	1
Minutes played:	1587	90
Percentage played:	43.0%	12.0%
Goals scored:	6	0
Percentage share:	15.4%	0%
Cards:	Y5, R0	Y0, R0
Strike rate:	264mins	-
Strike rate ranking:	83rd	-

AGE 32   **DREAM TEAM RANKING** 985

ONE TO WATCH

STEVEN PIENAAR EVERTON

Voted as South Africa's player of the year in 2009, Steven Pienaar is one of the few players of proven top class in the hosts' side.

Able to play anywhere across midfield, Pienaar is quick, skilful and is equally at home scoring goals or creating them. He is susceptible to injury but providing he stays fit, he will be the main man for South Africa.

Playing record	12 months lge	wcq
Appearances:	30	7
Minutes played:	2643	497
Percentage played:	75.3%	66.1%
Goals scored:	4	0
Clean sheets:	11	3
Cards:	Y6, R0	Y2, R0
Strike rate:	661mins	-
Midfielder ranking:	118th	-

AGE 28   **MIDFIELDER**   **DREAM TEAM RANKING** 168

ROUTE TO THE FINALS

Qualifying from the South American zone is always a tough task.

Ten teams – including Brazil and Argentina – and eighteen games, with only the top four guaranteed a place at the World Cup. Despite some mixed results they had their destiny in their own hands but failed to beat Argentina in the last game of qualifying. That set up a do-or-die showdown with Costa Rica and Uruguay sealed their place, winning the away leg thanks to a goal by captain Diego Lugano before securing a 1-1 draw in the second leg to take the tie 2-1.

For final qualification table see Paraguay.

				Avge FIFA ranking			
1	13 Oct 07	Home	Bolivia	66	W	5 0	Suarez 4, Forlan 38, Abreu 48, Sanchez 67, Bueno 82
2	17 Oct 07	Away	Paraguay	20	L	1 0	
3	18 Nov 07	Home	Chile	32	D	2 2	Suarez 41, Abreu 81
4	21 Nov 07	Away	Brazil	4	L	2 1	Abreu 8
5	14 Jun 08	Home	Venezuela	60	D	1 1	Lugano 12
6	17 Jun 08	Home	Peru	76	W	6 0	Forlan 8, 38pen, 57, Bueno 61, 69, Abreu 90
7	07 Sep 08	Away	Colombia	38	W	0 1	Eguren 15
8	10 Sep 08	Home	Ecuador	44	D	0 0	
9	11 Oct 08	Away	Argentina	6	L	2 1	Lugano 39
10	14 Oct 08	Away	Bolivia	66	D	2 2	Bueno 63, Abreu 88
11	28 Mar 09	Home	Paraguay	20	W	2 0	Forlan 29, Lugano 57
12	01 Apr 09	Away	Chile	32	D	0 0	
13	06 Jun 09	Home	Brazil	4	L	0 4	
14	11 Jun 09	Away	Venezuela	60	D	2 2	Suarez 60, Forlan 72
15	05 Sep 09	Away	Peru	76	L	1 0	
16	09 Sep 09	Home	Colombia	38	W	3 1	Suarez Diaz 7, Scotti 77, Eguren 87
17	10 Oct 09	Away	Ecuador	44	W	1 2	Suarez 69, Forlan 90 pen
18	14 Oct 09	Home	Argentina	6	L	0 1	
19	15 Nov 09	Away	Costa Rica	53	W	0 1	Lugano 21
20	18 Nov 09	Home	Costa Rica	53	D	1 1	Abreu 70
	Average FIFA ranking of opposition			**40**			

MAIN PLAYER PERFORMANCES IN QUALIFICATION

Match: 1 2 3 4 5 6 7 8 9 10 11 12 13 14 15 16 17 18 19 20
Venue: H A H A H H A H A A H A H A A H A H A H
Result: W L D L D W W D L D W D L D L W W L W D

	Appearances	Started	Subbed on	Subbed off	Mins played	% played	Goals	Yellow	Red
Goalkeepers									
Fabian Carini	5	5	0	0	450	25.0	0	0	0
Juan Castillo	8	8	0	0	720	40.0	0	1	0
Nestor Muslera	4	4	0	0	360	20.0	0	0	0
Sebastian Viera	3	3	0	0	270	15.0	0	0	0
Defenders									
Martin Caceres	12	12	0	1	1062	59.0	0	4	1
Jorge Fucile	9	8	1	1	683	37.9	0	2	0
Diego Godin	16	16	0	1	1430	79.4	0	4	0
Diego Lugano	17	17	0	0	1530	85.0	4	4	0
Cristian Rodriguez	15	13	2	6	1150	63.9	0	3	1
Andres Scotti	9	7	2	2	641	35.6	1	3	0
Bruno Silva	6	5	1	1	455	25.3	0	2	0
Midfielders									
Sebastian Eguren	12	9	3	2	826	45.9	2	4	0
Alvaro Fernandez	6	2	4	1	249	13.8	0	1	0
Walter Gargano	11	11	0	2	925	51.4	0	0	0
Alvaro Gonzalez	5	3	2	1	269	14.9	0	1	0
Ignacio Gonzalez	5	4	1	3	330	18.3	0	0	0
Alvaro Pereira	10	10	0	2	854	47.4	0	1	0
Maximiliano Pereira	15	12	3	1	1169	64.9	0	2	1
Diego Perez	14	14	0	6	1058	58.8	0	7	0
Forwards									
Sebastian Abreu	16	6	10	2	699	38.8	6	0	0
Carlos Bueno	8	3	5	2	322	17.9	4	1	0
Diego Forlan	15	15	0	3	1285	71.4	7	2	0
Jorge Martinez	3	2	1	1	188	10.4	0	0	0
Vicente Sanchez	7	2	5	1	279	15.5	1	0	0
Luis Suarez	19	17	2	12	1352	75.1	5	3	0

FINAL PROSPECTS

If the FIFA rankings are to be believed, then Uruguay have a real chance of qualifying for the last 16 from Group A. Unlike Group rivals Mexico and France they have precious little recent World Cup pedigree.

This is only the second finals they have qualified for since 1990 and in Japan and Korea 2002, they went home early having failed to win a game.

In qualifying for this tournament they needed a play-off win against Costa Rica having finished fifth in the CONMEBOL behind Brazil and Argentina but did so relatively comfortably, and the two-time champions have shown snatches of real quality in the past 18 months.

Their relatively inexperienced side is maturing with every game and, aided by talented campaigners such as Atletico Madrid's prolific striker Diego Forlan and captain Diego Lugano of Fenerbahce, they could easily cause an upset against an erratic France on the opening day of the tournament. If they can get a result in that game they could well find themselves in a strong position to reach the knock out stages.

DREAM TEAM | **TOP 15 RANKING** | 12

THE MANAGER

Oscar Washington Tabarez is a vastly experienced manager who has been at the helm at an impressive list of clubs including AC Milan, Boca Juniors and Cagliari.

Tabarez, 62, is in his second spell at the helm of Uruguay having managed them first twenty years ago. Back at Italia 90, his side made it into the knockout stages where they lost to the hosts Italy and a similar run would exceed expectations in South Africa with a tough group to get through.

Tabarez definitely has the ability to take Uruguay to the latter stages but he may be lacking the resources this time around.

GROUP FIXTURES

FRANCE	Thur 11 June 1930 BST
SOUTH AFRICA	Tue 16 June 1930 BST
MEXICO	Mon 22 June 1500 BST

Montevideo

Zone	South America
Population	3.5m
Language	Spanish
Top league	Uruguay Primera Division
Playing season	August - May

Major clubs and capacities
Nacional (20,000/76,000), Penarol (10,000), Defensor Sporting (18,000)

Where probable squad players play:

Premier League	-	Ligue 1	1
Serie A	3	Eredivisie	2
La Liga	3	Other Europe	7
Bundesliga	1	Outside Europe	6

Number of Uruguayan players playing:

Premier League	1	Bundesliga	1
Serie A	13	Ligue 1	1
La Liga	13	Eredivisie	2

World Cup record   ** best performance*

1930 - * Champions	1974 -	Round 1
1934 - Withdrew	1978 -	Did not qualify
1938 - Did not enter	1982 -	Did not qualify
1950 - * Champions	1986 -	Last 16
1954 - Semi Finals	1990 -	Last 16
1958 - Did not qualify	1994 -	Did not qualify
1962 - Round 1	1998 -	Did not qualify
1966 - Quarter Finals	2002 -	Round 1
1970 - Semi Finals	2006 -	Did not qualify

THE SQUAD

Goalkeepers	Club side	Age	QG
Fabian Carini	Atletico Mineiro	30	5
Juan Castillo	Botafogo	32	8
Nestor Muslera	Lazio	23	4
Sebastian Viera	Larissa	27	3
Defenders			
Martin Caceres	Juventus	23	12
Jorge Fucile	Porto	25	9
Diego Godin	Villarreal	24	16
Diego Lugano	Fenerbahce	29	17
Cristian Rodriguez	Porto	24	15
Andres Scotti	Argentinos Juniors	34	9
Bruno Silva	Ajax	30	6
Midfielders			
Edinson Cavani	Palermo	23	7
Sebastian Eguren	Villarreal	29	12
Alvaro Fernandez	Uni de Chile	24	6
Walter Gargano	Napoli	25	11
Alvaro Gonzalez	Nacional Montevideo	25	5
Ignacio Gonzalez	Levadiakos	27	5
Alvaro Pereira	Porto	25	10
Maximiliano Pereira	Benfica	26	15
Diego Perez	AS Monaco	30	14
Forwards			
Sebastian Abreu	Botafogo	33	16
Carlos Bueno	Real Sociedad	30	8
Diego Forlan	Atl Madrid	31	15
Jorge Martinez	Catania	27	3
Vicente Sanchez	Schalke	30	7
Luis Suarez	Ajax	23	19

■ Probable ■ Possible **QG** Qualification Games

KEY PLAYER

DIEGO FORLAN ATLETICO MADRID

One of the top strikers in Europe for some years now, Diego Forlan is Uruguay's ace up the sleeve with his eye for goal and proven ability against top-class opposition.

While some might remember his frustrating spell at Manchester United, it is during his time in Spain that he has become the player that Sir Alex Ferguson thought he would.

He finished the top scorer of all the European leagues, winning the coveted 'European Golden Shoe' award twice, in 2004/5 whilst with Villarreal and in 2008/9 with Atletico Madrid scoring 35 goals in 45 games. The clinical striker will need to be on top of his game if Uruguay are to progress to the latter stages of the competition.

Forlan is a Top 12 Striker.

AGE 31   STRIKER   DREAM TEAM RANKING 34

Position	1st	2nd	3rd	4th	5th	6th	7th	8th
Group	E	D	**B**	H	A	G	C	F
Total FIFA ranking	88	89	**98**	104	130	147	160	161

SOUTH KOREA V GREECE
Port Elizabeth, Saturday 12 June 1330 BST

While the first match of the group may not be one for the neutrals, it could be a defining game of the opening stage. A win for either South Korea or Greece would see them in with a great chance of making the knockout stages, with the beatable Nigerians and inconsistent group favourites Argentina still to come. Two superbly organised defensive sides threaten to stifle this match as a spectacle, but fingers crossed that both managers go for the win.

ARGENTINA V NIGERIA
Johannesburg JEP, Saturday 12 June 1600 BST

With question marks hanging over Argentina after a disappointing qualifying campaign, this game will set the tone for their tournament. A victory would see them become clear favourites to top the group, but Nigeria have some dangerous attacking options and could cause the South American's suspect defence some problems. A win for the Super Eagles, who finished third in the 2010 Africa Cup of Nations, against one of the giants of world football would be a great way to help start the continent's first World Cup.

ARGENTINA V SOUTH KOREA
Johannesburg JSC, Thursday 17 June 1230 BST

KEY MATCH

The stand-out game in the group, South Korea have a lot to live up to after their exploits in 2002, where they made it through to the semi-finals, but a win against Diego Maradona's Argentina would go a long way to matching those achievements of eight years ago. The Koreans prefer to defend deep and in numbers, which could be a blessing against Argentina's tricky creative unit, while a handy counter-attacking game, led by Manchester United's Ji-Sung Park, has the potential to embarrass the South Americans' flaky defence. Victory in this one would be a major stepping stone to the knock-out stage for either side, but if either had failed to win in their opening game then defeat would see them facing an early exit from the tournament.

South Korea's Ji-Sung Park

GREECE V NIGERIA
Bloemfontein, Thursday 17 June 1500 BST

If either Greece or Nigeria bagged three points in their first game of the tournament, this match could have great significance. With Argentina being the obvious favourites in the group, a second win for either side is likely to take them through to the knockout stages. Nigeria have the more attacking options in their squad but could still struggle to break down a solid Greece defence.

NIGERIA V SOUTH KOREA
Durban, Tuesday 22 June 1930 BST

Regardless of their match against Greece, if Nigeria are still in with a shout of qualifying entering their third match then expect this game to have an incredible atmosphere. A win will then give them the possibility of making the next stage. Expect a nervy encounter – unless the few creative players on show embrace the occasion.

GREECE V ARGENTINA
Polokwane, Tuesday 22 June 1930 BST

If Argentina's fate in Group B is still hanging in the balance coming down to their final game, then the two-time World Cup winners will not be relishing the prospect of needing a win against arguably the most formidable defensive outfit at the tournament. The Euro 2004 Champions relish these sort of games, and are often at their best against the better attacking teams. Depending on results earlier in the group, Greece could be still in the mixer at this stage, but needing a result against one of the biggest football nations on the planet could be too tough an ask for a team who work well together, but lack stand-out individual quality. This is a match that Argentina should win if they are to be feared.

VIEW FROM THE EXPERTS

ARGENTINA: Should win the group comfortably. It all depends whether mercurial coach Diego Maradona has the nous to pick the right team and a settled team. I'd still like to see a more experienced managerial figure in there to help him.
HARRY'S VERDICT: Semi-finals.
NIGERIA: Not as good as they were. The Super Eagles, who reached the semi-finals of the 2010 Africa Cup of Nations, still rely on old King Kanu who played for me at Portsmouth and Yakubu who made up the Pompey strike line. They could be dangerous as it's in Africa though.
HARRY'S VERDICT: Last 16.
SOUTH KOREA: I don't know much about this squad other than Manchester United's Ji-sung Park has Premier League quality. But you can guarantee they will be well organised, work their socks off and be incredibly hard to beat.
HARRY'S VERDICT: Group stage.
GREECE: Great European champions in the past. And if anyone is going to upset the top two teams in this group it will be them. Well-organised with great application but not sure it will be enough.
HARRY'S VERDICT: Group stage.

ARGENTINA: In my book, the most fascinating country in the tournament. Will they show their class like they did in 1978 and 1986? Or will they implode like they almost did in qualification? It all depends, of course, on what coach Diego Maradona does and whether he can get World Player of the Year Lionel Messi to perform for his country like he does for Barcelona.
TEL'S VERDICT: Argentina advance.
NIGERIA: Have some talented players in their ranks, such as Joseph Yobo, Jon Obi Mikel, Obafemi Martins and Yakubu, but the hard work they made of qualifying with a last-gasp win over Kenya in Nairobi, raises cause for concern. Will not be a pushover but I wonder if they have the quality of previous campaigns.
TEL'S VERDICT: No plans for Nigeria.
SOUTH KOREA: Huh Jung-Moo's men secured a seventh successive appearance at the finals and their qualification record of four wins, four draws and just four goals conceded shows what a well-drilled outfit they are. Skipper and Manchester United midfielder Ji-sung Park is their talisman, but he may not be able to stop them from boarding the early plane home.
TEL'S VERDICT: Close but no cigar in group stage.

GREECE: After reaching their first World Cup since 1994, I fancy Greece to accompany Argentina out of this group. They have a coach in German Otto Rehhagel who has managed to get the very best out of his squad of players, and in captain and midfielder Giorgos Karagounis they have a player who could become one of the unsung heroes of the tournament.
   TEL'S VERDICT: Greece slide through.

ARGENTINA: Argentina's success this summer depends mainly on the performances of two men: Diego Maradona and Lionel Messi. If coach Maradona can keep his erratic behaviour in check and World Player of the Year Messi can play for his country like he does for Barcelona then it could be quite a tournament for them both.
   WRIGHTY'S VERDICT: Quarters at the very least.

NIGERIA: The Super Eagles have a wealth of experience and no shortage of talent, with their squad boasting the likes of Joseph Yobo, Jon Obi Mikel, Obafemi Martins and Yakubu. As with all African nations, though, much depends on their discipline and preparation.
   WRIGHTY'S VERDICT: A most unpredictable threat.

SOUTH KOREA: A seventh successive finals appearance, they are sure to be well organised, very disciplined and fit. They famously made it to the semi-finals in 2002 on home soil. Although strong opposition nobody expects Huh Jung-Moo's squad to repeat those heroics this time.
   WRIGHTY'S VERDICT: No mugs.

GREECE: Did well to beat Ukraine in a play-off to secure their place at their first World Cup finals for 16 years, but I believe they used up most of their luck at a major tournament when they won Euro 2004. That was a big footballing moment for them and I can't see it happening for the Greeks again, certainly not in South Africa.
   WRIGHTY'S VERDICT: Early exit.

"Can World Player of the Year Lionel Messi perform for his country like he does for Barcelona?"

THE LIKELY ROUTES FOR THE TOP TWO TEAMS FROM THE GROUP

For the full draw please see page 80

GROUP STAGE
FIRST GROUP B

> ARGENTINA

LAST SIXTEEN
v SECOND GROUP A

> ARGENTINA v SOUTH AFRICA

QUARTER-FINALS
v FIRST GROUP D or SECOND GROUP C

> ARGENTINA v SERBIA

SECOND GROUP B

> NIGERIA

v FIRST GROUP A

> NIGERIA v FRANCE

v FIRST GROUP C or SECOND GROUP D

> FRANCE v ENGLAND

GROUP B
ARGENTINA, NIGERIA, SOUTH KOREA (KOREAN REPUBLIC), GREECE

GROUP A
SOUTH AFRICA, MEXICO, URUGUAY, FRANCE

GROUP C
ENGLAND, USA, ALGERIA, SLOVENIA
GROUP D
GERMANY, AUSTRALIA, SERBIA, GHANA

ROUTE TO THE FINALS

South American qualifying is always tough, but rarely have Argentina struggled as much as they did this time round.

A run of three wins in the first ten games was enough to see off coach Alfio Basile, who was replaced by Diego Maradona. However, after a 4-0 victory over Venezuela in Maradona's first game, the Albicelestes were hammered 6-1 away in Bolivia and a poor run saw them outside of the qualification places with two games remaining.

A late Peru equaliser looked to have held Argentina to a draw in their penultimate game, only for Martin Palermo to score a 92nd minute winner to spark jubilant scenes in a storm-drenched Buenos Aires. A 1-0 win in Uruguay wrapped up qualification.

For final qualification table see Paraguay.

Avge FIFA ranking

#	Date	Venue	Opponent	Rank	Result			Scorers
1	13 Oct 07	Home	Chile	32	W	2	0	Riquelme 26, 45
2	16 Oct 07	Away	Venezuela	60	W	0	2	G.Milito 15, Messi 18
3	17 Nov 07	Home	Bolivia	66	W	3	0	Aguero 41, Riquelme 57, 74
4	21 Nov 07	Away	Colombia	38	L	2	1	Messi 36
5	15 Jun 08	Home	Ecuador	44	D	1	1	Palacio 89
6	19 Jun 08	Away	Brazil	4	D	0	0	
7	06 Sep 08	Home	Paraguay	20	D	1	1	Aguero 61
8	11 Sep 08	Away	Peru	76	D	1	1	Cambiasso 84
9	11 Oct 08	Home	Uruguay	22	W	2	1	Messi 5, Aguero 12
10	16 Oct 08	Away	Chile	32	L	1	0	
11	28 Mar 09	Home	Venezuela	60	W	4	0	Messi 25, Tevez 47, Rodriguez 51, Aguero 72
12	01 Apr 09	Away	Bolivia	66	L	6	1	L.Gonzalez 25
13	06 Jun 09	Home	Colombia	38	W	1	0	Diaz 55
14	10 Jun 09	Away	Ecuador	44	L	2	0	
15	06 Sep 09	Home	Brazil	4	L	1	3	Datolo 65
16	10 Sep 09	Away	Paraguay	20	L	1	0	
17	10 Oct 09	Home	Peru	76	W	2	1	Higuain 48, Palermo 90
18	14 Oct 09	Away	Uruguay	22	W	0	1	Bolatti 84
	Average FIFA ranking of opposition			**40**				

MAIN PLAYER PERFORMANCES IN QUALIFICATION

Key: ■ played 90 mins « subbed off » subbed on ▨ on bench

Match	1 2 3 4 5 6 7 8 9 10 11 12 13 14 15 16 17 18	Appearances	Started	Subbed on	Subbed off	Mins played	% played	Goals	Yellow	Red
Venue	H A H A H A H A H A H A H A H A H A									
Result	W W W L D D D D W L W L W L L L W W									
Goalkeepers										
Roberto Abbondanzieri		7	7	0	1	554	34.2	0	0	0
Mariano Gonzalo Andujar		3	3	0	0	270	16.7	0	0	0
Juan Pablo Carrizo		6	5	1	0	526	32.5	0	0	0
Sergio German Romero		3	3	0	0	270	16.7	0	1	0
Defenders										
Nicolas Burdisso		6	5	1	2	368	22.7	0	0	0
Fabricio Coloccini		3	3	0	0	270	16.7	0	0	0
Martin Demichelis		14	13	1	0	1193	73.6	0	5	0
Daniel Alberto Diaz		6	2	4	0	317	19.6	1	1	0
Gabriel Ivan Heinze		14	14	0	2	1206	74.4	0	2	0
Hugo Benjamin Ibarra		3	3	0	1	248	15.3	0	1	0
Gabriel Milito		4	4	0	0	360	22.2	1	0	0
Rolando Schiavi		3	2	1	0	191	11.8	0	0	0
Javier Zanetti		16	15	1	0	1395	86.1	0	1	0
Midfielders										
Esteban Cambiasso		8	8	0	4	670	41.4	1	0	0
Angel Di Maria		5	3	2	2	235	14.5	0	0	1
Fernando Gago		12	8	4	2	772	47.7	0	3	0
Jonas Gutierrez		7	7	0	1	557	34.4	0	3	0
Javier Mascherano		16	16	0	1	1412	87.2	0	5	0
Nicolas Hernan Otamendi		3	3	0	0	270	16.7	0	1	0
Juan Riquelme		9	9	0	2	784	48.4	4	2	0
Maxi Rodriguez		8	6	2	5	407	25.1	1	1	0
Juan Sebastian Veron		7	5	2	1	443	27.3	0	1	1
Forwards										
Sergio Aguero		12	8	4	6	692	42.7	4	0	0
Gonzalo Higuain		2	2	0	2	146	9.0	1	0	0
Lionel Andres Messi		18	18	0	4	1604	99.0	4	1	0
Carlos Tevez		12	11	1	8	726	44.8	1	2	2
Martin Palermo		2	0	2	0	78	4.8	1	1	0

FINAL PROSPECTS

One of the all-time great footballing nations, Argentina go into this World Cup in the worst state they've been in for many years.

One of the favourites for the last World Cup, the Albicelestes were knocked out at the quarter-final stage by Germany, continuing a very disappointing run of World Cup performances that had seen them reach the last eight just one other time since 1990.

England and Sweden ensured they didn't make it out of the group stage in 2002, while Nigeria and Bulgaria did likewise in 1994, with a quarter-final defeat to the Netherlands in 1998 the nation's best World Cup performance in the last 20 years. In other words: they're due a big tournament.

Current manager Diego Maradona inspired Argentina to their most recent World Cup triumph – in 1986 – but his introduction to management got off to a stuttering start, as his lack of experience showed in the second half of a qualification campaign that almost ended in disaster.

> **Any side with World Player of the Year Lionel Messi in their midst should never be discounted.**

Maradona called up an incredible number of players to represent the nation during his first year in charge. His failure to find a settled first-team line-up is the main reason why Argentina are not considered amongst the favourites to triumph in South Africa.

That said, any side with World Player of the Year Lionel Messi in their midst should never be discounted, and there's no shortage of quality available in addition to Barcelona's fleet-footed star.

The father of Maradona's grandchild, Sergio Aguero, is a quality option up front, as is Carlos Tevez. Gonazalo Higuain's stunning form with Real Madrid has also seen him come into contention for a starting spot. Javier Mascherano, Fernando Gago and Esteban Cambiasso are defensive midfield options that cannot be matched by any other side in the world. The back line is unlikely to be as strong as in past years – despite the likely presence of Javier Zanetti.

There is still the chance that Argentina can defy their disappointing recent form and be a major threat to the more in-form nations. But they'll have to up their game from qualifying to avoid a major upset at the hands of three dangerously underrated sides.

DREAM TEAM	TOP 15 RANKING	8

GROUP FIXTURES

NIGERIA	Sat 12 June 1500 BST
SOUTH KOREA	Thur 17 June 1230 BST
GREECE	Tue 22 June 1930 BST

Buenos Aires●

Zone	South America
Population	41m
Language	Spanish
Top league	Primera Division
Playing season	February - June

Major clubs and **Capacities**
Boca Juniors (49,000), Racing (51,389), San Lorenzo (43,494)

Where probable squad players play:

Premier League	3	Ligue 1	1
Serie A	3	Eredivisie	1
La Liga	6	Other Europe	3
Bundesliga	1	Outside Europe	5

Number of Argentinian players playing:

Premier League	5	Bundesliga	4
Serie A	38	Ligue 1	14
La Liga	30	Eredivisie	2

World Cup record ** best performance*

1930 - Second place		1974 -	Round 2
1934 - Round 1		1978 -	*Champions
1938 - Withdrew		1982 -	Round 2
1950 - Withdrew		1986 -	*Champions
1954 - Withdrew		1990 -	Runners up
1958 - Round 1		1994 -	Last 16
1962 - Round 1		1998 -	Quarter finals
1966 - Quarter finals		2002 -	Round 1
1970 - Did not qualify		2006 -	Quarter finals

THE SQUAD

Goalkeepers	Club side	Age	QG
Roberto Abbondanzieri	Boca Juniors	37	7
Mariano Andujar	Catania	26	3
Juan Pablo Carrizo	Real Zaragoza	26	6
Sergio Romero	AZ Alkmaar	23	3
Defenders			
Nicolas Burdisso	Roma	29	6
Fabricio Coloccini	Newcastle	28	3
Martin Demichelis	Bayern Munich	29	14
Daniel Alberto Diaz	Getafe	30	6
Gabriel Ivan Heinze	Marseille	32	14
Hugo Benjamin Ibarra	Boca Juniors	36	3
Gabriel Milito	Barcelona	29	4
Rolando Schiavi	Newells Old Boys	37	3
Javier Zanetti	Inter Milan	36	16
Midfielders			
Esteban Cambiasso	Inter Milan	29	8
Angel Di Maria	Benfica	22	5
Fernando Gago	Real Madrid	24	12
Jonas Gutierrez	Newcastle	26	7
Javier Mascherano	Liverpool	26	16
Nicolas Otamendi	Velez Sarsfield	22	3
Juan Riquelme	Boca Juniors	31	9
Maxi Rodriguez	Liverpool	29	8
Juan Sebastian Veron	Estudiantes La Plata	35	7
Forwards			
Sergio Aguero	Atl Madrid	22	12
Gonzalo Higuain	Real Madrid	22	2
Lionel Messi	Barcelona	22	18
Carlos Tevez	Man City	26	12

■ Probable ■ Possible **QG** Qualification Games

KEY PLAYER

LIONEL MESSI BARCELONA

Argentina's Diego Maradona has described Lionel Messi as his 'successor' in the national team, but it is no exaggeration to suggest that the Barca star might even eclipse Maradona's success.

Before he even turned 22, Messi had two Champions League titles, three La Liga titles, an Olympic Gold Medal and the World Player of the Year award to his name. Originally seen as a winger, he has blossomed in Barcelona's three-pronged attack, although he has yet to replicate that form on the international stage. The national side do tend to rely on Messi to create chances out of nothing in tight games, but Argentina will have a great chance if he is on form.

Messi is a Top 12 Striker.

AGE 22 **STRIKER**

DREAM TEAM RANKING 15

KEY GOALKEEPERS

JUAN PABLO CARRIZO
REAL ZARAGOZA

Playing record	12 months lge	wcq
Appearances:	16	6
Minutes played:	1440	526
Percentage played:	94.1%	32.5%
Goals conceded:	30	9
Clean sheets:	4	2
Cards:	Y2, R0	Y0, R0
Minutes between goals:	48mins	58mins
Goalkeeper ranking:	34th	29th

AGE 26	DREAM TEAM	RANKING 1379

ROBERT ABBONDANZIERI
BOCA JUNIORS

Playing record	12 months lge	wcq
Appearances:	-	7
Minutes played:	-	554
Percentage played:	-	34.2%
Goals conceded:	-	5
Clean sheets:	-	3
Cards:	-	Y0, R0
Minutes between goals:	-	111mins
Goalkeeper ranking:	-	20th

AGE 37	DREAM TEAM	RANKING 98

KEY DEFENDERS

GABRIEL HEINZE
MARSEILLE

Capable of playing at left-back or in the centre of defence, Gabriel Heinze has had an illustrious career, winning the Premier League with Manchester United and La Liga with Real Madrid.

A regular on the left of the Argentina defence but his versatility will prove vital.

Heinze is a Top 12 Defender.

NICOLAS BURDISSO
ROMA

A highly experienced defender with an eye for a tackle - and a short fuse - Nicolas Burdisso made a name for himself at Boca Juniors, before moving to Europe to join Inter Milan in 2004, where he won four straight Serie A titles.

A versatile member of the Argentina squad, Burdisso can be used both in the centre and at right-back and could prove to be a vital part of Maradona's team in South Africa.

Playing record	12 months lge	wcq
Appearances:	27	6
Minutes played:	1944	368
Percentage played:	52.7%	22.7%
Goals conceded:	29	2
Clean sheets:	10	4
Cards:	Y5, R0	Y0, R0
Minutes between goals:	67mins	184mins
Defender ranking:	127th	36th

AGE 29	DREAM TEAM	RANKING 742

FABRICIO COLOCCINI
NEWCASTLE

Instantly recognisable, with his mop of curly hair and aggressive playing style, Fabricio Coloccini has spent the last season in the second tier of English football with Newcastle United.

A four-year spell at Deportivo La Coruna apart, Coloccini's club career has been a pale reflection of his form for Argentina over the years, with a five-year stay at AC Milan notable for his lack of appearances for the Rossoneri, while relegation with Newcastle in 2009 was a career low-point.

However, he has put in some top-class displays in central defence for his country, showing quality on the ball as well as his usual commanding presence in the air.

Despite being in and out of the side over the last few years, Argentina's defensive weaknesses mean that Coloccini will expect to play a large part in the Albicelestes' World Cup campaign in South Africa – even if he starts the tournament as back-up centre-half.

This could be a big tournament for Coloccini especially if he wants a move to a larger club.

Playing record	12 months lge	wcq
Appearances:	14	3
Minutes played:	1259	270
Percentage played:	77.7%	16.7%
Goals conceded:	24	2
Clean sheets:	2	1
Cards:	Y2, R0	Y0, R0
Minutes between goals:	52mins	135mins
Defender ranking:	163rd	61st

AGE 28	DREAM TEAM	RANKING 1436

THE MANAGER

One of the game's most famous and vibrant personalities, Diego Maradona has mixed the majestic and the controversial throughout his career, as both a player and manager.

Considered by many to be one of, if not the greatest player of all time, Maradona inspired Argentina to consecutive World Cup finals, and was voted player of the tournament as the Albicelestes triumphed in 1986.

A string of personal problems saw the attacking genius' playing career come to an undignified end, and his circus-like private life was aptly described by international team-mate Jorge Valdano as 'an ordeal that should not be imitated'.

With no real managerial experience of note, Maradona was a surprise choice to replace Alfio Basile in 2008. Just four wins in his first eight games in charge during qualifying were notable for his displays of tactical naivety and inconsistent selection. His relief as Argentina bagged a late win in their penultimate game was clear for all to see, as he slid along on the touchline on his knees in celebration of Martin Palermo's goal.

However, a furious outburst at reporters live on television after the final qualification game saw the coach banned for two months at the end of 2009, bringing a disappointing opening year in charge to a fittingly controversial end.

JAVIER ZANETTI
INTER MILAN

The most capped Argentina player of all time, Javier Zanetti has already written his name into the nation's footballing history, and it is testament to his outstanding ability that he remains a regular even at the age of 36.

The full-back is still a first team option for Inter Milan – 16 years after moving to the Italian club – and continues to combine consistently strong defensive work with his trademark forays further forward. He bagged a first Serie A title in 2006 and hasn't looked back since.

Ignored by Argentina coach Jose Pekerman for the 2006 World Cup, Zanetti will be keen to make up for an eight year absence from the world's biggest stage since he captained the Albicelestes in 2002 – when he was also left disappointed, as his side crashed out at the first hurdle.

A favourite of Diego Maradona, the defender will expect to be one of the first names on the team sheet in South Africa and he will be key to any success in the tournament.

Zanetti is a Top 12 Defender.

AGE 36	DREAM TEAM RANKING 25

KEY PLAYER

JAVIER MASCHERANO LIVERPOOL

There are few bigger fans of Javier Mascherano than Argentina manager Diego Maradona, who made him captain in November 2008 and described the national side as 'Mascherano and ten more'.

Arguably the world's best defensive midfielder, his move to Liverpool in 2007 exposed the 26-year-old to the highest level of club football. The fulcrum of both his club and international sides, Mascherano is a tough tackling presence in the centre of the park, who leaves the 'Hollywood passing' and creative play to those more suited to that role. The skipper's form and fitness alongside Fernando Gago in midfield will be vital to the side's hopes.

Mascherano is a Top 12 Midfielder.

AGE 26	MIDFIELDER	DREAM TEAM RANKING 45

KEY MIDFIELDERS

FERNANDO GAGO
REAL MADRID

Prodigious young midfielder Fernando Gago featured regularly in qualifying, forming a defensive midfield partnership with Javier Mascherano.

After bagging two league titles at Boca Juniors, Gago moved to Real Madrid in 2006, aged just 20, where he played a key role in both of the club's La Liga titles in his first two years at the club.

Cultured on the ball, with an eye for a pass, good defensive positioning and a decent challenge on him, Gago seems to have it all, with his flowing locks and boyish looks also making him the female fans' favourite.

The influx of players to the Bernabeu in 2009 limited Gago's playing time over the last season, but he looks likely to remain a key part of the national side.

Playing record	12 months lge	wcq
Appearances:	21	12
Minutes played:	1600	772
Percentage played:	45.6%	47.7%
Goals scored:	0	0
Clean sheets:	13	6
Cards:	Y9, R1	Y3, R0
Strike rate:	-	-
Midfielder ranking:	153rd	127th

AGE 24	DREAM TEAM	RANKING 663

ESTEBAN CAMBIASSO
INTER MILAN

Midfielder Esteban Cambiasso has dropped behind Fernando Gago in the Argentina pecking order, but the Inter Milan legend put in another impressive season for his club to stake a decent claim for a starting berth.

An Inter legend and consistent performer for his country over the last decade, Cambiasso was originally seen as a midfield 'destroyer' but has developed a more cultured side to his game. He endured mixed fortunes at the last World Cup, finishing off one of the great team goals against Serbia, but missing the decisive penalty against Germany in the quarter-finals.

Playing record	12 months lge	wcq
Appearances:	34	8
Minutes played:	2850	670
Percentage played:	79.2%	41.4%
Goals scored:	6	1
Clean sheets:	14	4
Cards:	Y2, R0	Y0, R0
Strike rate:	475mins	670mins
Midfielder ranking:	87th	61st

AGE 29	DREAM TEAM	RANKING 177

MAXI RODRIGUEZ
LIVERPOOL

Skilful attacking midfielder Maxi Rodriguez has a rounded creative game, developed during an eight-year spell in La Liga.

Pace, trickery and a powerful shot make the Liverpool man a constant threat, and he has that precious ability of being able to fashion a chance – or a goal – out of nothing. Scorer of one of the great World Cup goals in extra-time of the last 16 clash with Mexico in 2006, Maxi will need to show that he's back to his best to play regularly in South Africa.

Playing record	12 months lge	wcq
Appearances:	32	8
Minutes played:	2027	407
Percentage played:	60.1%	25.1%
Goals scored:	2	1
Clean sheets:	6	3
Cards:	Y5, R0	Y1, R0
Strike rate:	1013mins	407mins
Midfielder ranking:	-	-

AGE 29	DREAM TEAM	RANKING 435

KEY STRIKERS

CARLOS TEVEZ
MAN CITY

One of the biggest names in world football and an impressive performer for Manchester City, Manchester Utd and West Ham in the Premier League over the last four years, Carlos Tevez has flattered to deceive for his country.

Two red cards and just one goal in a disappointing qualifying campaign saw his position in the national side come under serious threat, although he did feature more regularly after the appointment of Diego Maradona as manager.

A hard-working yet skilful forward who isn't afraid to voice his opinions, Tevez is capable of leading the line if need be, but performs at his best when used either as a support striker in a front-two or as a wide player in a three-pronged strike force.

However, with the inspirational Lionel Messi guaranteed to start if fit, and Sergio Aguero, Gonzalo Higuain and Maxi Rodriguez among those competing for the remaining attacking positions, Tevez will be hoping that his form in a star-studded City team has been good enough to help him force his way into an Argentina side who have the individual talent to leave a real mark on the tournament.

Tevez is a Top 12 Striker.

AGE 26	DREAM TEAM	RANKING 67

GONZALO HIGUAIN
REAL MADRID

Young striker Gonzalo Higuain offers Argentina the natural finishing ability they need to complement the squad's wide range of deep-lying creative talents.

Since signing for Madrid at the age of just 19, Higuain has developed a fearsome goal-scoring record at club level. He managed to tie down a regular starting place for Los Blancos in 2009/10, despite the arrival of flagship signings Kaka, Cristiano Ronaldo and Karim Benzema. Ignored by Maradona until the penultimate game of South American qualifying, Higuain scored the opener in Argentina's vital 2-1 win over Peru and should feature in South Africa.

Playing record	12 months lge	wcq
Appearances:	34	2
Minutes played:	2423	146
Percentage played:	69.0%	9.0%
Goals scored:	22	1
Percentage share:	24.18%	4.35%
Cards:	Y3, R0	Y0, R0
Strike rate:	110mins	-
Strike rate ranking:	8th	-

AGE 22   **DREAM TEAM RANKING 188**

ONE TO WATCH

SERGIO AGUERO ATL MADRID

One of the most promising talents in world football, the diminutive Sergio Aguero combines pace, skill and clinical finishing.

Capable of playing as a lone front man but more effective alongside another forward, Aguero failed to tie down a regular berth under manager Diego Maradona, but will be a dangerous option coming off the bench.

Playing record	12 months lge	wcq
Appearances:	36	12
Minutes played:	2741	692
Percentage played:	78.1%	42.7%
Goals scored:	16	4
Percentage share:	23.19%	17.39%
Cards:	Y6, R0	Y0, R0
Strike rate:	171mins	173mins
Strike rate ranking:	34th	28th

AGE 22   **STRIKER**   **DREAM TEAM RANKING 82**

ROUTE TO THE FINALS

Greece qualified for the World Cup for only the second time in their history, but did so the hard way being forced to go through the play-offs after missing out on automatic qualification by just a single point.

The surprise Euro 2004 champions would have been confident of qualifying automatically when they were drawn in one of the easier European groups, but lost twice to Switzerland and dropped two crucial points in a shock draw with minnows Moldova, ensuring that the Swiss finished top of Group Two.

Successive victories in their final two games – including a 5-2 defeat of nearest challengers Latvia – wrapped up second place for Otto Rehhagel's side. They reaped the rewards of FIFA's seeding system when they picked out Ukraine in one of the more favourable play-off ties. A string of wasted chances in the home leg left Greece needing a win in Donetsk, but they duly delivered thanks to a first half goal by Dimitrios Salpigidis and a characteristically impressive defensive display to keep Ukraine out in the second half.

**FINAL QUALIFYING TABLE
EUROPE GROUP 2**

	P	W	D	L	F	A	Pts
Switzerland	10	6	3	1	18	8	21
Greece *	10	6	2	2	20	10	20
Latvia	10	5	2	3	18	15	17
İsrael	10	4	4	2	20	10	16
Luxembourg	10	1	2	7	4	25	5
Moldova	10	0	3	7	6	18	3

* Greece beat Ukraine in the play-offs.

	Date		Opposition	Avge FIFA ranking				
1	06 Sep 08	Away	Luxembourg	131	W	0 3	Torosidis 36, Gekas 45, Charisteas 77pen
2	10 Sep 08	Away	Latvia	63	W	0 2	Gekas 17, 50
3	11 Oct 08	Home	Moldova	78	W	3 0	Charisteas 31, 51, Katsouranis 40
4	15 Oct 08	Home	Switzerland	27	L	1 2	Charisteas 68
5	28 Mar 09	Away	Israel	21	D	1 1	Gekas 42
6	01 Apr 09	Home	Israel	21	W	2 1	Salpigidis 32, Samaras 67pen
7	05 Sep 09	Away	Switzerland	27	L	2 0	
8	09 Sep 09	Away	Moldova	78	D	1 1	Gekas 33
9	10 Oct 09	Home	Latvia	63	W	5 2	Gekas 4, 47pen, 57, 90, Samaras 73
10	14 Oct 09	Home	Luxembourg	131	W	2 1	Torosidis 30, Gekas 33
11	14 Nov 09	Home	Ukraine	22	D	0 0	
12	18 Nov 09	Away	Ukraine	22	W	0 1	Salpigidis 31

Average FIFA ranking of opposition	57

MAIN PLAYER PERFORMANCES IN QUALIFICATION

Match	1 2 3 4 5 6 7 8 9 10 11 12	Appearances	Started	Subbed on	Subbed off	Mins played	% played	Goals	Yellow	Red
Venue	A A H H A H A A H H H A									
Result	W W W L D W L D W W D W									
Goalkeepers										
Konstantinos Chalkias		8	8	0	0	720	66.7	0	0	0
Michail Sifakis		1	1	0	0	90	8.3	0	0	0
Alexandros Tzorvas		3	3	0	0	270	25.0	0	0	0
Defenders										
Traianos Dellas		5	5	0	0	450	41.7	0	1	0
Sotirios Kyrgiakos		11	11	0	2	880	81.5	0	3	0
Evangelos Moras		7	6	1	1	554	51.3	0	0	0
Avraam Papadopoulos		8	6	2	0	591	54.7	0	2	0
Sokratis Papastathopoulos		4	4	0	1	298	27.6	0	1	0
Christos Patsatzoglou		9	3	6	0	446	41.3	0	1	0
Giourkas Seitaridis		7	7	0	0	630	58.3	0	2	0
Nikolaos Spiropoulos		6	5	1	0	460	42.6	0	1	0
Vassillis Torosidis		8	8	0	0	720	66.7	2	0	0
Loukas Vyntra		4	4	0	1	302	28.0	0	2	1
Midfielders										
Ioannis Amanatidis		4	1	3	1	160	14.8	0	0	0
Angelos Basinas		6	4	2	2	322	29.8	0	0	0
Giorgos Karagounis		10	9	1	4	771	71.4	0	0	0
Konstantinos Katsouranis		10	10	0	1	881	81.6	1	3	0
Vassilios Pliatsikas		3	0	3	0	109	10.1	0	1	0
Alexandros Tziolis		4	3	1	2	242	22.4	0	1	0
Forwards										
Angelos Charisteas		10	9	1	3	791	73.2	4	1	0
Theofanis Gekas		12	10	2	6	771	71.4	10	0	0
Nikolaos Liberopoulos		4	1	3	1	158	14.6	0	0	0
Dimitrios Salpigidis		8	6	2	3	488	45.2	2	0	0
Georgios Samaras		10	7	3	4	653	60.5	2	1	0

FINAL PROSPECTS

One of the most defensive teams in world football, Greece are unlikely to repeat their shock Euro 2004 success in South Africa, but will fancy their chances of qualifying from what should be an extremely competitive and evenly matched Group B.

The Greeks have made just one previous World Cup appearance, in 1994. They lost all three games on that occasion, conceding ten goals without reply against the collective might of Bulgaria and two of the countries that they will face again in South Africa – Nigeria and Argentina. However, with the combination of a formidable defence and a dangerous group of strikers, spearheaded by Europe's top goal-scorer in qualification, Theofanis Gekas, Greece are rightly expected to improve that record in South Africa.

Under the guidance of the impressive tactician and long-serving manager Otto Rehhagel, they have what it takes to hurt South Korea and Nigeria in their opening two games. They could also spring a surprise in their final game in the group against an Argentina side who limped through qualifying, so the last 16 is a realistic target.

DREAM TEAM	TOP 15 RANKING	29

THE MANAGER

Manager of the Greek side since 2001, Otto Rehhagel oversaw one of the great football shocks as Greece won the Euro 2004 title.

With almost 30 years of managerial experience in the Bundesliga prior to his switch to international football, Rehhagel has developed a reputation as a manager who puts together defensive teams that are more effective than they are entertaining. That is exactly what he has done with this Greek side, and while the fans won't be queuing up to watch them play, don't bet against Rehhagel leading Greece into the knock out stages.

GROUP FIXTURES

SOUTH KOREA	Sat 12 June 1230 BST
NIGERIA	Thur 17 June 1500 BST
ARGENTINA	Tue 22 June 1930 BST

Athens

Zone	Europe
Population	10.7m
Language	Greek
Top league	Super League Greece
Playing season	August - May

Major clubs and capacities
Panathinaikos FC (71,030), AEK Athens (71,030), Olympiacos FC (33,334)

Where probable squad players play:

Premier League	2	Ligue 1	-
Serie A	2	Eredivisie	-
La Liga	-	Other Europe	14
Bundesliga	5	Outside Europe	-

Number of Greek players playing:

Premier League	2	Bundesliga	6
Serie A	2	Ligue 1	1
La Liga	-	Eredivisie	1

World Cup record   * best performance

1930 - Did not enter	1974 -	Did not qualify
1934 - Withdrew	1978 -	Did not qualify
1938 - Did not qualify	1982 -	Did not qualify
1950 - Did not enter	1986 -	Did not qualify
1954 - Did not qualify	1990 -	Did not qualify
1958 - Did not qualify	1994 -	* Round 1
1962 - Did not qualify	1998 -	Did not qualify
1966 - Did not qualify	2002 -	Did not qualify
1970 - Did not qualify	2006 -	Did not qualify

THE SQUAD

Goalkeepers	Club side	Age	QG
Konstantinos Chalkias	PAOK Salonika	36	8
Michail Sifakis	Aris	25	1
Alexandros Tzorvas	Panathinaikos	27	3
Defenders			
Traianos Dellas	Anorthosis	34	5
Sotirios Kyrgiakos	Liverpool	30	11
Evangelos Moras	Bologna	28	7
Avraam Papadopoulos	Olympiakos	25	8
Sokr Papastathopoulos	Genoa	22	4
Christos Patsatzoglou	Omonia Nicosia	31	9
Giourkas Seitaridis	Panathinaikos	29	7
Nikolaos Spiropoulos	Panathinaikos	26	6
Vassillis Torosidis	Olympiakos	25	8
Loukas Vyntra	Panathinaikos	29	4
Midfielders			
Ioannis Amanatidis	Eintr Frankfurt	28	4
Angelos Basinas	Portsmouth	34	6
Georgios Fotakis	PAOK Salonika	28	1
Giorgos Karagounis	Panathinaikos	33	10
Konstan Katsouranis	Panathinaikos	30	10
Vassilios Pliatsikas	Schalke	22	3
Alexandros Tziolis	Panathinaikos	25	4
Forwards			
Angelos Charisteas	Nurnberg	30	10
Theofanis Gekas	B Leverkusen	30	12
Nikolaos Liberopoulos	Eintr Frankfurt	34	4
Konstantinos Mitroglou	Olympiakos	22	1
Dimitrios Salpigidis	Panathinaikos	28	8
Georgios Samaras	Celtic	25	10

■ Probable ■ Possible **QG** Qualification Games

KEY PLAYER

GIORGOS KARAGOUNIS PANATHINAIKOS

A legend of Greek football, Giorgos Karagounis may be better known for his physicality, but he also has a refined and underrated creative game that makes the Greece team tick.

A powerful shot and good ability from set-pieces also mean Karagounis is a real danger from distance. If Greece do progress then Karagounis will play a major role.

Playing record 12 months	lge	wcq
Appearances:	-	10
Minutes played:	-	771
Percentage played:	-	71.38%
Goals scored:	-	0
Clean sheets:	-	5
Cards:	-	Y0, R0
Strike rate:	-	-
Midfielder ranking:	-	-

AGE 33   **MIDFIELDER**   **DREAM TEAM** **RANKING** 500

ROUTE TO THE FINALS

Despite going through the whole of the lengthy African qualification campaign unbeaten, Nigeria left it extremely late to seal a place at the World Cup.

The Super Eagles steam rollered their way through round two of African qualifying, winning all six group games – including home and away against World Cup hosts South Africa – and conceding just one goal in the process.

However, a draw against Mozambique in their first game of the third and final stage of qualification left Shaibu Amodu's side with a tough task to finish top of Group B, and two draws against Tunisia left Nigeria trailing behind the North Africans in the race for the solitary qualification space with two games remaining.

A 93rd minute winner from Victor Obinna against Mozambique ensured there was a glimmer of hope going into the final round of games. Nigeria still needed to win and hope that Mozambique pulled off a shock by beating Tunisia in Maputo.

However, that is exactly what happened, with goals from Obafemi Martins and Yakubu Aiyegbeni drawing Nigeria level against Kenya, before Martins bagged a late winner to send the Super Eagles to their fourth World Cup.

FINAL QUALIFYING TABLE
AFRICA ROUND 3 GROUP B

	P	W	D	L	F	A	Pts
Nigeria	6	3	3	0	9	4	12
Tunisia	6	3	2	1	7	4	11
Mozambique	6	2	1	3	3	5	7
Kenya	6	1	0	5	5	11	3

Avge FIFA ranking

	Date		Opposition		Result			Scorers
1	01 Jun 08	Home	South Africa	74	W	2	0	I.Uche 10, Nwaneri 44
2	07 Jun 08	Away	Sierra Leone	126	W	0	1	Yobo 89
3	15 Jun 08	Away	Equatorial Guinea	-	W	0	1	Yobo 5
4	21 Jun 08	Home	Equatorial Guinea	-	W	2	0	Yakubu 45, I.Uche 84
5	06 Sep 08	Away	South Africa	74	W	0	1	I.Uche 69
6	11 Oct 08	Home	Sierra Leone	126	W	4	1	Obodo 20, Obinna 34, Odemwingie 45, Odiah 50
7	29 Mar 09	Away	Mozambique	91	D	0	0	
8	07 Jun 09	Home	Kenya	97	W	3	0	I.Uche 2, Obinna 72pen, 77
9	20 Jun 09	Away	Tunisia	49	D	0	0	
10	06 Sep 09	Home	Tunisia	49	D	2	2	Odemwingie 24, Eneramo 80
11	11 Oct 09	Home	Mozambique	91	W	1	0	Obinna 90
12	14 Nov 09	Away	Kenya	97	W	2	3	Martins 60, 81, Yakubu 64

Average FIFA ranking of opposition	106

MAIN PLAYER PERFORMANCES IN QUALIFICATION

Match	1 2 3 4 5 6 7 8 9 10 11 12	Appearances	Started	Subbed on	Subbed off	Mins played	% played	Goals	Yellow	Red
Venue	H A A H A H A H A H H A									
Result	W W W W W W D W D D W W									
Goalkeepers										
Dele Aiyenugba		2	2	0	0	180	16.7	0	0	0
Vincent Enyeama		10	10	0	0	900	83.3	0	0	0
Defenders										
Olubayo Adefemi		2	2	0	0	180	16.7	0	1	0
Dele Adeleye		3	3	0	0	270	25.0	0	0	0
Obinna Nwaneri		8	8	0	0	720	66.7	1	2	0
Chidi Odiah		5	5	0	1	439	40.6	1	0	0
Daniel Olusola Shittu		4	3	1	0	329	30.5	0	0	0
Taye Ismaila Taiwo		9	9	0	0	810	75.0	0	0	0
Joseph Yobo		9	9	0	0	810	75.0	2	0	0
Midfielders										
Yussuf Atanda Ayila		7	6	1	1	570	52.8	0	1	0
Elderson Uwa Echiejile		3	3	0	0	270	25.0	0	2	0
Sani Kaita		2	2	0	0	180	16.7	0	1	0
Yusuf Mohamed		4	4	0	1	301	27.9	0	0	0
John Obi Mikel		7	6	1	1	541	50.1	0	1	0
Oluwaseyi George Olofinjana		9	7	2	2	590	54.6	0	0	0
Forwards										
Yakubu Aiyegbeni		8	7	1	3	561	51.9	2	0	0
Michael Eneramo		5	3	2	3	231	21.4	1	1	0
Nwankwo Kanu		6	2	4	2	258	23.9	0	0	0
Obafemi Martins		3	1	2	0	170	15.7	2	0	0
Victor Nsofor Obinna		9	3	6	3	415	38.4	4	0	0
Peter Odemwingie		10	9	1	2	798	73.9	2	2	0
Ikechukwu Uche		10	9	1	5	735	68.1	4	1	0
Kalu Uche		9	8	1	4	639	59.2	0	1	0
John Utaka		4	3	1	1	234	21.7	0	0	0

FINAL PROSPECTS

Africa's most consistently successful World Cup nation of the last two decades, Nigeria will once again have aspirations of qualifying for the knock out stages in South Africa.

2010 will be the Super Eagles' fourth taste of World Cup football and the first of those four occasions, in 1994, remains their most successful. They qualified top of a group that included Argentina and Greece, two of their group opponents again in South Africa. Then they were heartbreakingly close to making the quarter-finals, being beaten by eventual runners-up Italy in extra time.

With Premier League regulars Joseph Yobo, John Obi Mikel and Seyi Olofinjana they are ensured that the Super Eagles are strong defensively. The collective talents of Yakubu Aiyegbeni, Obafemi Martins and Lokomotiv Moscow's Peter Odemwingie are to choose from up front.

On their day Nigeria can be a match for anyone. It would be no real surprise if they did progress from Group B, but as one of the less-fancied African teams at the 2010 finals, it would be a huge surprise if they improved on their last 16 best - but never say never.

DREAM TEAM   TOP 15 RANKING   16

THE MANAGER

Shaibu Amodu has been manager of Nigeria on three separate occasions, leading the Super Eagles through successful qualifying campaigns to reach both the 2002 and the 2010 World Cup Finals.

Despite their reputation as one of the most famous and successful African football nations, Nigeria's current side lack the quality of old and it took all of Amodu's managerial nous to guide the current squad to South Africa.

After guiding Nigeria to third place at the 2010 Africa Cup of Nations Amodu was relieved of his duties in February.

GROUP FIXTURES

ARGENTINA	Sat 12 June 1500 BST
GREECE	Thur 17 June 1500 BST
SOUTH KOREA	Tue 22 June 1930 BST

Abuja

Zone	Africa
Population	149m
Language	English
Top league	Nigerian Premier League
Playing season	August - May

Major clubs and capacities
Enyimba FC (25,000), Kano Pillars FC (25,000),
Bayelsa United FC (5,000)

Where probable squad players play:

Premier League	6	Ligue 1	2
Serie A	1	Eredivisie	1
La Liga	3	Other Europe	6
Bundesliga	1	Outside Europe	3

Number of Nigerian players playing:

Premier League	11	Bundesliga	3
Serie A	2	Ligue 1	6
La Liga	3	Eredivisie	4

World Cup record   *best performance*

1930 - Did not enter	1974 - Did not qualify
1934 - Did not enter	1978 - Did not qualify
1938 - Did not enter	1982 - Did not qualify
1950 - Did not enter	1986 - Did not qualify
1954 - Did not enter	1990 - Did not qualify
1958 - Did not enter	1994 - * Last 16
1962 - Did not qualify	1998 - * Last 16
1966 - Withdrew	2002 - Round 1
1970 - Did not qualify	2006 - Did not qualify

KEY PLAYER

JOHN OBI MIKEL CHELSEA

**One of the young stars of African
football, John Obi Mikel has become a
vital member of the Nigeria team.**

With a solid defensive game and an
impressive passing range that rarely gets
seen at Chelsea, Mikel's contribution could
be key in both defence and attack. If Mikel
is in good form for his nation then they
might very well make the latter stages.

Playing record	12 months lge	wcq
Appearances:	30	7
Minutes played:	2145	541
Percentage played:	61.1%	50.1%
Goals scored:	0	0
Clean sheets:	16	5
Cards:	Y4, R0	Y1, R0
Strike rate:	-	-
Midfielder ranking:	159th	114th

AGE 23   **MIDFIELDER**   **DREAM TEAM RANKING 277**

THE SQUAD

Goalkeepers	Club side	Age	QG
Dele Aiyenugba	Bnei Yehuda	26	2
Vincent Enyeama	Hapoel Tel-Aviv	27	10
Defenders			
Olubayo Adefemi	Boulogne	24	2
Dele Adeleye	S Rotterdam	21	3
Obinna Nwaneri	Sion	28	8
Chidi Odiah	CSKA Moscow	26	5
Daniel Olusola Shittu	Bolton	29	4
Taye Ismaila Taiwo	Marseille	25	9
Joseph Yobo	Everton	29	9
Midfielders			
Yussuf Atanda Ayila	Dinamo Kiev	25	7
Elderson Uwa Echiejile	Rennes	22	3
Sani Kaita	Kuban Krasnodar	24	2
Yusuf Mohamed	Sion	26	4
John Obi Mikel	Chelsea	23	7
Chinedu Obasi	TSG Hoffenheim	24	2
Christian Obodo	Udinese	26	2
Oluwaseyi Olofinjana	Hull City	29	9
Forwards			
Yakubu Aiyegbeni	Everton	27	8
Michael Eneramo	Sportive de Tunis	24	5
Nwankwo Kanu	Portsmouth	33	6
Obafemi Martins	Wolfsburg	25	3
Victor Nsofor Obinna	Malaga	23	9
Peter Odemwingie	Lokomotiv Moscow	28	10
Ikechukwu Uche	Real Zaragoza	26	10
Kalu Uche	Almeria	27	9
John Utaka	Portsmouth	28	4

■ Probable ■ Possible **QG** Qualification Games

ROUTE TO THE FINALS

South Korea qualified for their seventh consecutive World Cup with ease, topping both qualification groups, going unbeaten in all 14 games and conceding just seven goals in the process.

The Red Devils were twice held by neighbours and fellow qualifiers North Korea in the third stage of Asian qualifying, but still managed to top the group on goal difference to go into the final group stage of AFC qualifying as joint top seeds.

Once again, South Korea were drawn alongside their Korean neighbours, but after a draw away from home, a 1-0 win in Seoul put Huh Jung-Moo's side in the driving seat to top Group B. Inspired by midfielder Ji-Sung Park, Korea finished top with four points to spare.

FINAL QUALIFYING TABLE
ASIA ROUND 4 GROUP 2

	P	W	D	L	F	A	Pts
Korea Republic	8	4	4	0	12	4	16
Korea DPR	8	3	3	2	7	5	12
Saudi Arabia	8	3	3	2	8	8	12
Iran	8	2	5	1	8	7	11
UA Emirates	8	0	1	7	6	17	1

	Date	Venue	Opponent	Avge FIFA ranking	Result		Scorers
1	06 Feb 08	Home	Turkmenistan	152	W	**4 0**	TH Kwak 43, Seol 57, 85, Ji-Sung Park 70
2	26 Mar 08	Away	Korea DPR	105	D	**0 0**	
3	31 May 08	Home	Jordan	120	D	**2 2**	Ji-Sung Park 39, CY Park 48
4	07 Jun 08	Away	Jordan	120	W	**0 1**	CY Park 24pen
5	14 Jun 08	Away	Turkmenistan	152	W	**1 3**	Do-Heon Kim 14, 81, 90pen
6	22 Jun 08	Home	Korea DPR	105	D	**0 0**	
7	10 Sep 08	Away	Korea DPR	105	D	**1 1**	Ki 69
8	15 Oct 08	Home	United Arab Emirates	113	W	**4 1**	TH Kwak 16, Keun-Ho Lee 20, 80, Ji-Sung Park 26
9	19 Nov 08	Away	Saudi Arabia	55	W	**0 2**	Keun-Ho Lee 77, CY Park 90
10	11 Feb 09	Away	Iran	50	D	**1 1**	Ji-Sung Park 81
11	01 Apr 09	Home	Korea DPR	105	W	**1 0**	CW Kim 86
12	06 Jun 09	Away	United Arab Emirates	113	W	**0 2**	CY Park 9, Ki 37
13	10 Jun 09	Home	Saudi Arabia	55	D	**0 0**	
14	17 Jun 09	Home	Iran	50	D	**1 1**	

Average FIFA ranking of opposition	100

MAIN PLAYER PERFORMANCES IN QUALIFICATION

Match	1 2 3 4 5 6 7 8 9 10 11 12 13 14	Appearances	Started	Subbed on	Subbed off	Mins played	% played	Goals	Yellow	Red
Venue	H A H A A H A H A A H A H H									
Result	W D D W W D D W W D W W D D									
Goalkeepers										
Sung-Ryong Jung		7	7	0	0	630	50.0	0	1	0
Woon-Jae Lee		6	6	0	0	540	42.9	0	0	0
Defenders										
Won-Hee Cho		10	6	4	1	592	47.0	0	1	0
Yong-Hyung Cho		10	8	2	1	774	61.4	0	3	0
Min-Soo Kang		9	9	0	0	810	64.3	0	1	0
Chi-Woo Kim		4	3	1	0	284	22.5	1	0	0
Dong-Jin Kim		7	4	3	1	424	33.7	0	1	0
Hee Ju Kwak		2	2	0	0	180	14.3	0	0	0
Young-Pyo Lee		10	9	1	4	723	57.4	0	2	0
Beom-Seok Oh		11	11	0	2	916	72.7	0	2	0
Midfielders										
Hyo-Jin Choi		3	1	2	0	147	11.7	0	0	0
Do-Heon Kim		6	3	3	0	430	34.1	3	0	0
Jung-Woo Kim		6	6	0	1	478	37.9	0	3	1
Nam-Il Kim		7	6	1	3	467	37.1	0	2	0
Chung Yong Lee		10	9	1	4	703	55.8	0	0	0
Jung Soo Lee		9	6	3	0	663	52.6	0	0	0
Keun-Ho Lee		10	9	1	7	735	58.3	3	0	0
Ji-Sung Park		11	11	0	1	982	77.9	4	2	0
Ki-Hun Yeom		4	1	3	1	128	10.2	0	0	0
Forwards										
Jung-Hwan Ahn		3	2	1	2	155	12.3	0	1	0
Jae-Jin Cho		2	2	0	2	104	8.3	0	0	0
Sung Hoon Jung		3	3	0	2	202	16.0	0	0	0
Sung-Yong Ki		8	8	0	2	693	55.0	2	2	0
Tae Hee Kwak		2	2	0	0	180	14.3	2	0	0
Chu Young Park		12	9	3	2	839	66.6	4	1	0
Ki-Hyeon Seol		4	4	0	2	305	24.2	2	0	0

FINAL PROSPECTS

Asia's most frequent representatives at the World Cup, South Korea shocked the footballing world when they beat Portugal, Italy and Spain en-route to the semi-finals and a fourth-place finish as hosts in 2002.

That performance was far and away South Korea and Asia's best at any World Cup. The Red Devils had failed to win a single game at any of their five previous tournaments. It is unlikely that they will come close to repeating that feat in South Africa. Led by Manchester United midfielder Ji-sung Park, Huh Jung-Moo's side are a well-drilled outfit, who are extremely hard to break down and concede very few goals as a result.

However, they lack the striking firepower that saw off those European 'giants' of eight years ago, which is likely to prove their undoing in South Africa. Drawn alongside Argentina, Nigeria and Greece, South Korea still certainly have a chance of progressing.

All three of their group opponents are not at all at their best going into the tournament. Even if they do make the last 16 it is unlikely that they will repeat their feats of 2002, despite having a good squad, they will be outclassed in the latter stages.

DREAM TEAM	TOP 15 RANKING	30

THE MANAGER

South Korean's head coach since 2007, Huh Jung-Moo has been involved in the national set-up on-and-off since 1989.

A full international in his playing days, Jung-Moo scored the goal that sent South Korea to the 1986 World Cup and trumped that by scoring again at the finals, against Italy.

He oversaw a comfortable qualification campaign as manager, picking up the Asian Coach of the Year award for 2009 in the process. Although his negative tactics are unpopular with the fans, he does get the most out of a squad that doesn't have a great deal of creative quality.

GROUP FIXTURES

GREECE	Sat 12 June 1230 BST
ARGENTINA	Thur 17 June 1230 BST
NIGERIA	Tue 22 June 1930 BST

KEY PLAYER

JI-SUNG PARK MAN UTD

Ji-Sung Park first made a splash in South Korea's outstanding run back in 2002, where he scored the winner against Portugal to secure a place in the knock out stages.

Hard-working, yet creative and with an eye for goal, Park's all-round game makes him the turn-to man for South Korea. He will be pivotal for the Red Devils..

Playing record	12 months lge	wcq
Appearances:	20	11
Minutes played:	1268	982
Percentage played:	34.4%	77.9%
Goals scored:	1	4
Clean sheets:	12	8
Cards:	Y3, R0	Y2, R0
Strike rate:	268mins	245mins
Midfielder ranking:	33rd	18th

AGE 29   **MIDFIELDER**   **DREAM TEAM RANKING 1109**

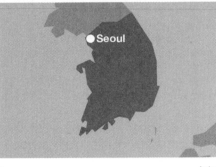

●Seoul

Zone	Asia
Population	49m
Language	Korean
Top league	K League
Playing season	March - November

Major clubs and capacities
FC Seoul (68,476), Suwon Bluewings (43,288), Seongnam Ilhwa Chunma (19,000), Incheon United FC (19,000), Jeonbuk Hyundai Motors (43,348)

Where probable squad players play:

Premier League	3	Ligue 1	1
Serie A	-	Eredivisie	-
La Liga	-	Other Europe	2
Bundesliga	-	Outside Europe	17

Number of South Korean players playing:

Premier League	4	Bundesliga	1
Serie A	-	Ligue 1	2
La Liga	-	Eredivisie	-

World Cup record   * best performance

1930 - Did not enter	1974 -	Did not qualify
1934 - Did not enter	1978 -	Did not qualify
1938 - Did not enter	1982 -	Did not qualify
1950 - Did not enter	1986 -	Round 1
1954 - Round 1	1990 -	Round 1
1958 - Banned from Fifa	1994 -	Round 1
1962 - Did not qualify	1998 -	Round 1
1966 - Did not enter	2002 -	*4th Place
1970 - Did not qualify	2006 -	Round 1

THE SQUAD

Goalkeepers	Club side	Age	QG
Sung-Ryong Jung	Seongnam Ilhwa	25	7
Woon-Jae Lee	Suwon Bluewings	37	6
Defenders			
Won-Hee Cho	Suwon Bluewings	27	10
Yong-Hyung Cho	Jeju Utd	26	10
Min-Soo Kang	Jeju Utd	24	9
Chi-Woo Kim	FC Seoul	26	4
Dong-Jin Kim	Zenit St Petersburg	28	7
Hee Ju Kwak	Samsung Bluewings	28	2
Young-Pyo Lee	Al-Hilal	33	10
Beom-Seok Oh	Krylia Sovetov	25	11
Midfielders			
Hyo-Jin Choi	Pohang Steelers	26	3
Do-Heon Kim	Suwon Bluewings	27	6
Jung-Woo Kim	Seongnam Ilhwa	28	6
Nam-Il Kim	Vissel Kobe	33	7
Chung Yong Lee	Bolton	21	10
Jung Soo Lee	Kyoto Sanga	30	9
Keun-Ho Lee	Jubilo Iwata	25	10
Ji-Sung Park	Man Utd	29	11
Ki-Hun Yeom	Ulsan Hyundai	27	4
Forwards			
Jung-Hwan Ahn	Dalian Shide	34	3
Jae-Jin Cho	Gamba Osaka	28	2
Sung Hoon Jung	Busan I'Park	30	3
Sung-Yong Ki	FC Seoul	21	8
Tae Hee Kwak	Chunnam Dragons	28	2
Chu Young Park	AS Monaco	24	12
Ki-Hyeon Seol	Fulham	31	4

■ Probable ■ Possible **QG** Qualification Games

DREAM TEAM WORLD RANKING

This book is packed with opinion from some of the biggest and most knowledgeable names in football, but our great game isn't always about what we think is true, it can also be analysed based on facts and statistics.

In an attempt to give you some key insights into what the numbers say about the players and teams involved in the 2010 World Cup, there are some overall and positional rankings inside every player's stats panel.

Two separate sets of rankings have been devised – a series of positional rankings based on league and qualification performances and an overall DREAM TEAM RANKING which takes a whole host of factors into the equation in rating the top players in world football.

In addition to the individual rankings, we have a TOP 15 TEAM RANKING – which looks to rank teams based on the strength of their top players – in stark contrast to the FIFA rankings which are based on team results.

All of the above is explained in detail over the next two pages and should you want to see any of the latest rankings – whether team or individual – in their totality, you can find them by logging on to the Dream Team site at:

www.dreamteamfc.com/worldcup

DREAM TEAM RANKING

The Dream Team Ranking is a comprehensive index that takes into account the most important factors when assessing a player and it works as follows:

Each player gets points for every match played.

These have three parts to their composition: Domestic League activity (12 months), UEFA Champions and Europa Leagues (12 months) and International activity (over the whole qualifying period).

Within each category players get points for each game they play based upon:
— strength of the league or competition
— strength of the opposition based upon the two teams' relative rankings at the time of the fixture
— time spent on the pitch
— cautions
— goals conceded
— goals scored by the player
— goals scored by the team
— who wins the match

This index is match based and therefore values activity as well as impact, so players who play more frequently will – as you might expect – be duly rewarded.

Where a player plays in a minor league not covered in depth we make an estimate for that category.

The results thrown up are fascinating and can be found in full on the Dream Team website – read on for some of the highlights.

STRENGTH IN DEPTH

The Rankings highlight an embarrassment of riches that some teams have in certain departments.

Take Euro 2008 champions, Spain, for example. Three of the top seven ranked goalkeepers are available to play for Spain. Iker Casillas rates as one of the best 12 players in the world, while Barcelona's Victor Valdes – who unbelievably has never been capped for Spain – and Jose Reina are the sixth and seventh best keepers in the world respectively.

Compare that to England and you start to understand why the lack of a world-class keeper is often a topic for conversation in the media. Robert Green is only rated the 18th best keeper, while David James is well down the list in 60th – partly due to missing games through injury.

See **page 154** for the **top four keepers** at the World Cup.

In terms of defenders, England fair rather better, however, with two players in the top five – John Terry ranked the second best in the world, Ashley Cole the fifth. But the next best ranked are unlikely to make the plane to South Africa – Liverpool's Jamie Carragher is the 15th best at the back but has retired from international football, while left-back Leighton Baines of Everton seems to be down Fabio Capello's pecking order.

Brazil also have a strong presence, with Inter Milan's Lucio and Maicon both in the top ten.

See **page 118** for the **top 12 defenders** at the World Cup.

Spain's dominance in the rankings is highlighted in particular by one look at the top midfielders. Barcelona's central midfield hub of Xavi and Andres Iniesta are first and seventh respectively, while Real Madrid's former Liverpool man Xabi Alonso is third in the table.

As might be expected, Brazil, too, are well represented in midfield and can boast two players in the top five – Real Madrid's Kaka is ranked second best in the world and Felipe Melo of Juventus is named fifth.

See **page 84** for the **top 12 midfielders** at the World Cup.

In terms of strikers there is far more of a mix of nationalities and it will be interesting to see if some of the star names in the top ten can do enough to fire their teams deep into the competition. Cameroon's Samuel Eto'o tops the list, closely followed by the world's most expensive player, Cristiano Ronaldo who plays as a striker for Portugal. The rest of the top 12 include players from France, Argentina, Ivory Coast and Uruguay.

See **page 38** for the top **12 strikers** at the World Cup.

TOP PLAYER SECTIONS

Using an algorithm based on the criteria above, each player in world football's major leagues has been assigned a Dream Team Ranking and the top players at the World Cup in each position are named in four sections. The next four pages count down the Top 12 strikers likely to be present in South Africa.

THE DREAM TEAM WORLD RANKING IS YOUR FORM GUIDE TO THE PLAYERS IN SOUTH AFRICA

TOP 15 RANKING

In order to assess a team, not only by their results, but also by the quality of personnel at their disposal, a TOP 15 RANKING has been attributed to each country in the tournament based on the Dream Team Ranking points picked up by each of their Top 15 players.

The results are revealing and show that sometimes teams are greater than the sum of their parts.

To see the full list of rankings by position, go to **www.dreamteamfc.com/worldcup**

POSITIONAL RANKINGS

The aim of the positional rankings is to provide a snapshot of a player's league form in the last 12 months and also their form throughout the World Cup qualifying campaign.

Goalkeepers and defenders have 'Minutes between goals' in their stat panel. This – as you might expect – is the average number of minutes between goals conceded while this player is on the pitch. A figure of 90 minutes, for example, would mean that this player's team concedes – on average – a goal a game when they are playing.

In terms of what is hot and what is not, in domestic football, anything over 90mins is pretty good – anything over 105 is special...

In World Cup qualifying, however, all bets are off. There are fewer games, a bigger gap between the quality of the teams and some crazy numbers are therefore possible.

Gerrard Pique managed to average a massive 240mins between goals – a goal conceded just once every two and a half games – while for The Netherlands, Joris Mathijsen banked a mammoth 360 minutes between goals – conceding on average just one goal every four games.

The 'Goalkeeper Ranking' and 'Defender Ranking' show how good each player's 'Minutes between goals' figure is for their respective position.

All midfielders and strikers have a 'Strike Rate' which is the average number of minutes between each goal they score. To work this out, the total number of minutes played are divided by the number of goals scored.

Each player also has a ranking based on their 'Strike Rate' compared to the other players in their position.

DIDN'T MAKE IT

Some of the unluckiest players in world football, it could be argued, are those good enough to mix it on the game's biggest stage, but who will be forced to watch from the side-lines along with the rest of the world come June?

Victor Valdes has already been mentioned and is the victim of a ridiculously strong goalkeeping line-up for Spain. In defence, Arsenal's **Thomas Vermaelen** can feel aggrieved Belgium couldn't make it, while up front, Worlsburg's **Edin Dzeko** – who has been scoring for fun in the Bundesliga – will be missed after he matched Wayne Rooney by netting nine times in the qualifiers for Bosnia & Herzegovina.

To see the full list of all players in the Dream Team Rankings – not just those heading to South Africa – go to:

www.dreamteamfc.com/worldcup

12th CARLOS TEVEZ
ARGENTINA & MAN CITY

A player who fuses English determination and hard work with South American flair, Carlos Tevez plays with a smile on his face and dynamite in both feet.

Surrounded by controversy following his move to West Ham and subsequent spat with Manchester United, Tevez has got back to his best playing for Manchester City. He hasn't been in the best goal-scoring form for Argentina in recent times but is definitely going to be a big part of the Argentinian set-up if they are to make it far in South Africa.

Playing record	12 mths lge	wcq
Appearances:	35	12
Minutes played:	2621	726
Percentage played:	72.8%	44.8%
Goals scored:	15	1
Percentage share:	24.19%	4.35%
Cards:	Y4, R0	Y2, R2
Strike rate:	175mins	726mins
Strike rate ranking:	36th	82nd

AGE 26 | **DREAM TEAM** | **RANKING 67**

11th LUIS FABIANO
BRAZIL & SEVILLA

A hungry centre-forward in great form, Luis Fabiano has been Brazil's first choice striker for the last year and his pace, strength and finishing ability make him the ideal focal point for Brazil's attacking ambitions.

After a three-year spell in the international wilderness, he returned in 2007 top-scoring for Brazil in qualifying and also in the 2009 Confederations Cup. As the man expected to deliver the firepower for the tournament favourites, Fabiano will be in the spotlight, but don't be too surprised if he rises to the occasion.

Playing record	12 mths lge	wcq
Appearances:	24	11
Minutes played:	1746	801
Percentage played:	51.1%	49.4%
Goals scored:	13	9
Percentage share:	22.4%	27.3%
Cards:	Y9, R0	Y4, R1
Strike rate:	134mins	89mins
Strike rate ranking:	17th	8th

AGE 29 | **DREAM TEAM** | **RANKING 58**

10th ALBERTO GILARDINO
ITALY & FIORENTINA

A clinical striker with an excellent goal return – both internationally and in Serie A – Alberto Gilardino has yet to set the world alight for the Azzurri but has the chance to do just that in South Africa.

In and out of the starting line-up in the qualifiers, Gilardino still managed to top score for Italy thanks to his good all-round game and ruthless eye for goal. With the options up front somewhat limited for Marcello Lippi, Gilardino may get an opportunity and if he can fire his way into the side, this could be his tournament.

Playing record	12 mths lge	wcq
Appearances:	37	6
Minutes played:	3190	414
Percentage played:	88.6%	46.0%
Goals scored:	16	4
Percentage share:	31.4%	22.2%
Cards:	Y4, R0	Y0, R0
Strike rate:	199mins	103mins
Strike rate ranking:	54th	9th

AGE 27 | **DREAM TEAM** | **RANKING 49**

9th DIEGO FORLAN
URUGUAY & ATL MADRID

There is no surprise that Diego Forlan is a Top 12 Striker – he has twice in the last six seasons scored more goals than any other striker in European football to earn himself the 'Golden Shoe'.

A naturally gifted all-round footballer, Forlan has added cutting edge to the ability he always possessed. While Uruguay are not going to win the tournament in South Africa, he can earn his country some glory in what could be his last World Cup and maybe land himself another chance with one of the biggest clubs in Europe.

Playing record	12 mths lge	wcq
Appearances:	36	13
Minutes played:	3142	1105
Percentage played:	91.9%	61.4%
Goals scored:	28	7
Percentage share:	43.1%	23.3%
Cards:	Y3, R0	Y2, R0
Strike rate:	112mins	158mins
Strike rate ranking:	9th	25th

AGE 31 | **DREAM TEAM** | **RANKING 35**

8th DAVID VILLA
SPAIN & VALENCIA

A predatory finisher of the highest order, David Villa scores goals at an incredible rate and has been one of the most prolific strikers in European football for half a decade.

A key part of Spain's success in the last few years, Villa fired himself to the Golden Boot at Euro 2008 and was Spain's top-scorer in their qualifying campaign. If the European Champions make it as far as expected in South Africa, then he will surely have played a major part in getting them there.

Playing record	12 mths lge	wcq
Appearances:	32	7
Minutes played:	2762	550
Percentage played:	80.8%	61.1%
Goals scored:	28	7
Percentage share:	42.4%	25.0%
Cards:	Y6, R1	Y0, R0
Strike rate:	99mins	79mins
Strike rate ranking:	4th	6th

AGE 28 **DREAM TEAM RANKING 25**

7th DIDIER DROGBA
IVORY COAST & CHELSEA

A centre-forward who on his day is simply unplayable, Didier Drogba is unorthodox, extremely athletic and capable of scoring and creating goals in abundance.

A big physical specimen, Drogba is also quick on his feet and comfortable on the ball. He might not be the most natural finisher in the game and is prone to going down dramatically, but he can score from anywhere. He was the top-scorer in qualifying and will be vital to the Ivorians' chances of progressing from arguably the toughest group in South Africa.

Playing record	12 mths lge	wcq
Appearances:	33	5
Minutes played:	2703	366
Percentage played:	79.0%	33.9%
Goals scored:	18	6
Percentage share:	24.7%	23.1%
Cards:	Y5, R0	Y0, R0
Strike rate:	150mins	61mins
Strike rate ranking:	26th	1st

AGE 32 **DREAM TEAM RANKING 23**

6th WAYNE ROONEY
ENGLAND & MANCHESTER UNITED

A whirlwind on the field and a creative talisman for England, Wayne Rooney will be hoping to add to his sack of domestic and European silverware in South Africa.

He was in superb form in the qualifiers, scoring nine goals in nine games as England strolled to the finals – only one player managed more in Europe. With outstanding vision and awareness, Rooney is the attacking hub of Fabio Capello's side and if he finds his rhythm and eye for goal, do not bet against the Manchester United star firing England a long way into this tournament.

Playing record	12 mths lge	wcq
Appearances:	33	9
Minutes played:	2639	757
Percentage played:	73.3%	84.1%
Goals scored:	22	9
Percentage share:	26.2%	26.5%
Cards:	Y7, R1	Y0, R0
Strike rate:	120mins	84mins
Strike rate ranking:	12th	7th

AGE 24 **DREAM TEAM RANKING 16**

5th LIONEL MESSI
ARGENTINA & BARCELONA

Destined, perhaps, to be considered one of the all-time greats of football, it is easy to forget that Lionel Messi has his best years ahead of him and will celebrate his 23rd birthday during the 2010 World Cup.

A prodigious talent with superb skill, pace and finishing ability, Messi has become the pre-eminent forward in world football and as well as the medals picked up with Barca, was named World Player of the Year in 2009. He played more minutes than any other Argentina player in qualifying and will be key to any success.

Playing record	12 mths lge	wcq
Appearances:	30	18
Minutes played:	2324	1604
Percentage played:	68.0%	99.0%
Goals scored:	22	4
Percentage share:	23.4%	17.4%
Cards:	Y1, R0	Y1, R0
Strike rate:	106mins	401mins
Strike rate ranking:	6th	70th

AGE 22 **DREAM TEAM RANKING 15**

4th

NICOLAS ANELKA

FRANCE & CHELSEA

Formerly the 'enfant terrible' of French football, Nicolas Anelka – having made his debut in 12 years ago – has finally settled into a steady role for Les Bleus, having found some stability in his career wearing the blue of Chelsea.

A quick, technically gifted striker with a real eye for goal, Anelka has scored goals consistently throughout his long career, but is now playing at a level for Chelsea that suggests he can make real impact for his country in South Africa up front alongside Thierry Henry.

Playing record	12 mths lge	wcq
Appearances:	33	8
Minutes played:	2674	626
Percentage played:	78.2%	56.4%
Goals scored:	10	3
Percentage share:	13.7%	15.0%
Cards:	Y0, R0	Y0, R0
Strike rate:	267mins	209mins
Strike rate ranking:	85th	41st

AGE 31	DREAM TEAM	RANKING 14

3rd

FERNANDO TORRES

SPAIN & LIVERPOOL

Often referred to as the best centre-forward in the world, Fernando Torres combines physical presence and appetite for a tussle with sublime skill and finishing ability.

Having cut his cloth with Atletico Madrid, Torres made a big money switch to Liverpool and did not disappoint, bagging 33 goals in his first season. He has been effective for Spain, too, scoring the only goal and being named man-of-the-match in the final of the European Championships in 2008 v Germany.

Playing record	12 mths lge	wcq
Appearances:	30	7
Minutes played:	2313	451
Percentage played:	67.6%	50.1%
Goals scored:	21	0
Percentage share:	26.6%	0%
Cards:	Y2, R0	Y0, R0
Strike rate:	110mins	-
Strike rate ranking:	7th	-

AGE 26	DREAM TEAM	RANKING 13

2nd

CRISTIANO RONALDO

PORTUGAL & REAL MADRID

A supremely gifted footballer and the most expensive player in history, Cristiano Ronaldo brings flair, drama and no small amount of ego to the World Cup, but Portugal will need all of his majestic talents to get out of a tough group that includes Brazil and the Ivory Coast.

His ability to run at players with the ball at pace is unparalleled in world football; add in his ability to score and create goals from open play and set-pieces and you get a player who could set the tournament alight.

Playing record	12 mths lge	wcq
Appearances:	27	7
Minutes played:	2216	565
Percentage played:	64.8%	52.3%
Goals scored:	17	0
Percentage share:	22.4%	0%
Cards:	Y5, R0	Y0, R0
Strike rate:	130mins	-
Strike rate ranking:	7th	-

AGE 25	DREAM TEAM	RANKING 4

THE TOP STRIKER

CAMEROON SAMUEL ETO'O

A prolific goal-scorer at the highest level for almost a decade, Samuel Eto'o is still one of the deadliest finishers in world football and has the ability to fire Cameroon through Group E.

Always passionate and often controversial, Eto'o left Barcelona with a sack of medals to join Inter Milan of Italy – and if he can inspire Cameroon past Japan and Denmark, it could well be Italy who lie in wait in the last 16.

Playing record	12 mths lge	wcq
Appearances:	37	11
Minutes played:	3072	967
Percentage played:	87.5%	89.5%
Goals scored:	23	9
Percentage share:	30.3%	39.1%
Cards:	Y4, R0	Y2, R0
Strike rate:	134mins	107mins
Strike rate ranking:	16th	12th

| AGE 29 | INTER MILAN | DREAM TEAM | RANKING 3 |

1st

Position	1st	2nd	3rd	4th	5th	6th	7th	8th
Group	E	D	B	H	A	G	C	F
Total FIFA ranking	88	89	98	104	130	147	160	161

ENGLAND V USA
Rustenburg, Saturday 12 June 1930 BST

Eagerly anticipated, this could be the key game in the group – if either side snatch a win they will fancy their chances of topping the pile, but a draw could mean Group C is wide open. This will be the first time the two sides have met at a World Cup finals since the USA's famous shock 1-0 victory in 1950 and while a repeat result would not be as surprising as it was 60 years ago, it would certainly be an upset.

England were magnificent in qualifying, while the USA have struggled since their Confederation Cup heroics. Bob Bradley's side are very well organised and they will hope to keep it tight and frustrate Fabio Capello's side with Everton goalkeeper Tim Howard a key figure. The longer it stays goalless the more the USA will fancy their chances but expect England to have a little too much quality.

ALGERIA V SLOVENIA
Polokwane, Sunday 13 June 1230 BST

Both sides will consider this as the ideal opener – the most winnable game of the group and an early chance to secure three points, in a relatively low-key fixture. The wider public will know little about either side but it does have the capacity to be a decent game of football – especially as both sides will be pushing for the win as their best chance of making it into the

last 16. Slovenia will start favourites and have certainly attained the more impressive results in the past 18 months – especially the way they played against Russia in the play-off game. Algeria have already played in one tournament in Africa this year – the Africa Cup of Nations – where their results were decidedly mixed. Any result is possible.

USA's Clint Dempsey

SLOVENIA V USA
Jo'burg JEP, Friday 18 June 1500 BST

Slovenia will be underdogs in this game – which tends to be the way that they like it – and the USA will know exactly what they need to do to reach the last 16. If they dropped points against England, a win is vital here and Bradley might have to ditch his usually conservative tactics and go for goals in this game. Whereas the defence were the key against England, the forward line will need to be in top form and two players capable of delivering goals are Landon Donovan and Clint Dempsey.

ENGLAND V ALGERIA
Cape Town, Friday 18 June 1930 BST

A must win game for England who, presuming they picked up at least a point against the USA, will not want to face Slovenia knowing that only a win will do if they are to progress further in the tournament. These two sides have never met in international football before and while

England will certainly not underestimate the North African side, they will be confident. Splitting the Desert Foxes' defence will therefore be key for Fabio Capello's side and expect Wayne Rooney to be the man looking to breach Algeria's back line.

SLOVENIA V ENGLAND
P Elizabeth, Wednesday 23 June 1500 BST

These two sides have only met once before and the 2-1 win for England in September 2009 was every bit as close as the scoreline suggests. True, the game was a friendly and England have been notoriously sloppy in non-competitive international fixtures for a long time, but Slovenia are not the same side when fighting tooth and nail either and they caused

significant problems for Fabio Capello's team. The Italian will be wily enough to have analysed the match and know exactly where the game will be won and lost but confidence could play a big factor and if England come into this game with four points or more, expect a decisive victory; but if England have stuttered against the USA and Algeria, it could be a tight game.

USA V ALGERIA
Pretoria, Wednesday 23 June 1500 BST

Chances are that one of these teams will need a victory to secure their participation in the last 16, so it could be a very open game. Algeria have never faced the USA in international

football before so there is no history to trade on but this game does pit two solid defensive units against each other so it will be a battle of the creative players.

VIEW FROM THE EXPERTS

ENGLAND: My choice for the winners of the whole shebang. We have the players and manager, even the weather in a South African winter will suit us. It's the best chance we'll ever have. Going all the way with the Three Lions.
HARRY'S VERDICT: Champions.

USA: Dangerous opponents and many have been unwise to write them off so easily following the draw. The Yanks don't stop working and will be super-fit.
HARRY'S VERDICT: Last 16.

ALGERIA: Saw their first game at the Africa Cup of Nations and wasn't impressed. Nadir Belhadj sprinkles a little stardust over the squad but put it this way he wouldn't get in the England team.
HARRY'S VERDICT: Group stage.

SLOVENIA: You only have to look at their run to the finals to see how dangerous this team will be. Poland, the Czechs and then Russia all knocked out in qualifying. They are no walkover and could be another team in the chase for the second place behind England.
HARRY'S VERDICT: Group stage only.

ENGLAND: I know we say it before every major tournament, but England have a real chance. Let's not get carried away, they are not as talented as maybe Brazil or Spain but with a bit of momentum and a couple of smiles from Lady Luck, who knows? We just need to pray that our top players steer clear of significant injuries.
TEL'S VERDICT: Semis at least.

USA: England's hardest opponents in the group. A great number of their players ply their trade in the Premier League. Ranked in FIFA's top 20, having finished top of the CONCACAF and lost to Brazil in last year's Confederations Cup final, Bob Bradley's side are no mugs.
TEL'S VERDICT: Amercian express to second stage...at least.

ALGERIA: The Desert Foxes are appearing at their first World Cup for 24 years, but are not your archetypal African side. They play a very European way and have gifted players in the form of Portsmouth's Nadir Belhadj and Lazio midfielder Mourad Meghni. They should not cause England too many problems.
TEL'S VERDICT: Will struggle to get past group.

SLOVENIA: Pulled off something of a shock by beating Russia in a play-off to book their place in South Africa, but I cannot see them shocking England. Fabio Capello's men beat them 2-1 in a friendly at Wembley in September. Well-organised and hard to break down, Matjaz Kek's men lack a little bit of quality.

TEL'S VERDICT: Nothing to fear.

ENGLAND: Capello has done a fantastic job getting us to South Africa, but as the finals approach I am getting more nervous about our chances. The potential routes through the tournament are not as cut and dried as some make out. We need to start well to build some momentum.

WRIGHTY'S VERDICT: Come on England!

USA: I played for England when the Americans beat us 2-0 in Boston in 1993. The game led to The Sun's famous back page headline: Yanks 2 Planks 0. Football in America has come a long way since then, but one thing has not changed: they still want to beat England. Bradley's squad contains a number of Premier League players to give the match against the Three Lions a bit of a derby feel.

WRIGHTY'S VERDICT: Not to be taken lightly.

ALGERIA: Did well at the African Nations Cup where they beat the much-fancied Ivory Coast 3-2 on the way to the semi-finals. With Pompey's Belhadj and Lazio midfielder Meghni in their ranks, it is maybe not surprising their play has been likened to that of a European nation. Hopefully that will suit England.

WRIGHTY'S VERDICT: Could spring the odd surprise.

SLOVENIA: Making their second appearance at the finals after winning their play-off against Russia on the away goals rule. They are more than capable of grinding out results in high-pressure situations. But realistically they should not pose too many problems.

WRIGHTY'S VERDICT: Very much run of the mill.

"It's the best chance we'll ever have. Going all the way with the Three Lions."

THE LIKELY ROUTES FOR THE TOP TWO TEAMS FROM THE GROUP

For the full draw please see page 80

GROUP STAGE	LAST SIXTEEN	QUARTER-FINALS
FIRST GROUP C	v SECOND GROUP D	v FIRST GROUP A or SECOND GROUP B
ENGLAND	ENGLAND v AUSTRALIA	ENGLAND v FRANCE
SECOND GROUP C	v FIRST GROUP D	v FIRST GROUP B or SECOND GROUP A
USA	USA v SERBIA	SERBIA v ARGENTINA

GROUP C
ENGLAND, USA, ALGERIA, SLOVENIA

GROUP D
GERMANY, AUSTRALIA, SERBIA, GHANA

GROUP A
SOUTH AFRICA, MEXICO, URUGUAY, FRANCE
GROUP B
ARGENTINA, NIGERIA, SOUTH KOREA (KOREAN REPUBLIC), GREECE

ROUTE TO THE FINALS

Fabio Capello not only guided England to one of the smoothest qualifying campaigns they have known in a long time, he also helped exorcise some of the ghosts accumulated during their ill-fated bid to make Euro 2008 by not just beating, but thrashing Croatia - the side that knocked them out in qualifying.

Comprehensive doesn't quite describe the 4-1 away win and 5-1 home victory over Slavan Bilic's team and with similar results home and away against Kazakhstan, Andorra and Belarus; it was no surprise that England topped the goalscoring chart in the European Zone. Usual suspects Steve Gerrard and Frank Lampard contributed from midfield with three and four goals respectively and up front, despite featuring sparingly, Peter Crouch with four goals and Jermain Defoe with three, both played their part but it was Wayne Rooney who stole the show with nine goals in as many games.

FINAL QUALIFYING TABLE
EUROPE GROUP 6

	P	W	D	L	F	A	Pts
England	10	9	0	1	34	6	27
Ukraine	10	6	3	1	21	6	21
Croatia	10	6	2	2	19	13	20
Belarus	10	4	1	5	19	14	13
Kazakhstan	10	2	0	8	11	29	6
Andorra	10	0	0	10	3	39	0

				Avge FIFA ranking			
1	06 Sep 08	Away	Andorra	192	W	**0 2**	J.Cole 49, 55
2	10 Sep 08	Away	Croatia	8	W	**1 4**	Walcott 26, 59, 82, Rooney 63
3	11 Oct 08	Home	Kazakhstan	130	W	**5 1**	Ferdinand 52, Kuchma 64og, Rooney 76, 85, Defoe 90
4	15 Oct 08	Away	Belarus	72	W	**1 3**	Gerrard 11, Rooney 50, 75
5	01 Apr 09	Home	Ukraine	22	W	**2 1**	Crouch 29, Terry 85
6	06 Jun 09	Away	Kazakhstan	130	W	**0 4**	Barry 39, Heskey 45, Rooney 73, Lampard 77pen
7	10 Jun 09	Home	Andorra	192	W	**6 0**	Rooney 4, 39, Lampard 29, Defoe 73, 75, Crouch 80
8	09 Sep 09	Home	Croatia	8	W	**5 1**	Lampard 7pen, 59, Gerrard 18, 66, Rooney 77
9	10 Oct 09	Away	Ukraine	22	L	**1 0**	
10	14 Oct 09	Home	Belarus	72	W	**3 0**	Crouch 4, 75, Wright-Phillips 60

Average FIFA ranking of opposition	85

MAIN PLAYER PERFORMANCES IN QUALIFICATION

Key: ■ played 90 mins ◀◀ subbed off ▶ subbed on ▦ on bench

Match	1 2 3 4 5 6 7 8 9 10	Appearances	Started	Subbed on	Subbed off	Mins played	% played	Goals	Yellow	Red
Venue	A A H A H A H H A H									
Result	W W W W W W W W L W									
Goalkeepers										
Ben Foster		1	1	0	0	90	10.0	0	0	0
Robert Green		4	4	0	0	283	31.4	0	0	1
David James		6	5	1	0	526	58.4	0	0	0
Defenders										
Wayne Bridge		3	2	1	1	194	21.6	0	0	0
Wes Brown		3	3	0	0	270	30.0	0	0	0
Ashley Cole		8	8	0	1	693	77.0	0	0	0
Rio Ferdinand		6	6	0	1	537	59.7	1	0	0
Philip Jagielka		1	0	1	0	3	0.3	0	0	0
Glen Johnson		7	7	0	1	615	68.3	0	1	0
Joleon Lescott		2	2	0	0	180	20.0	0	0	0
John Terry		8	8	0	1	718	79.8	1	1	0
Matthew Upson		5	4	1	0	362	40.2	0	0	0
Midfielders										
Gareth Barry		8	8	0	1	675	75.0	1	2	0
David Beckham		9	1	8	0	214	23.8	0	1	0
Michael Carrick		1	1	0	0	90	10.0	0	0	0
Joe Cole		2	1	1	1	99	11.0	2	0	0
Stewart Downing		1	1	0	1	45	5.0	0	0	0
Steven Gerrard		7	7	0	4	530	58.9	3	0	0
Jermaine Jenas		1	0	1	0	36	4.0	0	0	0
Frank Lampard		10	10	0	1	889	98.8	4	0	0
Aaron Lennon		4	0	4	0	207	23.0	0	0	0
James Milner		3	0	3	0	68	7.6	0	0	0
Theo Walcott		6	6	0	4	454	50.4	3	0	0
Shaun Wright-Phillips		5	1	4	0	215	23.9	1	0	0
Forwards										
Gabriel Agbonlahor		1	1	0	1	65	7.2	0	0	0
Carlton Cole		2	0	2	0	44	4.9	0	0	0
Peter Crouch		4	3	1	1	279	31.0	4	0	0
Jermain Defoe		5	1	4	0	136	15.1	3	0	0
Emile Heskey		7	6	1	4	504	56.0	1	1	0
Wayne Rooney		9	9	0	3	757	84.1	9	0	0
Ashley Young		1	0	1	0	45	5.0	0	0	0

FINAL PROSPECTS

Whisper it quietly, but there is a genuine swell of feeling from the serious pundits as well as the casual fans, that this England side - under the stewardship of Fabio Capello - can make a real impact in South Africa and should, perhaps, be considered serious contenders for the title.

OK, so we have been here before and England's chances are always hyped up but there is something genuinely different about things this time around - and not just the impressive style in which they qualified, sweeping away Croatia and Ukraine and topping the 'goals for' column in the European Zone in the process.

With talent in abundance in midfield and Capello having found the right mix to get the most out of Steven Gerrard and Frank Lampard, the key areas for England will be up front and at the back.

Up front, it is all about Wayne Rooney. He has been banging in the goals this season

At the back, a fit and in-form Rio Ferdinand and John Terry playing together in central defence will be very important. The two have formed a good understanding over the years and their presence would make up for England's lack of a truly world class keeper.

Up front, it is all about Wayne Rooney. He has been banging in the goals this season but with Rooney you always get so much more, with his vision and ability to split the defence a huge asset - especially with the goalscoring potential that England possess in midfield.

When the draw for this tournament was announced, the media almost universally proclaimed it a dream group and while England could certainly have done worse, the USA can never be underestimated, Slovenia gave England a good game in a friendly in 2009 and Algeria made it to the semi-finals of the Africa Cup of Nations, beating the Ivory Coast along the way.

Saying all that, though, England should make it through the group without having to hit the high gears and would probably face Serbia or Germany in the last 16 followed by France or Argentina in the quarters.

One of the best things about this side, however, is the fact they look more of a unit than any England squad in a long time and much of this is down to Capello and his regime.

DREAM TEAM	TOP 15 RANKING	3

GROUP FIXTURES

USA	Sat 12 June 1930 BST
ALGERIA	Fri 18 June 1930 BST
SLOVENIA	Wed 23 June 1500 BST

London

Zone	Europe
Population	51m
Language	English
Top league	The Premier League
Playing season	August - May

Major clubs and capacities
Manchester United (76,212), Chelsea (41,181),
Arsenal (60,355), Liverpool (45,276)

Where probable squad players play:

Premier League	22	Ligue 1	-
Serie A	1	Eredivisie	-
La Liga	-	Other Europe	-
Bundesliga	-	Outside Europe	-

Number of English players playing:

Premier League	260	Bundesliga	-
Serie A	1	Ligue 1	-
La Liga	1	Eredivisie	-

World Cup record   *** best performance**

1930 - Did not enter	1974 - Did not qualify
1934 - Did not enter	1978 - Did not qualify
1938 - Did not enter	1982 - Round 2
1950 - Round 1	1986 - Quarter finals
1954 - Quarter finals	1990 - Fourth place
1958 - Round 1	1994 - Did not qualify
1962 - Quarter finals	1998 - Round of 16
1966 - * Champions	2002 - Quarter finals
1970 - Quarter finals	2006 - Quarter finals

KEY PLAYER

WAYNE ROONEY MAN UTD

Although the departure of Cristiano Ronaldo to Real Madrid may have been to the detriment of Manchester United, and perhaps the Premier League, it might end up being to the benefit of England.

With the Portuguese hogging the limelight and scoring most of the goals, Rooney was often dropping deep to find the ball and get involved in the action. But with Ronaldo's departure, Rooney is being deployed as an out-and-out striker and asked to weigh-in with more goals - and he has duly delivered for United. He has also been in cracking form for England, being the second highest in Europe with nine goals in nine qualifying games.

Rooney is a Top 12 Striker

AGE 24   **STRIKER**   **DREAM TEAM**   **RANKING** 16

THE SQUAD

Goalkeepers	Club side	Age	QG
Paul Robinson	Blackburn	30	0
Ben Foster	Man Utd	27	1
Robert Green	West Ham	30	4
David James	Portsmouth	39	6
Joe Hart	Birmingham	23	0
Defenders			
Wayne Bridge	Man City	29	3
Wes Brown	Man Utd	30	3
Ashley Cole	Chelsea	29	8
Rio Ferdinand	Man Utd	31	6
Glen Johnson	Liverpool	25	7
John Terry	Chelsea	29	8
Matthew Upson	West Ham	31	5
Midfielders			
Gareth Barry	Man City	29	8
David Beckham	AC Milan	35	9
Michael Carrick	Man Utd	28	1
Joe Cole	Chelsea	28	2
Steven Gerrard	Liverpool	30	7
Frank Lampard	Chelsea	31	10
Aaron Lennon	Tottenham	23	4
James Milner	Aston Villa	24	3
Theo Walcott	Arsenal	21	6
Shaun Wright-Phillips	Man City	28	5
Forwards			
Carlton Cole	West Ham	26	2
Peter Crouch	Tottenham	29	4
Jermain Defoe	Tottenham	27	5
Emile Heskey	Aston Villa	32	7
Wayne Rooney	Man Utd	24	9
Ashley Young	Aston Villa	24	1

■ Probable ■ Possible **QG** Qualification Games

ROBERT GREEN
WEST HAM

A big, imposing goalkeeper and impressive shot-stopper, Robert Green is probably one of only two keepers in with a chance of making the starting line-up in South Africa alongside David James.

Having broken through at Championship side Norwich City he became their first choice at the relatively tender age at 21. Four seasons later he was a regular in the England squad and the Canaries were in the Premier League but the season after, Green joined West Ham. He was injured for the 2006 World Cup.

Playing record	12 months lge	wcq
Appearances:	38	4
Minutes played:	3402	283
Percentage played:	94.5%	31.4%
Goals conceded:	54	1
Clean sheets:	10	3
Cards:	Y0, R0	Y0, R1
Minutes between goals:	63mins	283mins
Goalkeeper ranking:	27th	4th

AGE 30	DREAM TEAM	RANKING 94

DAVID JAMES
PORTSMOUTH

A hardened veteran of 18 years of top-flight football, David James - even at 39 - continues to show flashes of brilliance between the posts and has made more appearances in the Premier League than any other player.

His international career spans an impressive 13 years but he has only been the England number one choice in sporadic bursts. Having played second fiddle to David Seaman until 2002, James wore the number one jersey at Euro 2004 and started in Capello's first game.

Playing record	12 months lge	wcq
Appearances:	28	6
Minutes played:	2504	526
Percentage played:	69.6%	58.4%
Goals conceded:	40	5
Clean sheets:	7	1
Cards:	Y1, R0	Y0, R0
Minutes between goals:	63mins	105mins
Goalkeeper ranking:	28th	21st

AGE 39	DREAM TEAM	RANKING 436

PAUL ROBINSON
BLACKBURN

The former England number one, Paul Robinson suffered from a drop in form and confidence at Spurs. Now settled at Blackburn, he has been looking the accomplished presence we all remember from a few years ago.

The feeling is, he still has to impress himself on Fabio Capello and there is little opportunity to do that. If all the other keepers are fit, he will probably miss out, but if form or fitness give him a chance, he will be given the opportunity to prove he is still the best in England.

Playing record	12 months lge	wcq
Appearances:	37	0
Minutes played:	3285	0
Percentage played:	96.1%	0%
Goals conceded:	58	-
Clean sheets:	11	-
Cards:	Y0, R0	-
Minutes between goals:	57mins	-
Goalkeeper ranking:	30th	-

AGE 30	DREAM TEAM	RANKING 169

JOE HART
BIRMINGHAM

One of the brightest jewels in England's goalkeeping crown, Joe Hart is fast maturing into one of the best young keepers in Europe and at just 23, is approaching 100 games in the top flight.

A big, brave, in-your-face character on-field, he has been superb for England's U-21's and has had a great season with Birmingham on loan from Manchester City. His experience in the England set up plus his form this season playing first team football make him a firm favourite to be on the plane to South Africa.

Playing record	12 months lge	wcq
Appearances:	22	0
Minutes played:	1980	0
Percentage played:	59.5%	0%
Goals conceded:	20	-
Clean sheets:	8	-
Cards:	Y2, R0	-
Minutes between goals:	99mins	-
Goalkeeper ranking:	7th	-

AGE 23   **DREAM TEAM** **RANKING** 615

THE MANAGER

Not only was Fabio Capello a good choice as England manager, he was a good choice at exactly the right time.

A man who demands respect from staff, press and players alike, he was the perfect tonic to the affable Steve McClaren who was widely accused of being too close to the players.

The respect Capello demands is based firmly on achievement. An accomplished midfielder, he scored the goal for Italy that consigned England to their first ever Wembley defeat in 1973. He won Serie A medals three times in his playing career. As manager of the all conquering AC Milan side that won Serie A three times on the bounce and four times in five years between 1991 and 1996, he also clinched the Champions League in 1994. Add to that Serie A titles at Juventus and Roma and La Liga honours twice with Real Madrid in two spells at the Bernabeu and you have a shrewd and very successful manager.

His appointment was greeted with cautious welcome by the English media but any negativity soon drifted away as England

> **"At this moment, the English players are in a really good moment of form. We hope it will be the same at the end of the season."**

strolled to qualification in emphatic fashion, thrashing Euro 2008 bogey side Croatia home and away and winning nine out of ten games - the sole loss against Ukraine once England had already qualified. Capello has made some simple changes to the side and

they have been extremely effective.

Firstly he has England playing as a cohesive unit when not in possession. The ability to press in unison from the front, close down teams and force mistakes is crucial in international football where even modest teams are comfortable at keeping the ball. It might not be the most attractive element of the game but it has been part of England's success under the Italian.

Secondly, he has Steven Gerrard and Frank Lampard playing well as part of the same midfield. Yes, Gerrard starts on the left but the presence of Gareth Barry means both players have freedom to get forward at will

> **"If everyone is fit, we have the quality to do it. Why not? The expectation is always the same for the England team. It is always very high."**

and Gerrard has the ability to make an impact no matter where he plays; and this was born out in the qualifiers with the pair netting almost 20% of England's goals between them.

Last, but by no means least, he has Wayne Rooney in the form of his life and the United striker is playing more as a genuine forward than ever - no longer chasing the ball in order to get involved. This has made a massive difference to his goal return with Rooney surpassing his previous season's goal tally by January in 09/10.

If any manager was ready to take England deep into this tournament, there could be few more qualified than Fabio Capello - and crucially for the Italian, he is doing so at just the right time.

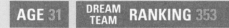

KEY DEFENDER

RIO FERDINAND MAN UTD

A classy, cultured centre-back, Rio Ferdinand has been one of the finest England defenders for a decade now, and would be pride of place in the defence of any top club in Europe.

  With great anticipation and the pace to get himself out of trouble, Ferdinand is a first-rate defender but has the added advantage of being comfortable on the ball.

Playing record	12 months lge	wcq
Appearances:	14	6
Minutes played:	1239	537
Percentage played:	33.6%	59.7%
Goals conceded:	17	5
Clean sheets:	5	1
Cards:	Y2, R0	Y0, R0
Minutes between goals:	73mins	107mins
Defender ranking:	107th	86th

AGE 31   **DREAM TEAM**   **RANKING** 353

JOHN TERRY
CHELSEA

One of the first names on the team sheet, John Terry is the heart and soul of Fabio Capello's England.

An old-school defender, Terry's awareness, instinct and no-nonsense approach have been vital for club and country over the years. The only England player named in Fifa's all-star squad - he was captain throughout qualifying, before being replaced by Rio Ferdinand. One of the best defenders in the world, Terry will play a big part if England make it to the latter stages.

Terry is a Top 12 Defender

Playing record	12 mths lge	wcq
Appearances:	37	8
Minutes played:	3327	718
Percentage played:	94.8%	79.8%
Goals conceded:	30	4
Clean sheets:	19	4
Cards:	Y7, R0	Y1, R0
Minutes between goals:	111mins	179mins
Defender ranking:	15th	38th

AGE 29 | **DREAM TEAM** | **RANKING** 7

GLEN JOHNSON
LIVERPOOL

One of the best right-backs in World football according to Fabio Capello, Glen Johnson is superb going forward and will be a certain pick providing he can avoid injury.

He is the first player to become an automatic pick at right-back since Gary Neville but he could not be further from the United stalwart in terms of style. With superb pace, and the ability to link up play and deliver from the by-line, his major assets are going forward - although his defending has improved over the years.

Playing record	12 months lge	wcq
Appearances:	32	7
Minutes played:	2831	615
Percentage played:	80.7%	68.3%
Goals conceded:	37	3
Clean sheets:	11	4
Cards:	Y7, R1	Y1, R0
Minutes between goals:	77mins	205mins
Defender ranking:	97th	28th

AGE 25 | **DREAM TEAM** | **RANKING** 87

ASHLEY COLE
CHELSEA

One of the finest left-backs in world football, Ashley Cole will be a certain starter for England in South Africa.

A veteran of two World Cups and a European Championship, Cole needs no tutoring on the demands of international football and has been in fine form for Chelsea this season. A complete full-back in that he is strong both going forward and defending, his ability to get down the left with no traditional left-winger playing in front of him will be an important weapon for England.

Cole is a Top 12 Defender

Playing record	12 months lge	wcq
Appearances:	35	8
Minutes played:	2990	693
Percentage played:	85.2%	77.0%
Goals conceded:	30	5
Clean sheets:	17	3
Cards:	Y6, R0	Y0, R0
Minutes between goals:	100mins	139mins
Defender ranking:	30th	57th

AGE 29 | **DREAM TEAM** | **RANKING** 19

MATTHEW UPSON
WEST HAM

Fabio Capello's first reserve at centre-back if either Rio Ferdinand or John Terry are unavailable, Upson is more similar in style to the latter.

Not the quickest, he is, however, superb in the air, a fine tackler and as brave as they come. Unfortunately, he is also somewhat injury prone, and his participation in this tournament will mean he has bucked the trend of the last few seasons and remained fit for six months at least. With all the main protagonists fit, Upson will start this tournament on the bench.

Playing record	12 months lge	wcq
Appearances:	32	5
Minutes played:	2752	362
Percentage played:	76.4%	40.2%
Goals conceded:	37	3
Clean sheets:	10	2
Cards:	Y3, R0	Y0, R0
Minutes between goals:	74mins	121mins
Defender ranking:	103rd	73rd

AGE 31 | **DREAM TEAM** | **RANKING** 245

GARETH BARRY
MAN CITY

An accomplished presence on the left or in the centre, Gareth Barry has excellent all-round skills and his passing ability and calmness under pressure have led to him occupying a holding role in central midfield for England.

His ability to pick a pass from midfield and shield the defence have been key in Capello's decision to play him there, as it has given licence to Steven Gerrard and Frank Lampard to get forward more and pick up goals from midfield, which was vital in qualifying.

Playing record	12 months lge	wcq
Appearances:	37	8
Minutes played:	3298	675
Percentage played:	91.6%	75.0%
Goals scored:	3	1
Clean sheets:	11	4
Cards:	Y5, R0	Y2, R0
Strike rate:	99mins	675mins
Midfielder ranking:	8th	62nd

AGE 29 | **DREAM TEAM** **RANKING** 115

STEVEN GERRARD
LIVERPOOL

One of the best midfielders of his generation, there are few teams in world football that Steven Gerrard wouldn't walk into, and it is no wonder.

He is a real-life Roy of the Rovers, a midfield tour de force, capable of the utterly spectacular, yet relentless enough to make a contribution in every game and inspire those around him. Not always at his fluent best playing in central midfield in partnership with Frank Lampard, he often starts on the left for Capello.

Gerrard is a Top 12 Midfielder

Playing record	12 months lge	wcq
Appearances:	30	7
Minutes played:	2580	530
Percentage played:	73.5%	58.9%
Goals scored:	13	3
Clean sheets:	14	2
Cards:	Y5, R0	Y0, R0
Strike rate:	198mins	177mins
Midfielder ranking:	17th	6th

AGE 30 | **DREAM TEAM** **RANKING** 71

JOE COLE
CHELSEA

He may have spent much of the last two seasons out injured, but Joe Cole offers something different to England's midfield - an extremely technically gifted and tricky player, comfortable with the ball at his feet, he can create something out of absolutely nothing.

With more than 50 caps, he also has a lot of international experience but perhaps the highlight was the 2006 World Cup, where he was one of the better players for England, scoring a spectacular volley against Sweden.

Playing record	12 months lge	wcq
Appearances:	11	2
Minutes played:	634	99
Percentage played:	18.1%	11.0%
Goals scored:	1	2
Clean sheets:	7	2
Cards:	Y0, R0	Y0, R0
Strike rate:	-	-
Midfielder ranking:	218th	189th

AGE 28 | **DREAM TEAM** **RANKING** 2076

DAVID BECKHAM
LA GALAXY/AC MILAN

The most capped England outfield player of all time, David Beckham needs little introduction and no matter what the naysayers claim - if fit and in form, he is worthy of a place in the squad.

He might be entering the second half of his 30s but he was never a player who relied on his pace and his fitness cannot be called into question. Neither too, can his ability to deliver the ball from the flank or from a set-piece. Although he is unlikely to start a game, his presence from the bench could be vital.

Playing record	12 months lge	wcq
Appearances:	20	9
Minutes played:	1593	214
Percentage played:	44.3%	23.8%
Goals scored:	2	0
Clean sheets:	10	8
Cards:	Y4, R0	Y1, R0
Strike rate:	796mins	-
Midfielder ranking:	138th	219th

AGE 35 | **DREAM TEAM** **RANKING** 899

KEY MIDFIELDER

FRANK LAMPARD CHELSEA

There can be few players in the history of modern football who have performed to such high standards as consistently as Frank Lampard and it is testament to his fitness and work ethic that he continues to deliver at the very highest level for both club and country.

He is a talisman for Chelsea, averaging just under a goal every three games and holding the Premier League record for consecutive appearances, with an amazing 164 straight games. An accomplished all-round footballer, Lampard was the only England player to start all ten of the qualifiers, scoring four times. Now in his early 30s, and with the experience of two major competition finals for England, Lampard is at the height of his powers and is well capable of taking England a long way in this tournament.

Lampard is a Top 12 Midfielder

| AGE 31 | DREAM TEAM | RANKING 9 |

KEY STRIKER

WAYNE ROONEY MAN UTD

The most gifted forward at England's disposal, Wayne Rooney has consistently proved himself to be one of the finest strikers in European football for Manchester United and England.

He has all of the skill you would associate with a top international but it is his vision and awareness that makes him stand head and shoulders above his peers and suits England's strong midfield. While he has been in fine goalscoring form for club and country for the last two years, his ability to set up goals and split defences will suit Steven Gerrard, Frank Lampard and company, and make him a massive asset for Fabio Capello in South Africa. Whether scoring or creating, Rooney's form will be critical to England's chances of making the latter stages.

Rooney is a Top 12 Striker

AGE 24	DREAM TEAM	RANKING 16

PETER CROUCH
TOTTENHAM

A tall, gangly handful of a centre-forward, Peter Crouch has a superb goalscoring record for England and even if he does not start, has the ability to make an impact in games coming off the bench.

Despite his height – Crouch is 2.01m / 6ft 7ins – heading the ball is not Crouch's speciality, with many of his goals relying on magnificent timing, using his long legs to hook volleys home from strange angles. Expect him to make a contribution somewhere along the line – especially if England go far.

Playing record	12 months lge	wcq
Appearances:	38	4
Minutes played:	2908	279
Percentage played:	82.8%	31.0%
Goals scored:	7	4
Percentage share:	10.45%	11.76%
Cards:	Y3, R0	Y0, R0
Strike rate:	415mins	70mins
Strike rate ranking:	110th	2nd

AGE 29	DREAM TEAM	RANKING 184

JERMAIN DEFOE
TOTTENHAM

The best out-and-out finisher in the squad, and perhaps the best England has seen since Gary Lineker, Jermain Defoe is a natural predator in and around the box and has been in fine form for Spurs.

Despite the goals he has put away in the last 18 months, he is not a guaranteed starter, with Fabio Capello preferring a big centre forward to partner Wayne Rooney but if given the chance – from the bench or perhaps if injuries come into play – he could fire England a long way into this tournament.

Playing record	12 months lge	wcq
Appearances:	26	5
Minutes played:	1918	136
Percentage played:	54.6%	15.1%
Goals scored:	17	3
Percentage share:	25.37%	8.82%
Cards:	Y1, R1	Y0, R0
Strike rate:	113mins	-
Strike rate ranking:	10th	-

AGE 27	DREAM TEAM	RANKING 451

EMILE HESKEY
ASTON VILLA

He might not have the goal record you would expect of a top striker but Emile Heskey brings more to the table than his stats might suggest.

A powerhouse centre forward with the pace to scare any defence, Heskey is a handful and his ability to hold up the ball and link up play make him an invaluable presence – especially in a team that relies on goals from midfield. Fabio Capello's preferred partner for Wayne Rooney, he might not score that many himself but he will increase the goal output of those around him.

Playing record	12 months lge	wcq
Appearances:	33	7
Minutes played:	1871	504
Percentage played:	52.0%	56.0%
Goals scored:	4	1
Percentage share:	8.00%	2.94%
Cards:	Y0, R0	Y1, R0
Strike rate:	468mins	504mins
Strike rate ranking:	113th	76th

AGE 32	DREAM TEAM	RANKING 897

GOALKEEPER

BEN FOSTER
MAN UTD

A promising young keeper with time on his side. Ben Foster has suffered injuries at key times in his short career although he has been a player who Fabio Capello has turned to in the past.

Playing record	12 months lge	wcq
Appearances:	10	1
Minutes played:	900	90
Percentage played:	24.4%	10.0%
Goals conceded:	9	0
Clean sheets:	4	1
Cards:	Y0, R0	Y0, R0
Minutes between goals:	-	-
Goalkeeper ranking:	-	-

AGE 27 | **DREAM TEAM RANKING** 1232

DEFENDERS

WES BROWN
MAN UTD

A dependable defender able to play at right-back and centre-back, Wes Brown is not the most talented player in England but he has plenty of experience at the highest level with Manchester United.

Playing record	12 months lge	wcq
Appearances:	15	3
Minutes played:	1132	270
Percentage played:	30.7%	30.0%
Goals conceded:	7	3
Clean sheets:	8	0
Cards:	Y2, R0	Y0, R0
Minutes between goals:	162mins	90mins
Defender ranking:	3rd	103rd

AGE 30 | **DREAM TEAM RANKING** 1580

WAYNE BRIDGE
MAN CITY

Playing record	12 months lge	wcq
Appearances:	30	3
Minutes played:	2604	194
Percentage played:	72.3%	21.6%
Goals conceded:	34	1
Clean sheets:	8	2
Cards:	Y2, R0	Y0, R0
Minutes between goals:	77mins	-
Defender ranking:	96th	-

AGE 29 | **DREAM TEAM RANKING** 221

MIDFIELDERS

MICHAEL CARRICK
MAN UTD

A deep-lying midfield playmaker with a superb range of passing, Michael Carrick has never really established himself as a midfield regular for England as he strives to flourish in the shadow of Steven Gerrard, Frank Lampard and Gareth Barry.

Unlikely to be a starter if all personnel are fit, Carrick is nonetheless an asset to England. Playing at the highest level with Manchester United, it is unfair to consider him as a back up only, but if ever a player was needed to step into the central midfield berth, you could not ask for better than Carrick. He will be an important part of England's campaign.

Playing record	12 months lge	wcq
Appearances:	35	1
Minutes played:	2601	90
Percentage played:	70.5%	10.0%
Goals scored:	4	0
Clean sheets:	17	0
Cards:	Y2, R0	Y0, R0
Strike rate:	650mins	-
Midfielder ranking:	116th	185th

AGE 28 | **DREAM TEAM RANKING** 74

JAMES MILNER
ASTON VILLA

Playing record	12 months lge	wcq
Appearances:	37	3
Minutes played:	3251	68
Percentage played:	90.3%	7.6%
Goals scored:	7	0
Clean sheets:	13	3
Cards:	Y6, R0	Y0, R0
Strike rate:	464mins	-
Midfielder ranking:	85th	176th

AGE 24 | **DREAM TEAM RANKING** 163

THEO WALCOTT
ARSENAL

A lightning quick right sided winger who can also play up front, Theo Walcott is fast enough to scare the life out of any defence and has already proven his potential worth to England.

It was September 2008 that the youngest player ever to play for England became the youngest to score a hat-trick as Walcott's three goals helped inflict a 4-1 defeat on Croatia in Zagreb in England's second qualifier for this World Cup. Walcott can cement himself as an England regular if he performs in South Africa.

Playing record	12 months lge	wcq
Appearances:	17	6
Minutes played:	801	454
Percentage played:	22.3%	50.4%
Goals scored:	2	3
Clean sheets:	-	-
Cards:	Y0, R0	Y0, R0
Strike rate:	-	151mins
Midfielder ranking:	-	22nd

AGE 21 | **DREAM TEAM RANKING** 1285

SHAUN WRIGHT-PHILLIPS
MAN CITY

Playing record	12 months lge	wcq
Appearances:	25	5
Minutes played:	2056	215
Percentage played:	57.1%	23.9%
Goals scored:	5	1
Clean sheets:	9	4
Cards:	Y3, R0	Y0, R0
Strike rate:	411mins	-
Midfielder ranking:	73rd	221st

AGE 28 | **DREAM TEAM RANKING** 338

ASHLEY YOUNG
ASTON VILLA

Playing record	12 months lge	wcq
Appearances:	35	1
Minutes played:	3090	45
Percentage played:	85.8%	5.0%
Goals scored:	5	0
Clean sheets:	10	1
Cards:	Y8, R1	Y0, R0
Strike rate:	618mins	-
Midfielder ranking:	111th	165th

AGE 24 | **DREAM TEAM RANKING** 252

STRIKERS

CARLTON COLE
WEST HAM

A physical centre forward with an eye for goal who has impressed as a sub.

Carlton Cole has been in fine form for West Ham this season and will hope to be part of the squad that heads for South Africa in the summer.

Playing record	12 months lge	wcq
Appearances:	23	2
Minutes played:	1839	44
Percentage played:	51.1%	4.9%
Goals scored:	12	0
Percentage share:	26.09%	0.00%
Cards:	Y4, R1	Y0, R0
Strike rate:	153mins	-
Strike rate ranking:	30th	-

AGE 26 | **DREAM TEAM** **RANKING** 680

DARREN BENT
SUNDERLAND

Playing record	12 months lge	wcq
Appearances:	34	0
Minutes played:	2651	0
Percentage played:	77.5%	0%
Goals scored:	18	-
Percentage share:	34.0%	-
Cards:	Y3, R0	-
Strike rate:	147mins	-
Strike rate ranking:	23rd	-

AGE 26 | **DREAM TEAM** **RANKING** 291

ONE TO WATCH

AARON LENNON TOTTENHAM

A diminutive, skilful and very quick right-winger, Aaron Lennon, on his day, could get the better of any defence in world football.

Fleet footed and lightweight, Lennon is an old fashioned wide player, intent on beating his man and delivering from the by-line. Much will depend on how Fabio Capello views his end of season form.

Playing record	12 months lge	wcq
Appearances:	33	4
Minutes played:	2876	207
Percentage played:	81.9%	23.0%
Goals scored:	7	0
Clean sheets:	11	3
Cards:	Y1, R0	Y0, R0
Strike rate:	411mins	-
Midfielder ranking:	72nd	216th

AGE 23 | **MIDFIELDER** | **DREAM TEAM** **RANKING** 112

ROUTE TO THE FINALS

It is a long hard road to qualify from the African Confederation.

Algeria started well, edging out Senegal and Gambia in the second round group stage and impressing further in the third round group stage, topping the pile ahead of reigning Africa Cup of Nation holders following a controversial one-off game after the sides could not be split on their overall or head-to-head record.

The last group game in Cairo spilled into violence and alleged crowd trouble in the playoff that took place in Sudan lead to political tension between the two countries with Algeria settling matters on the pitch and staking their claim to a berth in South Africa courtesy of a 1-0 win. There were a few standout players, but Bochum centre-half Anthar Yahia was impressive as any, scoring three times including the crucial goal against Egypt in the play-off.

FINAL QUALIFYING TABLE
AFRICA ROUND 3 GROUP C

	P	W	D	L	F	A	Pts
Algeria*	7	5	1	1	10	4	16
Egypt	7	4	1	2	9	5	13
Zambia	6	1	2	3	2	5	5
Rwanda	6	0	2	4	1	8	2

*Algeria beat Egypt in tiebreaking play-off.

#	Date	Venue	Opponent	Avge FIFA ranking	Result			Scorers
1	31 May 08	Away	Senegal	60	L	1	0	
2	06 Jun 08	Home	Liberia	142	W	3	0	Djebbour 16, Ziani 20, 47pen
3	14 Jun 08	Away	Gambia	87	L	1	0	
4	20 Jun 08	Home	Gambia	87	W	1	0	Yahia 33
5	05 Sep 08	Home	Senegal	60	W	3	2	Gueye 60og, Saifi 66, Yahia 72
6	11 Oct 08	Away	Liberia	142	D	0	0	
7	28 Mar 09	Away	Rwanda	95	D	0	0	
8	07 Jun 09	Home	Egypt	28	W	3	1	Matmour 60, Ghezzal Abdel 64, Djebbour 77
9	20 Jun 09	Away	Zambia	79	W	0	2	M.Bougherra 21, Saifi 66
10	06 Sep 09	Home	Zambia	79	W	1	0	Saifi 59
11	11 Oct 09	Home	Rwanda	95	W	3	1	Ghezzal Abdel 22, Belhadj 45, Ziani 90pen
12	14 Nov 09	Away	Egypt	28	L	2	0	
13	18 Nov 09	Home	Egypt	28	W	1	0	Yahia 40

Average FIFA ranking of opposition	78

MAIN PLAYER PERFORMANCES IN QUALIFICATION

Match	1 2 3 4 5 6 7 8 9 10 11 12 13	Appearances	Started	Subbed on	Subbed off	Mins played	% played	Goals	Yellow	Red
Venue	A H A H H A A H A H H A H									
Result	L W L W W D D W W W W L W									
Goalkeepers										
Faouzi Chaouchi		1	1	0	0	90	7.7	0	0	0
Lounes Gaouaoui		12	12	0	0	1080	92.3	0	2	0
Defenders										
Nadir Belhadj		11	11	0	1	985	84.2	1	4	0
Madjid Bougherra		10	10	0	0	900	76.9	1	1	0
Slimane Raho		7	7	0	0	630	53.8	0	0	0
Anthar Yahia		11	11	0	3	936	80.0	3	3	0
Samir Zaoui		6	4	2	0	396	33.8	0	1	0
Abderaouf Zarabi		3	2	1	0	185	15.8	0	0	0
Midfielders										
Cherif Abdesslam		2	2	0	0	180	15.4	0	1	0
Yacine Bezzaz		8	3	5	3	308	26.3	0	1	0
Hameur Bouazza		5	0	5	0	107	9.1	0	0	0
Rafik Djebbour		9	7	2	5	592	50.6	2	1	0
Lamouri Djediat		6	2	4	0	285	24.4	0	1	0
Brahim Hemdani		2	2	0	1	158	13.5	0	0	0
Kaled Lemmouchia		10	10	0	2	900	76.9	0	2	0
Yazid Mansouri		11	11	0	0	990	84.6	0	3	0
Karim Matmour		7	6	1	2	523	44.7	1	1	0
Mourad Meghni		3	3	0	2	218	18.6	0	0	0
Hassan Yebda		2	1	1	0	108	9.2	0	0	0
Karim Ziani		12	12	0	2	1028	87.9	3	4	0
Forwards										
Kader Ghezzal Abdel		7	5	2	4	469	40.1	2	2	0
Kamel Ghilas		6	3	3	3	201	17.2	0	0	0
Rafik Halliche		9	7	2	1	641	54.8	0	0	0
Rafik Saifi		11	10	1	6	838	71.6	3	3	0

FINAL PROSPECTS

Algeria are hardly the biggest name in this competition but do not be deceived – they are an extremely capable side.

Having walked though fire to make it to South Africa, this will be a highly motivated group of players and while they cannot boast the star names of some of their competitors, they are not to be underestimated. Central defender Antar Yahia is a regular at Bundesliga side Bochum and the rock of Algeria's defence and is joined in the back four by Glasgow Rangers' Madjid Bougherra and Nadir Belhadj of Portsmouth. Add Lorient playmaker Yazid Mansouri and striker Karim Ziani of Wolfsburg and you have a side with the kind of experience that will prove invaluable come June. In January they proved exactly what they are capable of in the pressure cooker environment of a short tournament, overcoming a horrendous start and knocking out the Ivory Coast en route to the semi-finals were they suffered a painful defeat to bitter rivals Egypt. They have a dream low-key start to the competition against Slovenia and if they win that, they will be definite contenders to make the last 16 where a likely tie with Germany or Serbia awaits.

DREAM TEAM	TOP 15 RANKING	21

THE MANAGER

A part of the backdrop of the Algerian national team for almost 20 years, Rabah Saadane is in his fifth stint at the helm and will be looking to make his mark with a team that impressed during qualifying.

He will also be looking to exorcise the ghosts of 1986, when he last lead Algeria to a World Cup, and they returned home, bottom of the group, without a point. Luck was against them in the draw with three strong teams - but they couldn't have asked for much more than an opening game against the weakest - and least fashionable of the three sides.

GROUP FIXTURES

SLOVENIA	Sun 13 June 1230 BST
ENGLAND	Fri 18 June 1930 BST
USA	Wed 23 June 1500 BST

KEY PLAYER

MADJID BOUGHERRA RANGERS

Madjid Bougherra is an all-action centre-half who manages to star from defence, often - as he did in the Africa Cup of Nations - with critical goals.

Having spent his early career playing in lower league football in France and then England, Bougherra started to turn heads until Rangers saw off the interest of a number of Premier League clubs to sign him.

Playing record	12 months lge	wcq
Appearances:	28	10
Minutes played:	2388	900
Percentage played:	69.8%	76.9%
Goals conceded:	15	6
Clean sheets:	14	6
Cards:	Y5, R2	Y1, R0
Minutes between goals:	159mins	150mins
Defender ranking:	4th	52nd

AGE 27   **DEFENDER**   **DREAM TEAM** **RANKING** 881

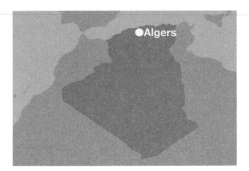

●Algers

Zone	Africa
Population	33.8m
Language	Arabic
Top league	Algeria Division 1
Playing season	August - May

Major clubs and capacities
MC Alger (80,200), JSM Bejaia (19,000), Belouizdad (20,000)

Where probable squad players play:

Premier League	3	Ligue 1	1
Serie A	2	Eredivisie	-
La Liga	-	Other Europe	6
Bundesliga	3	Outside Europe	8

Number of Algerian players playing:

Premier League	1	Bundesliga	1
Serie A	-	Ligue 1	2
La Liga	1	Eredivisie	-

World Cup record   ** best performance*

1930 - Did not enter	1974 - Did not qualify
1934 - Did not enter	1978 - Did not qualify
1938 - Did not enter	1982 - * Round 1
1950 - Did not enter	1986 - * Round 1
1954 - Did not enter	1990 - Did not qualify
1958 - Did not enter	1994 - Did not qualify
1962 - Did not enter	1998 - Did not qualify
1966 - Withdrew	2002 - Did not qualify
1970 - Did not qualify	2006 - Did not qualify

THE SQUAD

Goalkeepers	Club side	Age	QG
Faouzi Chaouchi	ES Setif	25	1
Lounes Gaouaoui	ASO Chlef	32	12
Defenders			
Nadir Belhadj	Portsmouth	27	11
Madjid Bougherra	Rangers	27	10
Nabil Hemani	ES Setif	30	3
Slimane Raho	ES Setif	34	7
Anthar Yahia	Bochum	28	11
Samir Zaoui	ASO Chlef	34	6
Abderaouf Zarabi	Nimes	31	3
Midfielders			
Cherif Abdesslam	USM Annaba	31	2
Yacine Bezzaz	Strasbourg	28	8
Hameur Bouazza	Blackpool	25	5
Rafik Djebbour	AEK Athens	26	9
Lamouri Djediat	ES Setif	29	6
Brahim Hemdani	Floating	32	2
Kaled Lemmouchia	ES Setif	28	10
Yazid Mansouri	Lorient	32	11
Karim Matmour	B M'gladbach	24	7
Mourad Meghni	Lazio	26	3
Mohamed Seguer	ES Setif	24	1
Hassan Yebda	Portsmouth	26	2
Karim Ziani	Wolfsburg	27	12
Forwards			
Kader Ghezzal Abdel	Siena	25	7
Kamel Ghilas	Hull City	26	6
Rafik Halliche	Nacional	23	9
Rafik Saifi	Al Khor	35	11

■ Probable ■ Possible **QG** Qualification Games

ROUTE TO THE FINALS

The US made light work of the second and third round of qualifying, thrashing Barbados 9-0 in a one-off game before losing just one game in six in the third round qualifying group to finish top and proceed to the group stage of the fourth qualifying round.

In a group containing Mexico, Costa Rica and Honduras, they had mixed results, beating Mexico at home but then losing away to Costa Rica and Trinidad and Tobago and it took strong home form and a superb 3-2 away to Honduras that sealed them top-spot in the group, qualifying alongside Mexico.

Jozy Altidore top-scored in the campaign with six goals but Landon Donavan and midfielders Clint Dempsey and Michael Bradley all weighed five apiece to prove the US have goalscorers throughout the team, a leaky defence could well be their downfall though.

For final qualification table see Honduras.

#	Date	Venue	Opposition	Avge FIFA ranking	W/L/D	Score	Scorers
1	15 Jun 08	Home	Barbados	118	W	8 0	Dempsey 1, 62, Bradley 12, Ching 20, 88, Donovan 58, Johnson 82, Ferguson 85og
2	22 Jun 08	Away	Barbados	118	W	0 1	Lewis 21
3	21 Aug 08	Away	Guatemala	106	W	0 1	Bocanegra 70
4	07 Sep 08	Away	Cuba	90	W	0 1	Dempsey 39
5	11 Sep 08	Home	Trinidad & Tobago	79	W	3 0	Bradley 10, Dempsey 18, Ching 57
6	12 Oct 08	Home	Cuba	90	W	6 1	Beasley 10, 30, Donovan 48, Ching 63, Altidore 87, Onyewu 89
7	16 Oct 08	Away	Trinidad & Tobago	79	L	2 1	Davies 74
8	20 Nov 08	Home	Guatemala	106	W	2 0	Cooper 54, Adu 69
9	12 Feb 09	Home	Mexico	24	W	2 0	Bradley 43, 90
10	29 Mar 09	Away	El Salvador	107	D	2 2	Altidore 77, Hejduk 88
11	02 Apr 09	Home	Trinidad & Tobago	79	W	3 0	Altidore 13, 71, 89
12	04 Jun 09	Away	Costa Rica	53	L	3 1	Donovan 90pen
13	07 Jun 09	Home	Honduras	43	W	2 1	Donovan 41pen, Bocanegra 67
14	12 Aug 09	Away	Mexico	24	L	2 1	Davies 9
15	06 Sep 09	Home	El Salvador	107	W	2 1	Dempsey 41, Altidore 45
16	10 Sep 09	Away	Trinidad & Tobago	79	W	0 1	Clark 61
17	11 Oct 09	Away	Honduras	43	W	2 3	Casey 54, 65, Donovan 71
18	15 Oct 09	Home	Costa Rica	53	D	2 2	Bradley 72, Bornstein 90

Average FIFA ranking of opposition	78

MAIN PLAYER PERFORMANCES IN QUALIFICATION

Match: 1 2 3 4 5 6 7 8 9 10 11 12 13 14 15 16 17 18
Venue: H A A A H H A H A H H A H A H A A H
Result: W W W W W W L W W D W L W L W W W D

Player	Appearances	Started	Subbed on	Subbed off	Mins played	% played	Goals	Yellow	Red
Goalkeepers									
Brad Guzan	5	5	0	0	450	27.8	0	0	0
Tim Howard	13	13	0	0	1170	72.2	0	2	0
Defenders									
Carlos Bocanegra	15	15	0	1	1330	82.1	2	1	0
Jonathan Bornstein	6	6	0	0	540	33.3	1	1	0
Danny Califf	3	3	0	0	270	16.7	0	0	0
Steven Cherundolo	7	6	1	0	510	31.5	0	2	1
Jay DeMerit	3	2	1	0	200	12.3	0	1	0
Frankie Hejduk	6	5	1	0	475	29.3	1	1	0
Pablo Mastroeni	6	6	0	4	389	24.0	0	2	0
Oguchi Onyewu	13	13	0	0	1170	72.2	1	2	0
Heath Pearce	9	9	0	3	753	46.5	0	0	0
Jonathan Spector	4	4	0	0	360	22.2	0	0	0
Midfielders									
DaMarcus Beasley	12	10	2	1	929	57.3	2	0	0
Michael Bradley	15	15	0	2	1325	81.8	5	4	0
Ricardo Clark	7	5	2	1	445	27.5	1	1	0
Clint Dempsey	13	13	0	7	1065	65.7	5	1	0
Maurice Edu	4	2	2	0	194	12.0	0	0	0
Benny Feilhaber	6	2	4	2	257	15.9	0	1	0
Stuart Holden	5	2	3	2	220	13.6	0	0	0
Sacha Kljestan	10	7	3	3	662	40.9	1	0	0
Eddie Lewis	4	2	2	1	188	11.6	1	0	0
Jose Francisco Torres	7	2	5	2	211	13.0	0	0	0
Forwards									
Freddy Adu	6	3	3	3	342	21.1	1	0	0
Jozy Altidore	13	8	5	2	773	47.7	6	2	0
Conor Casey	3	3	0	3	232	14.3	2	1	0
Brian Ching	11	9	2	5	744	45.9	4	0	0
Charlie Davies	6	4	2	4	332	20.5	2	0	0
Landon Donovan	15	15	0	1	1339	82.7	5	1	0

FINAL PROSPECTS

The USA are no longer the team of college kids they were when they first strode into the world's footballing consciousness as hosts in 1994.

The stereotype was one of an athletic and willing side with little in the way of the skill, guile and 'soccer' savvy needed to do really well in international football. Things have changed since then and while the USA have not suddenly become a Brazil or an Italy, they are certainly a more tasty proposition. Improvement in the last 16 years has been born out with a quarter-final appearance in the 2002 World Cup and a FIFA ranking high of four in 2006.

> ... while the USA have not suddenly become a Brazil or an Italy, they are certainly a more tasty proposition

With the MLS still developing as a competition, one of the biggest changes has been the number of US players playing overseas. The experience of mixing it in some of the most competitive leagues in the world has added an extra dimension to the personnel available and allowed coach Bob Bradley to bring in some young players to learn from their more experienced peers. The problem, however, is that with his best players playing in Europe, they are not always available to him.

They also have a number of injury worries. Two of their most important players centre back Oguchi Onyewu and forward Clint Dempsey have been out for long periods this season. Both players will be critical to the USA's chances, particularly Dempsey who is one of the key sources of goals.

The other frustration for Bradley is that for every USA player starring on foreign shores, for example Landon Donovan, he has players who are not getting regular football.

It is difficult therefore, to accurately gauge how the US will fare. They did well in the 2009 Confederations Cup, beating Spain and losing the final 3-2 having lead 2-0 against Brazil but their form since has been quite poor.

They face England in the much anticipated opening game - drawing comparison with the 1950 World Cup when they famously triumphed 1-0 - and then take on the underrated Slovenia.

They will need to have won at least one match by the time they face Algeria in their final group game if they are to go through.

DREAM TEAM   TOP 15 RANKING   19

GROUP FIXTURES

ENGLAND	Sat 12 June 1930 BST
SLOVENIA	Fri 18 June 1500 BST
ALGERIA	Wed 23 June 1500 BST

Washington D.C.●

Zone	North, Central America & Caribbean
Population	303m
Language	English
Top league	Major League Soccer
Playing season	March - November

Major clubs and capacities
Chicago (20,000), LA Galaxy (27,000), Columbus (23,425)

Where probable squad players play:

Premier League	5	Ligue 1	2
Serie A	1	Eredivisie	-
La Liga	-	Other Europe	3
Bundesliga	2	Outside Europe	10

Number of American players playing:

Premier League	9	Bundesliga	1
Serie A	1	Ligue 1	2
La Liga	-	Eredivisie	-

World Cup record   * best performance

1930 - * Semi finals	1974 - Did not qualify
1934 - Round 1	1978 - Did not qualify
1938 - Withdrew	1982 - Did not qualify
1950 - Round 1	1986 - Did not qualify
1954 - Did not qualify	1990 - Round 1
1958 - Did not qualify	1994 - Round 2
1962 - Did not qualify	1998 - Round 1
1966 - Did not qualify	2002 - Quarter finals
1970 - Did not qualify	2006 - Round 1

THE SQUAD

Goalkeepers	Club side	Age	QG
Brad Guzan	Aston Villa	25	5
Tim Howard	Everton	31	13
Defenders			
Carlos Bocanegra	Rennes	31	15
Jonathan Bornstein	Chivas	25	6
Danny Califf	Midtjylland	30	3
Steven Cherundolo	Hannover 96	31	7
Frankie Hejduk	Columbus Crew	35	6
Pablo Mastroeni	Colorado Rapids	33	6
Oguchi Onyewu	AC Milan	28	13
Heath Pearce	FC Dallas	25	9
Jonathan Spector	West Ham	24	4
Midfielders			
DaMarcus Beasley	Rangers	28	12
Michael Bradley	B M'gladbach	22	15
Ricardo Clark	Houston Dynamo	27	7
Clint Dempsey	Fulham	27	13
Maurice Edu	Rangers	24	4
Benny Feilhaber	AGF Aarhus	25	6
Stuart Holden	Houston Dynamo	24	5
Sacha Kljestan	Chivas	24	10
Eddie Lewis	Los Angeles Galaxy	36	4
Jose Francisco Torres	Pachuca	22	7
Forwards			
Freddy Adu	Aris	21	6
Jozy Altidore	Hull City	20	13
Brian Ching	Houston Dynamo	32	11
Charlie Davies	Sochaux	23	6
Landon Donovan	LA Galaxy/Everton	28	15

■ Probable ■ Possible **QG** Qualification Games

KEY PLAYER

LANDON DONOVAN LA GALAXY/EVERTON

A compact, skilful attacking midfielder, Landon Donovan is quick and incisive, can play up front as a second striker and is the all-time leading goalscorer for the USA.

Donovan plays for LA Galaxy but recently showed his potential effectiveness in European football with a successful ten-week loan spell at Everton.

Playing record	12 months lge		wcq
Appearances:		7	15
Minutes played:		227	1339
Percentage played:		6.5%	82.7%
Goals scored:		0	5
Percentage share:		0.00%	11.90%
Cards:		Y0, R0	Y1, R0
Strike rate:		-	268mins
Strike rate ranking:		-	56th

AGE 28   **STRIKER**   **DREAM TEAM**   **RANKING** 228

KEY GOALKEEPER

TIM HOWARD
EVERTON

A dominant keeper with excellent shot-stopping skills, Tim Howard is one of the finest American keepers to ever wear the gloves for his country and has become one of the most consistent performers in the English Premier League for Everton.

A key performer for the States, Howard has proved his worth against top opposition, making a string of crucial saves as the USA beat European Champions Spain in the semi-finals of the 2009 Confederations Cup.

Howard is a Top 4 goalkeeper

AGE 31	DREAM TEAM	RANKING 17

THE MANAGER

An intelligent and composed manager, USA coach Bob Bradley has had a torrid time of late but will be hoping to rediscover the form his side showed early in his reign in time for the World Cup.

Appointed as the interim manager following the USA's poor showing in the 2006 World Cup, he was made permanent boss when he guided his side to ten games unbeaten but it was the 14-month purple patch from August 2008 that really turned heads. The USA cruised through World Cup qualifying, in the meantime, they went to the 2009 Confederation Cup in South Africa and had a phenomenal tournament, beating European Champions Spain and making the final where they were 2-0 up against Brazil at half time, only to lose the match 3-2. Since then they have had some poor results, suffering an embarrassing 5-0 loss to arch-rivals Mexico on home soil in the final of the Gold Cup and losing to Slovakia, Denmark and Honduras.

KEY DEFENDERS

JONATHAN SPECTOR
WEST HAM

A defender who can play anywhere along the back-line, Jonathan Spector usually plays at left-back but has the innate skill and defensive ability to play in the middle - or as a defensive midfielder. He is an integral part of West Ham's defence.

Playing record	12 months lge	wcq
Appearances:	18	4
Minutes played:	1275	360
Percentage played:	35.4%	22.2%
Goals conceded:	23	4
Clean sheets:	6	1
Cards:	Y1, R0	Y0, R0
Minutes between goals:	55mins	-
Defender ranking:	154th	-

OGUCHI ONYEWU
AC MILAN

A towering centre-back, Oguchi Onyewu has spent his entire professional career playing in Europe, with Metz, Standard Liege and currently with AC Milan. Onyewu is a big, quick and strong defender and who is a certain starter if fit.

Playing record	12 months lge	wcq
Appearances:	0	13
Minutes played:	0	1170
Percentage played:	0.0%	72.2%
Goals conceded:	0	11
Clean sheets:	0	7
Cards:	Y0, R0	Y2, R0
Minutes between goals:	-	106mins
Defender ranking:	-	88th

AGE 28	DREAM TEAM	RANKING 1230

KEY MIDFIELDERS

CLINT DEMPSEY
FULHAM

A tenacious wide player who can also play as a striker, Clint Dempsey, is a fierce competitor but also has some superb skills - and frequently looks to go past defenders.

One of the few USA players playing in Europe who is a first team regular, Dempsey became the most expensive export from the MLS when Fulham paid around £2m to secure his services in 2006. He soon cemented his place in the side and top scored in 2007/8 as the Cottagers miraculously avoided relegation on the last day of the season. Entering his prime at 27, the experienced international will be a key player for the USA if he is fit.

Playing record	12 months lge	wcq
Appearances:	39	13
Minutes played:	3397	1065
Percentage played:	89.9%	65.7%
Goals scored:	9	5
Clean sheets:	14	7
Cards:	Y3, R0	Y1, R0
Strike rate:	377mins	213mins
Midfielder ranking:	62nd	13th

MICHAEL BRADLEY
BORUSSIA MONCHENGLADBACH

Playing record	12 months lge	wcq
Appearances:	30	15
Minutes played:	2555	1325
Percentage played:	83.5%	81.8%
Goals scored:	6	5
Clean sheets:	6	8
Cards:	Y6, R0	Y4, R0
Strike rate:	426mins	265mins
Midfielder ranking:	77th	21st

AGE 22	DREAM TEAM	RANKING 237

KEY STRIKER

BRIAN CHING
HOUSTON DYNAMO

An experienced campaigner with a knack for finding the back of the net, Brian Ching might not be the most talented or the most well known striker in Bob Bradley's squad but he is likely to be on hand in South Africa to provide firepower if needed.

Say what you want about Ching - the one thing he has done throughout his career is score goals.

Averaging almost a goal every other game in more than 150 senior appearances in the MLS, his international record at a goal every four games is not quite as impressive. But he did find the net four times in the qualifiers.

Playing record	12 months lge	wcq
Appearances:	-	11
Minutes played:	-	744
Percentage played:	-	45.9%
Goals scored:	-	4
Percentage share:	-	9.52%
Cards:	-	Y0, R0
Strike rate:	-	186mins
Strike rate ranking:	-	32nd

AGE 32   **DREAM TEAM** **RANKING** 2380

ONE TO WATCH

JOZY ALTIDORE HULL CITY

A talented young centre forward with bags of skill and energy, Jozy Altidore is the great American hope and despite featuring sparingly for current club side Hull City, looks destined to lead the line for the USA.

Having starred in the 2007 U-20 World Cup, Villarreal paid around £6m in 2008 making him the most expensive MLS player in history.

Playing record	12 months lge	wcq
Appearances:	15	13
Minutes played:	725	773
Percentage played:	20.7%	47.7%
Goals scored:	0	6
Percentage share:	0.00%	14.29%
Cards:	Y1, R0	Y2, R0
Strike rate:	-	129mins
Strike rate ranking:	-	17th

AGE 20   **STRIKER**   **DREAM TEAM** **RANKING** 975

ROUTE TO THE FINALS

Group 3 proved one of the more curious UEFA groups and it threw up its fair share of surprises, the fact that neither Poland or the Czech Republic came remotely close to qualifying is one of them.

Slovakia ended up group winners but having drawn with Poland in the opening game, Slovenia beat them at home 2-1. A win against Northern Ireland followed but that was the last of the positive cheer in 2008 as Slovenia lost away and then played out a goalless draw against the Czech Republic in a double header. 2009 started no better, with a 1-0 defeat in Belfast against Northern Ireland but the rot was stopped with a 5-0 thrashing of San Marino and Slovenia did not look back, comfortably winning their last three games - including another 2-0 win over Slovakia - to finish just two points behind the group leaders. This led to a play-off tie with Russia and despite going two goals down away from home, Nejc Pecnik headed one back and they won 1-0 at home to pull off the shock of the round on away goals.

FINAL QUALIFYING TABLE EUROPE GROUP 3

	P	W	D	L	F	A	Pts
Slovakia	10	7	1	2	22	10	22
Slovenia*	10	6	2	2	18	4	20
Czech Republic	10	4	4	2	17	6	16
Northern Ireland	10	4	3	3	13	9	15
Poland	10	3	2	5	19	14	11
San Marino	10	0	0	10	1	47	0

***Slovenia beat Russia in the play-offs.**

Avge FIFA ranking

1	06 Sep 08	Away	Poland	35	D	1 1	Dedic 35
2	10 Sep 08	Home	Slovakia	51	W	2 1	Novakovic 22, 81
3	11 Oct 08	Home	N Ireland	109	W	2 0	Novakovic 84, Ljubijankic 85
4	15 Oct 08	Away	Czech Republic	12	L	1 0	
5	28 Mar 09	Home	Czech Republic	12	D	0 0	
6	01 Apr 09	Away	N Ireland	109	L	1 0	
7	12 Aug 09	Home	San Marino	201	W	5 0	Koren 19, 73, Radosavljevic 38, Kirm 54, Ljubijankic 90
8	09 Sep 09	Home	Poland	35	W	3 0	Dedic 13, Novakovic 44, Birsa 63
9	10 Oct 09	Away	Slovakia	51	W	0 2	Birsa 56, Pecnik 90
10	14 Oct 09	Away	San Marino	201	W	0 3	Novakovic 24, Stevanovic 67, Suler 81
11	14 Nov 09	Away	Russia	11	L	2 1	Pecnik 88
12	18 Nov 09	Home	Russia	11	W	1 0	Dedic 44

Average FIFA ranking of opposition	70

MAIN PLAYER PERFORMANCES IN QUALIFICATION

Match	Venue	Result	Appearances	Started	Subbed on	Subbed off	Mins played	% played	Goals	Yellow	Red
1 2 3 4 5 6 7 8 9 10 11 12	A H H A H A H H A A A H	D W W L D L W W W W L W									
Goalkeepers											
Jasmin Handanovic			3	3	0	0	270	25.0	0	0	0
Samir Handanovic			9	9	0	0	810	75.0	0	1	0
Defenders											
Miso Brecko			11	11	0	3	974	90.2	0	3	0
Bostjan Cesar			10	10	0	0	900	83.3	0	2	0
Branko Ilic			5	4	1	0	366	33.9	0	2	0
Bojan Jokic			9	8	1	0	732	67.8	0	0	0
Mitja Morec			1	1	0	0	90	8.3	0	0	0
Marko Suler			10	10	0	0	900	83.3	1	2	0
Midfielders											
Armin Bacinovic			1	0	1	0	17	1.6	0	1	0
Suad Filekovic			2	2	0	0	180	16.7	0	1	0
Andraz Kirm			12	11	1	5	990	91.7	1	1	0
Andrej Komac			6	5	1	2	457	42.3	0	2	0
Robert Koren			11	11	0	0	990	91.7	2	3	0
Matej Mavric			3	3	0	0	270	25.0	0	0	0
Nejc Pecnik			6	1	5	1	95	8.8	2	0	0
Aleksandar Radosavljevic			7	7	0	2	610	56.5	1	0	0
Mirnes Sisic			5	5	0	4	399	36.9	0	2	0
Dalibor Stevanovic			4	1	3	1	100	9.3	1	1	0
Anton Zlogar			3	0	3	0	21	1.9	0	0	0
Forwards											
Valter Birsa			9	6	3	4	551	51.0	2	1	0
Zlatko Dedic			11	11	0	11	777	71.9	3	3	0
Zlatan Ljubijankic			8	1	7	0	276	25.6	2	0	0
Ales Mejac			3	0	3	0	16	1.5	0	0	0
Milivoje Novakovic			12	11	1	0	1009	93.4	5	0	0
Etien Velikonja			1	1	0	1	71	6.6	0	0	0

FINAL PROSPECTS

The serial overachievers of Europe, Slovenia make yet another World Cup finals appearance having left Poland, the Czech Republic and Russia in their wake during qualifying.

There is barely a known name amongst Matjaz Kek's squad but that has not prevented his team from producing some amazing results and that is down to the organisation and team spirit he has installed in his side.

They boast a very consistent selection strategy and this clearly means the players know their roles and in West Bromwich Albion's Robert Koren, they have a talented playmaker and captain.

Up front, Cologne's Milivoje Novakovic scored five times in qualifying. At the back, full-back Miso Brecko, also of Cologne, and centre-back Marko Suler of Gent, were almost ever present in qualifying and will be important players when the action starts.

The good news for Slovenia is that their first game is against the unfancied but talented Algeria, giving them an excellent chance to get points on the board before they face their daunting tasks against USA and England.

DREAM TEAM TOP 15 RANKING 24

THE MANAGER

It's hard to overestimate how impressive it is that a country of just two million people has not only competed in Europe but also managed - for the second time in eight years - to make it to the World Cup finals.

Matjez Kek was managing his hometown club Maribor when the national team were competing in the 2002 World Cup, a club where he spent much of his playing career and won the title as player and manager before taking over as national coach in 2007. A fiercely determined character, he has proven he knows his fair share about management and opponents should beware.

GROUP FIXTURES

ALGERIA	Sun 13 June 1230 BST
USA	Fri 18 June 1500 BST
ENGLAND	Wed 23 June 1500 BST

KEY PLAYER

ROBERT KOREN WEST BROM

A talented creative midfielder, Robert Koren is Slovenia's current captain and their pivotal player going forward.

Having stood head and shoulders above those around him playing at Norwegian side Lillestrom, English club West Bromwich Albion took a chance on him in 2007 and he helped them out of the Championship and into the Premier League.

Playing record	12 months lge	wcq
Appearances:	17	11
Minutes played:	1442	990
Percentage played:	89.0%	91.7%
Goals scored:	1	2
Clean sheets:	-	-
Cards:	Y1, R0	Y3, R0
Strike rate:	787mins	495mins
Midfielder ranking:	-	-

AGE 29   **MIDFIELDER**   **DREAM TEAM**   **RANKING** 2938

Ljubljana

Zone	Europe
Population	2m
Language	Slovene
Top league	Prva Liga
Playing season	August - May

Major clubs and capacities
Interblock Ljubljana (5,000), Drava Ptuj (2,200), NK Rudar Velenje (2,500)

Where probable squad players play:

Premier League	-	Ligue 1	3
Serie A	3	Eredivisie	1
La Liga	-	Other Europe	15
Bundesliga	1	Outside Europe	-

Number of Slovenian players playing:

Premier League	-	Bundesliga	3
Serie A	2	Ligue 1	3
La Liga	-	Eredivisie	3

World Cup record * best performance

1930 - Did not enter	1974 - Did not enter
1934 - Did not enter	1978 - Did not enter
1938 - Did not enter	1982 - Did not enter
1950 - Did not enter	1986 - Did not enter
1954 - Did not enter	1990 - Did not enter
1958 - Did not enter	1994 - Did not enter
1962 - Did not enter	1998 - Did not qualify
1966 - Did not enter	2002 - * Round 1
1970 - Did not enter	2006 - Did not qualify

THE SQUAD

Goalkeepers	Club side	Age	QG
Jasmin Handanovic	AC Mantova	32	3
Samir Handanovic	Udinese	25	9
Defenders			
Miso Brecko	Cologne	26	11
Bostjan Cesar	Grenoble	27	10
Branko Ilic	FC Moscow	27	5
Bojan Jokic	Sochaux	24	9
Mitja Morec	Slavia Sofia	27	1
Marko Suler	Gent	27	10
Midfielders			
Armin Bacinovic	Maribor	20	1
Suad Filekovic	Floating	31	2
Andraz Kirm	Domzale	25	12
Andrej Komac	Djurgarden	30	6
Robert Koren	West Brom	29	11
Matej Mavric	Koblenz	31	3
Nejc Pecnik	Nacional	24	6
Aleksr Radosavljevic	Tom Tomsk	31	7
Mirnes Sisic	Crvena Zvezda	28	5
Dalibor Stevanovic	Vitesse Arnhem	25	4
Anton Zlogar	Omonia Nicosia	32	3
Forwards			
Valter Birsa	Auxerre	23	9
Zlatko Dedic	Bochum	26	11
Zlatan Ljubijankic	Gent	26	8
Darijan Matic	Interblock Ljubljana	27	3
Ales Mejac	Koper	27	3
Milivoje Novakovic	Cologne	31	12
Etien Velikonja	Gorica	21	1

■ Probable ■ Possible **QG** Qualification Games

Position	1st	2nd	3rd	4th	5th	6th	7th	8th
Group	E	D	B	H	A	G	C	F
Total FIFA ranking	88	89	98	104	130	147	160	161

SERBIA V GHANA

Pretoria, Sunday 13 June 1500 BST

Two highly-rated sides both likely to be going all-out for a win to get their tournament off to a good start and give them a decent chance of making it out of the group. Ghana will expect to control central midfield, but Serbia will be confident of doing more damage when they have the ball. Defeat for either side would leave them with a mountain to climb – with a crunch match against Germany still ahead – and the result of this game is likely to set the tone for the group. One for the neutrals, there's enough world-class quality in these two sides to ensure that this game should continue a strong start to the tournament.

GERMANY V AUSTRALIA

Durban, Sunday 13 June 1930 BST

Traditional slow-starters and talked of as one of the big teams that might not make it out of the group stages, Germany will be desperate to win their opener to silence the doubters and give them a decent shout of qualification with two tricky games to come. However, Australia's solid defence may prove tricky to break down, and the Socceroos' direct attacking game has the potential to expose their European opponents' frailties at the back. While the smart money will be on a win for the group favourites here, it wouldn't be a surprise to see Australia get a result to throw Group D wide open. Expect it to be a decent match to watch.

KEY MATCH

GERMANY V SERBIA

Port Elizabeth, Friay 18 June 1230 BST

One the biggest games of the entire group stage, Germany against Serbia has all the hallmarks of a potential classic. Depending on results in the first set of matches, qualification or an early exit could be on the cards for either of these sides. A win here might not necessarily guarantee qualification, but defeat would certainly see them needing something from their last game – a position that neither team would want to be in. It should be another cracking game to watch. If Vidic is available then he will have a huge role to play in keeping the likes of Klose and Podolski quiet.

Germany's Lukas Podolski

GHANA V AUSTRALIA

Rustenburg, Saturday 19 June 1500 BST

If either of these teams managed three points in the opening round of games then they could qualify today, but the reverse is also true – two defeats usually means that a team's tournament is over. The Africans may struggle to break down an organised Aussie defence, while the likes of Cahill and Kewell will fancy their chances against Ghana's back-line.

GHANA V GERMANY

Jo'burg JSC, Wed 23 June 1930 BST

If Ghana are still in with a chance of qualifying at this stage then expect the atmosphere to be buzzing for this one, particularly if Germany have still not qualified. Low will not want to still be needing points going into a game against the Ghanaians, who will hope to control the centre of the park to prevent Germany's attacking players getting too much of the ball.

AUSTRALIA V SERBIA

Nelspruit, Wednesday 23 June 1930 BST

Both could be looking to secure a place in the knock-out stage when they meet in Nelspruit. They have strong defences and the match is likely to be won or lost in midfield. Everton powerhouse Cahill could be the key for the Socceroos, especially with his runs from the middle and a talent for getting goals in crucial matches. It should be tough and physical with plenty on both sides plying their trades with top European clubs. Vidic and Ivanovic will offer a muscular presence in the Serbia defence. However, Raddy Antic's team can also play good football and have enough skill to unlock any defence. Australia will not give up without a fight and will battle to the death if there is a place in the next round to play for.

VIEW FROM THE EXPERTS

GERMANY: Everyone always fancies them to do well but I think this is a very mediocre Germany team. Not potential winners to me this time around, they will do well to last beyond three matches. A poor show by their standards.
HARRY'S VERDICT: Group stage only.
AUSTRALIA: With the likes of Tim Cahill and Lucas Neill the Socceroos have some fearsome competitors in their squad. Slowly and steadily improving as the sport becomes more popular Down Under. Hard done by against Italy in the 2006 World Cup.
HARRY'S VERDICT: Last 16.
SERBIA: Nemanja Vidic is the headline act. The Manchester United defender is an awesome presence. And when you throw in the traditional Slav way of playing football - on the ground with technically skilful players - they could be a handful.
HARRY'S VERDICT: Quarters.
GHANA: Sulley Muntari cost Inter Milan £15 million to buy him off me at Portsmouth. That shows there is real quality in the Black Stars' squad. The key will be whether Michael Essien's knee injury has the last say as the Chelsea midfielder is world class.
HARRY'S VERDICT: Group stage only.

GERMANY: Winners three times and runners-up on four occasions, the Germans always seem to rise for the big World Cup occasions. Maybe not as powerful as they once were, but still a force to be reckoned with.
TEL'S VERDICT: Last eight at least.
AUSTRALIA: The Aussies sailed through their final qualifying phase. They do not have the easiest of groups, but you can guarantee Pim Verbeek's squad, which will contain plenty of faces familiar to Premier League fans, will not fall short when it comes to preparation, fitness and desire.
TEL'S VERDICT: No one will want to play them.
SERBIA: The fact Serbia finished above a below-par France in their qualifying group possibly offers no indication of the progress the team has made under their coach, former Luton star Raddy Antic. They have two quality defenders in Nemanja Vidic and Branislav Ivanovic, while Nenad Milijas has performed well at Wolves, but inexperience could be their undoing.
TEL'S VERDICT: Not to be taken lightly.

GHANA: With an engine room of Chelsea's Michael Essien and Inter Milan's former Portsmouth midfielder Sulley Muntari, there will be no shortage of stamina and enthusiasm in the Black Stars squad. But the lack of a quality striker raises questions about whether they will be able to qualify from the group like they did in 2006.

TEL'S VERDICT: Second phase at best.

GERMANY: Apart from Michael Ballack and Miroslav Klose, Joachim Low's squad might not contain the big international names of previous German campaigns, but their strong performance in qualifying suggests they will be as ruthless and efficient as always.

WRIGHTY'S VERDICT: Never write them off.

AUSTRALIA: The Socceroos have come a long way in recent years with many players plying their trades in the Premier League and across Europe. All of their squad will be super fit, totally prepared and blessed with that Australian winning mentality.

WRIGHTY'S VERDICT: I wouldn't want to play them.

SERBIA: Still relatively an unknown quantity in European football, but any country that produces Manchester United defender Nemanja Vidic has to command respect. Their opponents will be hoping there are not too many more like him in their ranks.

WRIGHTY'S VERDICT: Tough nuts to crack.

GHANA: Blessed with flair and boundless athleticism, the Black Stars will never give up the ghost. They were the only African side to progress beyond the first round of the last World Cup and they could do so again, thanks to their talismen Sulley Muntari and Michael Essien.

WRIGHTY'S VERDICT: Ready to shock a few.

"Nemanja Vidic is the headline act. The Manchester United defender is an awesome presence"

THE LIKELY ROUTES FOR THE TOP TWO TEAMS FROM THE GROUP

For the full draw please see page 80

GROUP STAGE
FIRST GROUP D

> **SERBIA**

LAST SIXTEEN
v SECOND GROUP C

> **SERBIA v USA**

QUARTER-FINALS
v FIRST GROUP B or SECOND GROUP A

> **SERBIA v ARGENTINA**

GROUP STAGE
SECOND GROUP D

> **AUSTRALIA**

LAST SIXTEEN
v FIRST GROUP C

> **AUSTRALIA v ENGLAND**

QUARTER-FINALS
v FIRST GROUP A or SECOND GROUP B

> **ENGLAND v FRANCE**

GROUP D
GERMANY, AUSTRALIA, SERBIA, GHANA

GROUP C
ENGLAND, USA, ALGERIA, SLOVENIA

GROUP A
SOUTH AFRICA, MEXICO, URUGUAY, FRANCE
GROUP B
ARGENTINA, NIGERIA, SOUTH KOREA (KOREAN REPUBLIC), GREECE

GERMANY

ROUTE TO THE FINALS

It may be a cliche, but Germany are always a threat when it comes to major championships and they will be again in South Africa after maintaining their record of qualifying for every World Cup that the country has been allowed to enter.

Drawn in a potentially tricky group alongside Euro 2008 surprise package Russia and the ever-dangerous Finland, Germany were ruthless throughout qualifying, going all ten games unbeaten and scoring 26 goals in the process.

They got the ball rolling with a 6-0 demolition of Liechtenstein before a Miroslav Klose hat-trick ensured they came from behind three times to claim a draw in Finland. This set-up a pivotal clash with the highly fancied Russians.

First half goals from Lukas Podolski and skipper Michael Ballack earned Germany a deserved victory, before a run of five straight wins without conceding put Joachim Low's side in pole position. A victory in the penultimate game in Russia secured top spot.

FINAL QUALIFYING TABLE
EUROPE GROUP 4

	P	W	D	L	F	A	Pts
Germany	10	8	2	0	26	5	26
Russia	10	7	1	2	19	6	22
Finland	10	5	3	2	14	14	18
Wales	10	4	0	6	9	12	12
Azerbaijan	10	1	2	7	4	14	5
Liechtenstein	10	0	2	8	2	23	2

#	Date	Venue	Opponent	Avge FIFA ranking	Result	Score	Scorers
1	06 Sep 08	Away	Liechtenstein	145	W	0 6	Podolski 21, 48, Rolfes 65, Schweinsteiger 66, Hitzlsperger 76fk, Westermann 87
2	10 Sep 08	Away	Finland	49	D	3 3	Klose 38, 45, 83
3	11 Oct 08	Home	Russia	11	W	2 1	Podolski 9, Ballack 28
4	15 Oct 08	Home	Wales	63	W	1 0	Trochowski 72
5	28 Mar 09	Home	Liechtenstein	145	W	4 0	Ballack 4, Jansen 9, Schweinsteiger 48, Podolski 50
6	01 Apr 09	Away	Wales	63	W	0 2	Ballack 11, A.Williams 48og
7	12 Aug 09	Away	Azerbaijan	137	W	0 2	Schweinsteiger 12, Klose 54
8	09 Sep 09	Home	Azerbaijan	137	W	4 0	Ballack 14pen, Klose 55, 66, Podolski 71
9	10 Oct 09	Away	Russia	11	W	0 1	Klose 34
10	14 Oct 09	Home	Finland	49	D	1 1	Podolski 90

Average FIFA ranking of opposition	81

MAIN PLAYER PERFORMANCES IN QUALIFICATION

Key: ■ played 90 mins « subbed off » subbed on ▦ on bench

Match	1 2 3 4 5 6 7 8 9 10	Appearances	Started	Subbed on	Subbed off	Mins played	% played	Goals	Yellow	Red
Venue	A A H H H A A H A H									
Result	W D W W W W W W W D									
Goalkeepers										
Rene Adler		5	5	0	0	450	50.0	0	0	0
Robert Enke		5	5	0	0	450	50.0	0	0	0
Defenders										
Andreas Beck		4	3	1	0	315	35.0	0	0	0
Jerome Boateng		1	1	0	0	68	7.6	0	1	1
Arne Friedrich		4	3	1	1	263	29.2	0	0	0
Clemens Fritz		3	2	1	0	197	21.9	0	0	0
Marcell Jansen		2	1	1	1	77	8.6	1	0	0
Philipp Lahm		10	10	0	0	900	100.0	0	0	0
Per Mertesacker		7	7	0	0	630	70.0	0	0	0
Marcel Schafer		2	2	0	1	135	15.0	0	0	0
Serdar Tasci		5	5	0	0	450	50.0	0	1	0
Heiko Westermann		8	7	1	0	642	71.3	1	0	0
Midfielders										
Mesut Ozil		4	2	2	1	213	23.7	0	0	0
Michael Ballack		8	8	0	1	675	75.0	4	0	0
Christian Gentner		1	0	1	0	45	5.0	0	0	0
Thomas Hitzlsperger		9	9	0	4	729	81.0	1	0	0
Marko Marin		2	0	2	0	35	3.9	0	0	0
Simon Rolfes		6	4	2	3	321	35.7	1	1	0
Bastian Schweinsteiger		9	9	0	3	778	86.4	3	0	0
Piotr Trochowski		9	6	3	2	566	62.9	1	0	0
Forwards										
Cacau		2	1	1	0	106	11.8	0	0	0
Mario Gomez		10	5	5	3	463	51.4	0	0	0
Patrick Helmes		4	0	4	0	86	9.6	0	0	0
Miroslav Klose		8	6	2	5	490	54.4	7	0	0
Lukas Podolski		9	9	0	4	762	84.7	6	0	0

FINAL PROSPECTS

Germany might not have the pool of world-class talent at their disposal that we've come to expect, but under manager Joachim Low they have developed into a formidable unit.

They play to their strengths with a decent batch of attacking players and remaining reasonably solid at the back, despite limited options.

One of the most successful World Cup nations of all-time, Germany have lifted the trophy on three occasions – most recently in 1990 – and travel to South Africa on the back of the terrific record of making at least the last 16 in each of the last seven tournaments.

Over recent years, Germany have developed a reputation for exceeding expectations at major tournaments and will need to do so again if they are to make the latter stages in South Africa.

Full-back Philipp Lahm, captain Michael Ballack and goal-poacher Miroslav Klose bring real quality to the side, while the likes of Bastian Schweinsteiger and Lukas Podolski are capable of causing opponents serious problems on their day.

> **Over recent years, Germany have developed a reputation for exceeding expectations at major tournaments**

However, the overall squad lacks the abundance of quality and strength in depth of other leading nations at the tournament, and Low will need to be at his tactical best to get the Germans any further than the last eight. The defence is a particular worry, and with out-of-favour Torsten Frings likely to miss out on the squad, there is a lack of solidity to the side – something you wouldn't expect from a German team.

Despite being drawn in a tricky group alongside Australia, a dangerous Ghana side and one of the most improved nations at the finals, Serbia, Germany will still expect to qualify. Australia – such a dangerous outfit in 2006 – aren't the side they once were, while their defensive mindset should invite Germany's attacking players on to them. For all the hype, Ghana are a beatable side, relying on a clutch of top-class midfielders to carry a team that lacks balance and quality in other areas of the pitch. Serbia are one of the 'dark horses' at this World Cup, but despite quality in all positions they are hardly a team to strike fear into German hearts.

DREAM TEAM TOP 15 RANKING 5

GROUP FIXTURES

AUSTRALIA	Sun 13 June 1930 BST
SERBIA	Fri 18 June 1230 BST
GHANA	Wed 23 June 1500 BST

KEY PLAYER

MIROSLAV KLOSE BAYERN MUNICH

One of the most feared finishers in world football, Miroslav Klose has had decent club careers with Kaiserslautern, Werder Bremen and Bayern Munich in the Bundesliga, but ups his game at international level.

The striker has bagged five goals in each of the last two World Cup finals – matching his 2002 haul to win the Golden Boot in 2006.

Playing record	12 months lge	wcq
Appearances:	21	8
Minutes played:	1191	490
Percentage played:	38.9%	54.4%
Goals scored:	4	7
Percentage share:	6.06%	26.92%
Cards:	Y0, R0	Y0, R0
Strike rate:	298mins	70mins
Strike rate ranking:	94th	3rd

AGE 32   STRIKER   DREAM TEAM   RANKING 1151

Berlin●

Zone	Europe
Population	82.3m
Language	German
Top league	Bundesliga
Playing season	August - May

Major clubs and capacities
Bayern Munich (69,900), Borussia Dortmund (80,552), Werder Bremen (80,552)

Where probable squad players play:

Premier League	1	Ligue 1	-
Serie A	-	Eredivisie	-
La Liga	-	Other Europe	-
Bundesliga	22	Outside Europe	-

Number of German players playing:

Premier League	3	Bundesliga	228
Serie A	1	Ligue 1	1
La Liga	1	Eredivisie	3

World Cup record   * best performance

1930 -	Withdrew	1974 -	* Champions
1934 -	3rd place	1978 -	2nd Round
1938 -	Round 1	1982 -	Runners up
1950 -	Banned	1986 -	Runners up
1954 -	* Champions	1990 -	* Champions
1958 -	4th place	1994 -	Quarter finals
1962 -	Quarter finals	1998 -	Quarter finals
1966 -	Runners up	2002 -	Runners up
1970 -	3rd place	2006 -	3rd place

THE SQUAD

Goalkeepers	Club side	Age	QG
Rene Adler	B Leverkusen	25	5
Manuel Neuer	Schalke	24	0
Defenders			
Andreas Beck	TSG Hoffenheim	23	4
Jerome Boateng	Hamburg	21	1
Arne Friedrich	Hertha Berlin	31	4
Clemens Fritz	W Bremen	29	3
Marcell Jansen	Hamburg	24	2
Philipp Lahm	Bayern Munich	26	10
Per Mertesacker	W Bremen	25	7
Marcel Schafer	Wolfsburg	26	2
Serdar Tasci	Stuttgart	23	5
Heiko Westermann	Schalke	26	8
Midfielders			
Mesut Ozil	W Bremen	21	4
Michael Ballack	Chelsea	33	8
Christian Gentner	Wolfsburg	24	1
Thomas Hitzlsperger	Stuttgart	28	9
Marko Marin	W Bremen	21	2
Simon Rolfes	B Leverkusen	28	6
Bastian Schweinsteiger	Bayern Munich	25	9
Piotr Trochowski	Hamburg	26	9
Forwards			
Cacau	Stuttgart	29	2
Mario Gomez	Bayern Munich	24	10
Patrick Helmes	B Leverkusen	26	4
Miroslav Klose	Bayern Munich	32	8
Kevin Kuranyi	Schalke	28	1
Lukas Podolski	Cologne	25	0

■ Probable ■ Possible **QG** Qualification Games

KEY GOALKEEPERS

RENE ADLER
BAYER LEVERKUSEN

Playing record	12 months lge	wcq
Appearances:	33	5
Minutes played:	2970	450
Percentage played:	97.1%	50.0%
Goals conceded:	38	2
Clean sheets:	10	3
Cards:	Y3, R0	Y0, R0
Minutes between goals:	78mins	225mins
Goalkeeper ranking:	16th	8th

AGE 25	DREAM TEAM	RANKING 191

MANUEL NEUER
SCHALKE

Playing record	12 months lge	wcq
Appearances:	33	0
Minutes played:	2970	0
Percentage played:	97.1%	0%
Goals conceded:	28	-
Clean sheets:	15	-
Cards:	Y2, R0	-
Minutes between goals:	106mins	-
Goalkeeper ranking:	6th	-

AGE 24	DREAM TEAM	RANKING 248

KEY DEFENDERS

HEIKO WESTERMANN
SCHALKE

A versatile defensive player, Westerman can be used across the back line and in a defensive midfield role.

Tall, athletic and with an eye for goal, the defender moved to the Bundesliga when he joined Arminia Bielefeld in 2005, before sealing a transfer to Schalke in 2007.

Playing record	12 months lge	wcq
Appearances:	34	8
Minutes played:	3015	642
Percentage played:	98.5%	71.3%
Goals conceded:	30	5
Clean sheets:	15	5
Cards:	Y4, R0	Y0, R0
Minutes between goals:	100mins	128mins
Defender ranking:	28th	67th

AGE 26	DREAM TEAM	RANKING 212

ARNE FRIEDRICH
HERTHA BERLIN

Playing record	12 months lge	wcq
Appearances:	23	4
Minutes played:	1927	263
Percentage played:	63.0%	29.2%
Goals conceded:	43	2
Clean sheets:	4	2
Cards:	Y6, R0	Y0, R0
Minutes between goals:	45mins	131mins
Defender ranking:	170th	66th

AGE 31	DREAM TEAM	RANKING 1071

PER MERTSACKER
WERDER BREMEN

Towering centre-back Per Mertesacker has been Germany's first-choice in defence since establishing himself in the team during qualification for the last World Cup. Still just 25, Mertesacker has already passed 50 caps for his country.

Strong in the air, he does lack the pace and physicality needed to rank him alongside the best defenders at the tournament, but his clean style sees him rarely give away free-kicks in dangerous areas of the pitch. A real threat presence from set-pieces at the other end of the pitch, Mertesacker is often used as a foil to allow the likes of Miroslav Klose and Lukas Podolski more space in the opposition box. The youngster started his career with local club Hanover, but an impressive string of performances at the 2006 World Cup saw him snapped up by Werder Bremen. Injured for much of qualification for this tournament, he strolled back into the starting line-up when back to full fitness. If Germany are to impress in South Africa, Mertesacker's performances are likely to be crucial.

Playing record	12 months lge	wcq
Appearances:	29	7
Minutes played:	2610	630
Percentage played:	85.3%	70.0%
Goals conceded:	30	1
Clean sheets:	10	6
Cards:	Y0, R0	Y0, R0
Minutes between goals:	87mins	630mins
Defender ranking:	61st	7th

AGE 25	DREAM TEAM	RANKING 84

THE MANAGER

The suave Joachim Low has shown enough managerial nous during his tenure as coach of Germany to suggest that the national side will once again be serious contenders for the World Cup title.

However, they lack the individual talent of some of the other leading football nations.

After a solid but unspectacular playing career and an equally unremarkable start to managing, Low was seen as a surprise choice when appointed as assistant coach of Germany in 2004 by personal friend Jurgen Klinsmann.

However, he excelled in the role, taking much of the credit as Germany finished third on home soil in the last World Cup, and his obvious tactical ability saw him emerge as the clear successor for the manager's job when Klinsmann stepped down in 2006. Low has since turned Germany into a potent attacking force, relying on a host of creative talent to take pressure off a shaky defence. He led them to the final of Euro 2008, before qualifying for South Africa with ease.

His innovative training methods and ability to make the most of the players at his disposal are two of the great strengths of the current Germany side, but he will need to be at his tactical best to get his team out of an extremely tough group.

PHILIPP LAHM

BAYERN MUNICH

One of the world's best attacking full-backs, Philipp Lahm – like a number of the Germany squad – ups his game at international level.

After playing all three games in Euro 2004, he established himself as the first-choice right-back, before excelling at the 2006 World Cup.

Switched to left-back in Euro 2008, Lahm also excelled on the other side of defence, proving the versatility that has seen him alternate between full-back positions during his time with Bayern Munich. An ever present in qualifying and the only German to play every minute of all ten games.

Playing record	12 months lge	wcq
Appearances:	32	10
Minutes played:	2869	900
Percentage played:	93.8%	100%
Goals conceded:	33	5
Clean sheets:	8	7
Cards:	Y2, R0	Y0, R0
Minutes between goals:	87mins	180mins
Defender ranking:	62nd	36th

AGE 26   **DREAM TEAM** **RANKING** 39

KEY PLAYER

MICHAEL BALLACK CHELSEA

Veteran Germany skipper Michael Ballack will play at his third World Cup in South Africa, having finished second in 2002 and third in 2006.

The three-time German Player of the Year has had a fantastic career, racking up a host of titles with FC Bayern and Chelsea, but has an unfortunate record of losing in major finals. This may well be his last chance.

Playing record	12 months lge	wcq
Appearances:	33	8
Minutes played:	2436	675
Percentage played:	69.4%	75.0%
Goals scored:	4	4
Clean sheets:	19	6
Cards:	Y2, R0	Y0, R0
Strike rate:	609mins	169mins
Midfielder ranking:	110th	4th

AGE 33   **MIDFIELDER**   **DREAM TEAM** **RANKING** 104

KEY MIDFIELDERS

THOMAS HITZLSPERGER
STUTTGART

Versatile midfielder Thomas Hitzlsperger is hard working, with an eye for a pass and a powerful shot, his defensive work allows the more attacking players in the midfield unit freedom to create.

Capable of playing in the middle or out on the left, the 28-year-old made a big impression at Aston Villa – where he started his career – earning the nickname of 'The Hammer' for his trademark long-range drive, before moving to Stuttgart in 2005.

The midfielder played in nine of the ten qualifying matches but is unlikely to retain his starting place at the tournament.

Playing record	12 months lge	wcq
Appearances:	27	9
Minutes played:	2189	729
Percentage played:	71.5%	81.0%
Goals scored:	5	1
Clean sheets:	11	6
Cards:	Y5, R0	Y0, R0
Strike rate:	438mins	729mins
Midfielder ranking:	79th	68th

AGE 28	DREAM TEAM	RANKING 396

SIMON ROLFES
BAYER LEVERKUSEN

A powerful and experienced central defensive midfielder, Simon Rofles made his Germany debut in 2007.

Joachim Low uses the midfielder in games against attacking sides, but the 28-year-old is far from a guaranteed starter for the national side. A powerful shot has seen him rack up a fair few goals in the Bundesliga with both Werder Bremen and Bayer Leverkusen – having made more than 100 appearances for both clubs. Tall, strong in the air, but lacking pace and the quality on the ball needed to stand out at the top level.

Playing record	12 months lge	wcq
Appearances:	25	6
Minutes played:	2189	321
Percentage played:	71.5%	35.7%
Goals scored:	5	1
Clean sheets:	7	5
Cards:	Y2, R0	Y1, R0
Strike rate:	438mins	321mins
Midfielder ranking:	80th	30th

AGE 28	DREAM TEAM	RANKING 583

PIOTR TROCHOWSKI
HAMBURG

An extremely talented attacking midfielder, Piotr Trochowski has emerged as a genuine first-team option for the German national side since his debut in 2006.

Let go by Bayern Munich in 2005 after becoming disillusioned with a lack of playing time, the playmaker excelled with a Hamburg side who have established themselves as a major force in the Bundesliga. Born in Poland, the diminutive Trochowski instead opted to represent Germany and has become a key member of Joachim Low's squad. A certainty for the World Cup finals if fit, Trochowski's creative skills can make the most of the collective talents of Lukas Podolski, Miroslav Klose and company.

Playing record	12 months lge	wcq
Appearances:	32	9
Minutes played:	2271	566
Percentage played:	74.2%	62.9%
Goals scored:	6	1
Clean sheets:	14	6
Cards:	Y5, R0	Y0, R0
Strike rate:	378mins	566mins
Midfielder ranking:	63rd	58th

AGE 26	DREAM TEAM	RANKING 185

KEY STRIKERS

LUKAS PODOLSKI
COLOGNE

Lukas Podolski is another Germany international who seems more at home when representing the national side.

The forward failed to tie down a regular first team place when he moved to Bayern Munich in 2006, forcing him into a return to Cologne – the club with whom he started his career. The Germany squad's youngest member at Euro 2004, Podolski made a name for himself in the 2006 World Cup, being named the Best Young Player at the tournament, ahead of the likes of Lionel Messi and Cristiano Ronaldo. Polish-born, the forward also excelled at Euro 2008. He can either be used in a partnership with Miroslav Klose or in an attacking left-wing position. Podolski is in his element when playing for Germany and his versatile qualities make him a real asset for Joachim Low's side.

Playing record	12 months lge	wcq
Appearances:	28	9
Minutes played:	2257	762
Percentage played:	73.8%	84.7%
Goals scored:	4	6
Percentage share:	15.38%	23.08%
Cards:	Y6, R0	Y0, R0
Strike rate:	564mins	127mins
Strike rate ranking:	118th	16th

AGE 25	DREAM TEAM	RANKING 703

MARIO GOMEZ
BAYERN MUNICH

A talented and prolific front man at club level, Mario Gomez has struggled to establish himself in the Germany side, with Joachim Low appearing to prefer a Lukas Podolski and Miroslav Klose partnership.

The tall and powerful forward did partner Klose in the group stages of Euro 2008 – at the expense of Bastian Schweinsteiger, with Podolski moving out wide – but he failed to replicate his sensational form with Stuttgart – his club at the time – and was relegated to the bench in the knockout stages. Gomez lacks the composure to be considered genuinely top class.

Playing record	12 months lge	wcq
Appearances:	33	10
Minutes played:	2464	463
Percentage played:	80.5%	51.4%
Goals scored:	25	0
Percentage share:	37.88%	0.00%
Cards:	Y1, R0	Y0, R0
Strike rate:	99mins	-
Strike rate ranking:	4th	-

AGE 24	DREAM TEAM RANKING 140

ONE TO WATCH

BASTIAN SCHWEINSTEIGER BAYERN MUNICH

Another of Germany's group of talented attacking midfielders, Bastian Schweinsteiger has excelled at major tournaments in the past.

Right-footed, but often used as a left-winger who cuts inside, Schweinsteiger has also been deployed in a more central creative role at club level. He has racked up over 200 appearances for Bayern Munich – the club with whom he started his career – but can't always replicate his form for Germany at club level. Supreme in Euro 2004 and impressive at the 2006 World Cup, Schweinsteiger was initially dropped from the Germany side for Mario Gomez, but regained his place in the knockout stages as Low's team reached the final.

Schweinsteiger is a Top 12 Midfielder

AGE 25	MIDFIELDER	DREAM TEAM RANKING 48

ROUTE TO THE FINALS

Serbia qualified for the World Cup as an independent nation at the first time of asking as they topped European qualification Group 7, forcing group favourites France into the play-offs.

Serbia is the FIFA recognised descendant of what was Serbia and Montenegro until 2006. The team did the country proud in a qualification campaign that saw them emerge as one of the potential dark horses for South Africa. Serbia's success was built on a solid defence, led by Nemanja Vidic and Branislav Ivanovic. But an attacking unit containing Nikola Zigic, Milos Krasic and the team's top-scorer in qualifying, Milan Jovanovic, was a handful for all their opponents in the group.

Despite picking up just a point from two games against the French, it was Serbia's consistency in their remaining matches that set them apart in the group. The only other game they failed to win was their final one in Lithuania, when top spot in the group was already assured. Nenad Milijas' penalty helped Serbia to a 1-1 draw with France in September 2009, a result that proved vital, leaving Raddy Antic's side four points clear at the top and needing just a win in one of the two remaining games to secure automatic qualification.

They did so in style, thrashing Romania 5-0 on a famous night in Belgrade. Dangerous front man Nicola Zigic opened the scoring in the first half, before Marko Pantelic and Zdravko Kuzmanovic wrapped up the win after the break, leaving winger Jovanovic to secure qualification in style with two late goals.

For final qualification table see France.

	Date	Venue	Opposition	Avge FIFA ranking	Result	Score	Scorers
1	06 Sep 08	Home	Faroe Islands	178	W	2 0	J.Jacobsen 30og, Zigic 88
2	10 Sep 08	Away	France	10	L	2 1	Ivanovic 76
3	11 Oct 08	Home	Lithuania	54	W	3 0	Ivanovic 6, Krasic 34, Zigic 82
4	15 Oct 08	Away	Austria	74	W	1 3	Krasic 15, M.Jovanovic 18, Obradovic 24
5	28 Mar 09	Away	Romania	21	W	2 3	M.Jovanovic 18, D.Stoica 44og, Ivanovic 59
6	06 Jun 09	Home	Austria	74	W	1 0	Milijas 7pen
7	10 Jun 09	Away	Faroe Islands	178	W	0 2	M.Jovanovic 44, Subotic 62
8	09 Sep 09	Home	France	10	D	1 1	Milijas 13pen
9	10 Oct 09	Home	Romania	21	W	5 0	Zigic 37, Pantelic 50, Kuzmanovic 78, M.Jovanovic 86, 90
10	14 Oct 09	Away	Lithuania	54	L	2 1	Z.Tosic 59
	Average FIFA ranking of opposition			67			

MAIN PLAYER PERFORMANCES IN QUALIFICATION

Match	1 2 3 4 5 6 7 8 9 10	Appearances	Started	Subbed on	Subbed off	Mins played	% played	Goals	Yellow	Red
Venue	H A H A A H A H H A									
Result	W L W W W W W D W L									
Goalkeepers										
Vladimir Disljenkovic		2	2	0	0	180	20.0	0	0	0
Vladimir Stojkovic		8	8	0	0	720	80.0	0	0	0
Defenders										
Ivica Dragutinovic		6	5	1	1	428	47.6	0	1	0
Branislav Ivanovic		9	9	0	0	810	90.0	3	1	0
Gojko Kacar		5	2	3	1	238	26.4	0	0	0
Mladen Krstajic		2	1	1	0	157	17.4	0	0	0
Ivan Obradovic		6	6	0	1	509	56.6	1	2	0
Antonio Rukavina		2	1	1	0	135	15.0	0	1	0
Neven Subotic		5	3	2	0	313	34.8	1	2	0
Dusko Tosic		1	1	0	0	90	10.0	0	0	0
Nemanja Vidic		8	8	0	2	657	73.0	0	1	0
Midfielders										
Bosko Jankovic		6	1	5	0	202	22.4	0	2	0
Aleksandar Kolarov		2	2	0	0	180	20.0	0	0	0
Milos Krasic		10	9	1	3	760	84.4	2	0	0
Zdravko Kuzmanovic		6	2	4	0	300	33.3	1	1	0
Aleksandar Lukovic		5	4	1	1	346	38.4	0	1	0
Nenad Milijas		8	8	0	4	605	67.2	2	1	0
Radoslav Petrovic		1	1	0	0	90	10.0	0	0	0
Dejan Stankovic		8	8	0	2	620	68.9	0	4	0
Zoran Tosic		3	1	2	1	147	16.3	1	0	0
Forwards										
Milan Jovanovic		8	8	0	4	650	72.2	5	1	0
Danko Lazovic		3	1	2	1	96	10.7	0	0	1
Marko Pantelic		9	9	0	5	681	75.7	1	0	0
Miralem Sulejmani		2	1	1	1	82	9.1	0	0	0
Nikola Zigic		9	8	1	0	754	83.8	3	2	0

FINAL PROSPECTS

Serbia could yet shape up to be one of the surprise packages in South Africa.

They earned the right to be there with some impressive performances in qualifying, consigning France to second place in Group 7. In terms of personnel, they are a talented squad and have a good crop of players in their prime – led by the vastly experienced midfielder Dejan Stankovic of Inter Milan. Manchester United's Nemanja Vidic is the most familiar face in a quality defensive unit that also includes Chelsea's underrated full-back Branislav Ivanovic.

Stankovic is joined in midfield by the talented CSKA Moscow playmaker Milos Krasic – who was superb in this season's Champions League – and Milan Jovanovic. Valencia marksman Nikola Zigic is the perfect target to lead the line.

Serbia's opener against the highly fancied Ghana in front of a partisan African crowd will be crucial, with both teams eyeing the knockout stages. Things won't get any easier when they face the ever-dangerous Germany in the following game. In a tough-to-call group, Raddy Antic's side will probably need a victory in their final game against Australia if they are to progress.

DREAM TEAM TOP 15 RANKING 15

THE MANAGER

Former manager of Real Madrid, Atletico Madrid and Barcelona – the only manager to have taken charge of all three Spanish giants – Radomir 'Raddy' Antic was made coach of Serbia in 2008.

He has turned a talented squad into a well-balanced unit that topped their qualification group. They are considered a major threat to the more established nations in South Africa. A talented player who forged a great reputation in England during a four-year spell with Luton Town. Antic has had even more success as a coach, with a league and cup double at Atletico Madrid in 1996 being the highlight to date.

GROUP FIXTURES

GHANA	Sun 13 June 1500 BST
GERMANY	Fri 18 June 1230 BST
AUSTRALIA	Wed 23 June 1930 BST

KEY PLAYER

NEMANJA VIDIC MANCHESTER UTD

Combative defender Nemanja Vidic has developed into a world-class centre-back at Manchester United.

The leader of Serbia's back-four, Vidic's ability in the air gives the side solidity at the back and a real threat in the opposition penalty box from set-pieces. No striker at the tournament will relish facing a fit and in-form Vidic who will be vital for Serbia.

Playing record	12 months lge	wcq
Appearances:	30	8
Minutes played:	2569	657
Percentage played:	69.6%	73.0%
Goals conceded:	18	6
Clean sheets:	17	4
Cards:	Y7, R2	Y1, R0
Minutes between goals:	143mins	109mins
Defender ranking:	7th	83rd

AGE 28   **DEFENDER**   **DREAM TEAM RANKING** 46

Zone	Europe
Population	7.4m
Language	Serbian
Top league	Prva Liga
Playing season	August - May

Major clubs and capacities
Crvena Zvezda (54,069), Partizan (30,887), Vojvodina (15,205)

Where probable squad players play:

Premier League	5	Ligue 1	-
Serie A	4	Eredivisie	3
La Liga	3	Other Europe	4
Bundesliga	4	Outside Europe	-

Number of Serbian players playing:

Premier League	6	Bundesliga	9
Serie A	10	Ligue 1	9
La Liga	3	Eredivisie	11

World Cup record   * *best performance*

1930 - * 4th place	1974 - Round 2
1934 - Did not qualify	1978 - Did not qualify
1938 - Did not qualify	1982 - Round 1
1950 - Round 1	1986 - Did not qualify
1954 - Quarter finals	1990 - Quarter finals
1958 - Quarter finals	1994 - Banned
1962 - * 4th place	1998 - Last 16
1966 - Did not qualify	2002 - Did not qualify
1970 - Did not qualify	2006 - Group stages

*including Serbia & Montenegro and Yugoslavia

THE SQUAD

Goalkeepers	Club side	Age	QG
Vladimir Disljenkovic	Metalurh Donetsk	28	2
Vladimir Stojkovic	Wigan	26	8
Defenders			
Ivica Dragutinovic	Sevilla	34	6
Branislav Ivanovic	Chelsea	26	9
Gojko Kacar	Hertha Berlin	23	5
Mladen Krstajic	Partizan	36	2
Ivan Obradovic	Real Zaragoza	21	6
Antonio Rukavina	1860 Munich	26	2
Neven Subotic	B Dortmund	21	5
Dusko Tosic	W Bremen	25	1
Nemanja Vidic	Man Utd	28	8
Midfielders			
Sasa Ilic	Salzburg	32	1
Bosko Jankovic	Genoa	26	6
Aleksandar Kolarov	Lazio	24	2
Milos Krasic	CSKA Moscow	25	10
Zdravko Kuzmanovic	Stuttgart	22	6
Aleksandar Lukovic	Udinese	27	5
Nenad Milijas	Wolverhampton	27	8
Radoslav Petrovic	Partizan	21	1
Dejan Stankovic	Inter Milan	31	8
Zoran Tosic	Man Utd	23	3
Forwards			
Milan Jovanovic	Standard Liege	29	8
Danko Lazovic	PSV Eindhoven	27	3
Marko Pantelic	Ajax	31	9
Miralem Sulejmani	Ajax	21	2
Nikola Zigic	Valencia	29	9

■ Probable ■ Possible **QG** Qualification Games

ROUTE TO THE FINALS

Australia reaped the rewards of a switch to the Asian qualifying process, topping both groups in the two-stage campaign and bagging an automatic qualification spot for the finals as a result.

Defeats to Iran and China in the first phase of qualifying left the Socceroos level on points with Qatar after all six games, but they topped the group on goal difference, picking up an all-important seeded place for the final stage of qualifying.

Drawn against Japan, Bahrain, Uzbekistan and Qatar once again in Group A, Australia cruised to victory, finishing top of the group by five points, and conceded just one goal in eight games – in their final game when top spot was already assured.

A 4-0 win over Qatar was the highlight of qualification, with goals from Tim Cahill, Joshua Kennedy and two from Brett Emerton wrapping up a fine win in Brisbane.

FINAL QUALIFYING TABLE
ASIA ROUND 4 GROUP 1

	P	W	D	L	F	A	Pts
Australia	8	6	2	0	12	1	20
Japan	8	4	3	1	11	6	15
Bahrain	8	3	1	4	6	8	10
Qatar	8	1	3	4	5	14	6
Uzbekistan	8	1	1	6	5	10	4

Avge FIFA ranking

#	Date	H/A	Opponent	Rank	Res	Score	Scorers
1	06 Feb 08	Home	Qatar	85	W	3 0	Kennedy 10, Cahill 18, Bresciano 33
2	26 Mar 08	Away	China PR	98	D	0 0	
3	01 Jun 08	Home	Iraq	81	W	1 0	Kewell 47
4	07 Jun 08	Away	Iraq	81	L	1 0	
5	14 Jun 08	Away	Qatar	85	W	1 3	Emerton 17, 56, Kewell 75
6	22 Jun 08	Home	China PR	98	L	0 1	
7	10 Sep 08	Away	Uzbekistan	71	W	0 1	Chipperfield 26
8	15 Oct 08	Home	Qatar	85	W	4 0	Cahill 8, Emerton 17pen, 58, Kennedy 76
9	19 Nov 08	Away	Bahrain	71	W	0 1	Bresciano 90
10	11 Feb 09	Away	Japan	36	D	0 0	
11	01 Apr 09	Home	Uzbekistan	71	W	2 0	Kennedy 66, Kewell 73pen
12	06 Jun 09	Away	Qatar	85	D	0 0	
13	10 Jun 09	Home	Bahrain	71	W	2 0	Sterjovski 55, Carney 88
14	17 Jun 09	Home	Japan	36	W	2 1	Cahill 59, 77

Average FIFA ranking of opposition 75

MAIN PLAYER PERFORMANCES IN QUALIFICATION

Match: 1 2 3 4 5 6 7 8 9 10 11 12 13 14
Venue: H A H A A H A H A A H A H H
Result: W D W L W L W W W D W D W W

Player	Appearances	Started	Subbed on	Subbed off	Mins played	% played	Goals	Yellow	Red
Goalkeepers									
Michael Petkovic	1	1	0	0	90	7.1	0	0	0
Mark Schwarzer	13	13	0	0	1170	92.9	0	2	0
Defenders									
Michael Beauchamp	5	5	0	0	450	35.7	0	0	0
David Carney	10	8	2	0	739	58.7	1	3	0
Chris Coyne	5	5	0	3	383	30.4	0	1	0
Mark Milligan	1	1	0	0	90	7.1	0	1	0
Craig Moore	3	3	0	1	256	20.3	0	1	0
Lucas Neill	9	9	0	0	810	64.3	0	2	0
Shane Steffanuto	1	1	0	0	90	7.1	0	0	0
Nikolai Topor-Stanley	1	1	0	0	90	7.1	0	0	0
Luke Wilkshire	11	11	0	0	990	78.6	0	5	0
Midfielders									
Mark Bresciano	9	9	0	4	748	59.4	2	1	0
Jacob Burns	3	1	2	0	109	8.7	0	0	0
Tim Cahill	6	6	0	5	498	39.5	4	0	0
Scott Chipperfield	5	5	0	1	405	32.1	1	1	0
Jason Culina	12	12	0	0	1080	85.7	0	0	0
Bruce Djite	4	1	3	0	111	8.8	0	0	0
Brett Emerton	6	6	0	1	535	42.5	4	1	0
Richard Garcia	3	1	2	0	118	9.4	0	0	0
Vincenzo Grella	7	6	1	2	505	40.1	0	2	0
Michael John Jedinak	3	2	1	2	149	11.8	0	1	0
Harry Kewell	9	9	0	6	733	58.2	3	0	0
Jade North	9	6	3	0	598	47.5	0	0	0
Matthew Spiranovic	1	1	0	0	90	7.1	0	0	0
Carl Valeri	11	9	2	1	854	67.8	0	3	0
Ruben Zadkovich	1	1	0	0	90	7.1	0	0	0
Forwards									
Brett Holman	12	4	8	3	550	43.7	0	1	0
Joshua Kennedy	8	5	3	1	492	39.0	3	0	0
Scott McDonald	7	5	2	3	406	32.2	0	0	0
Mile Sterjovski	5	2	3	0	243	19.3	1	0	0

FINAL PROSPECTS

A far more defensive side than the Australian team that reached the last 16 under Guus Hiddink in 2006, the Aussie outfit that travels to South Africa will still feel confident that they can qualify from Group D and maybe even improve on their efforts of four years ago.

The tactical genius of Hiddink inspired the Socceroos to a second-place group finish in Germany four years ago. A win over Japan and a late Harry Kewell penalty against Croatia was enough to see them through to the second round. A gut-wrenching defeat to a 95th-minute penalty winner against the eventual winners Italy was a cruel way to go out of the tournament. Progress to the knockout stages represented a huge step forward for the country after they had failed to score in all three games of their only other World Cup appearance back in 1974.

Their quality proved too much for the Asian teams in qualification for South Africa

A comfortable qualification campaign this time out saw a squad of predominantly European-based players dominate their Asian opponents, as the Socceroos competed in AFC qualifying for the first time.

The ageing Australian team is set up in a much more orthodox way than it was under Hiddink, with manager Pim Verbeek tending to prefer either a 4-4-2 system, or a 4-5-1 formation with Tim Cahill supporting the lone forward. Big target man Joshua Kennedy or the nippier alternative Brett Holman allow the likes of Cahill and Kewell the opportunity to get on the ball in the final third. Their quality proved too much for the Asian teams, and is likely to cause many of the world's best some problems. Emerton and Mark Bersciano add steel and quality in midfield, with Verbeek often using two defensively minded central players to shield the back line. Scott Chipperfield and Lucas Neill lead an experienced defensive unit in front of Mark Schwarzer, one of the most underrated goalkeepers at the finals. However, their big-name players will need to be at their best to lead Verbeek's side out of a group that contains Germany and two of the most highly-fancied 'dark horses', Ghana and Serbia.

Germany's defensive weaknesses may offer an upset in the opening game, but Serbia's all-round game and Ghana's strong midfield will really test the Socceroos.

DREAM TEAM	TOP 15 RANKING	18

GROUP FIXTURES

GERMANY	Sun 13 June 1930 BST
GHANA	Sat 19 June 1500 BST
SERBIA	Wed 23 June 1930 BST

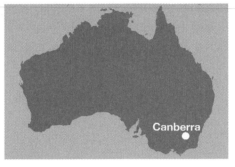

Canberra

Zone	Asia
Population	20.1m
Language	English
Top league	The A League
Playing season	August - March

Major clubs and capacities
Melbourne Victory (56,347), Sydney FC (45,503), Newcastle Jets (26,164)

Where probable squad players play:

Premier League	5	Ligue 1	-
Serie A	1	Eredivisie	2
La Liga	-	Other Europe	10
Bundesliga	-	Outside Europe	5

Number of Australian players playing:

Premier League	7	Bundesliga	-
Serie A	1	Ligue 1	-
La Liga	-	Eredivisie	3

World Cup record * best performance

1930 - Did not enter	1974 - Round 1
1934 - Did not enter	1978 - Did not qualify
1938 - Did not enter	1982 - Did not qualify
1950 - Did not enter	1986 - Did not qualify
1954 - Did not enter	1990 - Did not qualify
1958 - Did not enter	1994 - Did not qualify
1962 - Did not enter	1998 - Did not qualify
1966 - Did not qualify	2002 - Did not qualify
1970 - Did not qualify	2006 - * Last 16

THE SQUAD

	Club side	Age	QG
Goalkeepers			
Michael Petkovic	Sivasspor	33	1
Mark Schwarzer	Fulham	37	13
Defenders			
Michael Beauchamp	Aalborg BK	29	5
David Carney	Twente	26	10
Chris Coyne	Perth Glory	31	5
Mark Milligan	Shanghai Shenhua	24	1
Craig Moore	AO Kavala	34	3
Lucas Neill	Galatasaray	39	9
Luke Wilkshire	Dinamo Moscow	28	11
Midfielders			
Mark Bresciano	Palermo	30	9
Jacob Burns	Perth Glory	32	3
Tim Cahill	Everton	30	6
Scott Chipperfield	Basel	34	5
Jason Culina	Gold Coast United	29	12
Bruce Djite	Genclerbirligi	23	4
Brett Emerton	Blackburn	30	6
Richard Garcia	Hull City	28	3
Vincenzo Grella	Blackburn	30	7
Michael John Jedinak	Antalayaspor	25	3
Harry Kewell	Galatasaray	31	9
Jade North	Incheon Utd	28	9
Carl Valeri	Grosseto	25	11
Forwards			
Brett Holman	AZ Alkmaar	26	12
Joshua Kennedy	Nagoya Grampus	27	8
Scott McDonald	Celtic	26	7
Mile Sterjovski	Perth Glory	31	5

■ Probable ■ Possible **QG** Qualification Games

KEY PLAYER

TIM CAHILL EVERTON

A vastly underrated attacking midfielder, Tim Cahill will have a major part to play if Australia are to progress from Group D, as long as the injury-prone Evertonian remains fit.

Despite his lack of height, Cahill is a threat in the air and is at his best when making late runs to support a lone striker or front-two.

Playing record	12 months lge	wcq
Appearances:	35	6
Minutes played:	2912	498
Percentage played:	83.0%	39.5%
Goals scored:	6	4
Clean sheets:	15	5
Cards:	Y7, R0	Y0, R0
Strike rate:	485mins	124mins
Midfielder ranking:	89th	2nd

AGE 30 **MIDFIELDER** **DREAM TEAM RANKING** 203

KEY GOALKEEPER

MARK SCHWARZER
FULHAM

Mark Schwarzer has had a great couple of years with overachieving Premier League side Fulham.

The 37-year-old's experience and ability to control his area make Australia a very strong defensive unit. His shot-stopping ability and terrific penalty saving record could make the difference between the Socceroos crashing out at the first hurdle or springing another World Cup surprise. With both Serbia and Germany dangerous going forward, Schwarzer will need to be at his best.

Playing record	12 months lge	wcq
Appearances:	38	13
Minutes played:	3420	1170
Percentage played:	90.5%	92.9%
Goals conceded:	41	3
Clean sheets:	13	10
Cards:	Y0, R0	Y2, R0
Minutes between goals:	83mins	390mins
Goalkeeper ranking:	14th	2nd

AGE 37	DREAM TEAM RANKING 40

KEY DEFENDERS

LUCAS NEILL
GALATASARAY

An experienced and reliable right-back, Lucas Neill brings proven quality to a solid Australian defence. Usually deployed as a full-back, the skipper can also play in the centre of defence if needed.

Playing record	12 months lge	wcq
Appearances:	29	9
Minutes played:	2450	810
Percentage played:	69.8%	64.3%
Goals conceded:	34	1
Clean sheets:	10	8
Cards:	Y6, R0	Y2, R0
Minutes between goals:	72mins	810mins
Defender ranking:	111th	4th

BRETT EMERTON
BLACKBURN

Another experienced member of the Australia side, Brett Emerton can play right-back, right midfield or in a central role. He will hope to avoid a repeat of the 2006 World Cup, where a late red card against Croatia saw him suspended for the second round defeat to Italy.

Playing record	12 months lge	wcq
Appearances:	16	6
Minutes played:	1088	535
Percentage played:	29.5%	42.5%
Goals conceded:	-	-
Clean sheets:	7	4
Cards:	Y2, R0	Y1, R0
Minutes between goals:	-	-
Defender ranking:	-	-

AGE 30	DREAM TEAM RANKING 1711

KEY MIDFIELDERS

VINCENZO GRELLA
BLACKBURN

Underrated defensive midfielder Vince Grella epitomises Pim Verbeek's Australia side. Hard-working and not a player likely to steal the headlines, Grella's role in shielding the Socceroos back line is key.

He excelled in that position to such an extent back in 2006 that he was named on the shortlist for Team of the Tournament. A team-mate of Brett Emerton at Blackburn Rovers for the past two seasons, the midfielder has struggled with injuries and has failed to tie down a first team place...at club level at least. He could play a major role in South Africa, if he is fit.

Playing record	12 months lge	wcq
Appearances:	23	7
Minutes played:	1651	505
Percentage played:	44.7%	40.1%
Goals scored:	0	0
Clean sheets:	11	5
Cards:	Y4, R1	Y2, R0
Strike rate:	-	-
Midfielder ranking:	178th	137th

JASON CULINA
GOLD COAST UNITED

Playing record	12 months lge	wcq
Appearances:	-	12
Minutes played:	-	1080
Percentage played:	-	85.7%
Goals scored:	-	0
Clean sheets:	-	9
Cards:	-	Y0, R0
Strike rate:	-	-
Midfielder ranking:	-	-

AGE 29	DREAM TEAM RANKING 1083

THE MANAGER

Assistant to Guus Hiddink with South Korea at the 2002 World Cup, Pim Verbeek faced a tough task when he took over as manager of the Socceroos in 2007.

Despite leading the country through qualification, Verbeek has come in for criticism for a perceived negative style that sees his side often use a lone front man and two holding midfielders, relying on crosses and knock-downs rather than the passing football that the fans had become accustomed to. An outspoken man, Verbeek has backed his tactics to the hilt, dismissing claims that Australia now play boring football.

Qualification for the country's third World Cup with an ageing squad of players – most of whom are based with clubs on the other side of the world – should have pacified most of the manager's critics. Hiddink's impressive feats at the 2006 World Cup were always going to be a tough act to follow, and he will need all his experience to get out of Group D.

KEY STRIKER

BRETT HOLMAN
AZ ALKMAAR

Brett Holman is another of Australia's talented attacking midfielders. However, having played for most of his career in Holland's Eredivisie, it is unclear whether the creative talent has enough quality to cut it at the top level of club football.

He certainly doesn't score enough goals for a player of his natural ability, but the combination of work-rate and spark that he brings to the side – from either a central or wide attacking midfield position – is perfect for an Australia team who prefer to play on the break. Holman could secure himself a move to a bigger team if he has a good tournament.

Playing record	12 months lge	wcq
Appearances:	16	12
Minutes played:	1050	550
Percentage played:	33.3%	43.7%
Goals scored:	3	0
Percentage share:	-	-
Cards:	Y3, R0	Y1, R0
Strike rate:	-	-
Strike rate ranking:	-	-

AGE 26	DREAM TEAM	RANKING 1471

ONE TO WATCH

HARRY KEWELL GALATASARAY

Still only 31 years old, Harry Kewell's career has been hampered by a string of injury problems.

Probably the stand out Australian player of his generation, Kewell is a skilful attacking midfield player, effective in either a wide or central role. Man of the Match as Australia beat Croatia to make the last 16 in 2006, Kewell will be a key member of the team.

Playing record	12 months lge	wcq
Appearances:	-	9
Minutes played:	-	733
Percentage played:	-	58.2%
Goals scored:	-	3
Percentage share:	-	15.8%
Cards:	-	Y0, R0
Strike rate:	-	244mins
Strike rate ranking:	-	51st

AGE 31	MIDFIELDER	DREAM TEAM	RANKING 1617

GHANA

ROUTE TO THE FINALS

Ghana wrapped up automatic qualification for the World Cup with two games to spare, despite suffering a scare in the first stage of the lengthy African qualification process.

Defeats to Gabon (2-0) and Libya (1-0) left the Black Stars in a three-way tie at the top of Group E, with just two teams set to go through, but they finished top courtesy of superior goal difference with Libya being the unfortunate team to miss out.

The second stage of qualification was far more straightforward, despite the fact that Milovan Rajevac's side were drawn in a group with the much-improved Mali and Benin.

Four wins from their first four games, with seven goals scored and not a single goal conceded, saw Ghana top the group with consummate ease. A hard-fought 2-2 draw with Mali was a strong way to finish the campaign. The most successful nation in African football history will have high hopes of building on their qualification successes in the first ever World Cup hosted in their continent.

FINAL QUALIFYING TABLE
AFRICA ROUND 3 GROUP D

	P	W	D	L	F	A	Pts
Ghana	6	4	1	1	9	3	13
Benin	6	3	1	2	6	6	10
Mali	6	2	3	1	8	7	9
Sudan	6	0	1	5	2	9	1

#	Date	Venue	Opponent	Avge FIFA ranking	Result			Scorers
1	01 Jun 08	Home	Libya	84	W	3	0	Tagoe 17, Agogo 54, L.Kingston 64
2	08 Jun 08	Away	Lesotho	160	W	2	3	L.Kingston 15, Agogo 41, 63
3	14 Jun 08	Away	Gabon	59	L	2	0	
4	22 Jun 08	Home	Gabon	59	W	2	0	Tagoe 31, Muntari 75
5	05 Sep 08	Away	Libya	84	L	1	0	
6	11 Oct 08	Home	Lesotho	160	W	3	0	Appiah 19, Agogo 24, M.Amoah 62
7	29 Mar 09	Home	Benin	91	W	1	0	Tagoe 1
8	07 Jun 09	Away	Mali	50	W	0	2	K.Asamoah 66, M.Amoah 78
9	20 Jun 09	Away	Sudan	97	W	0	2	M.Amoah 6, 52
10	06 Sep 09	Home	Sudan	97	W	2	0	Muntari 14, Essien 53
11	11 Oct 09	Away	Benin	91	L	1	0	
12	15 Nov 09	Home	Mali	50	D	2	2	M.Amoah 65, Annan 83

Average FIFA ranking of opposition	90

MAIN PLAYER PERFORMANCES IN QUALIFICATION

Match	1 2 3 4 5 6 7 8 9 10 11 12	Appearances	Started	Subbed on	Subbed off	Mins played	% played	Goals	Yellow	Red
Venue	H A A H A H H A A H A H									
Result	W W L W L W W W W W L D									
Goalkeepers										
Richard Kingson		12	12	0	0	1080	100.0	0	1	0
Defenders										
Harrison Afful		10	10	0	0	900	83.3	0	0	0
Samuel Inkoom		4	4	0	0	360	33.3	0	0	0
John Mensah		8	8	0	1	707	65.5	0	1	0
John Paintsil		11	11	0	1	988	91.5	0	2	0
Jonathan Quartey		4	4	0	0	360	33.3	0	0	0
Midfielders										
Eric Addo		11	11	0	1	945	87.5	0	1	0
Emmanuel Agyemang-Badu		3	1	2	1	103	9.5	0	1	0
Anthony Annan		12	12	0	1	1074	99.4	1	1	0
Stephen Appiah		6	5	1	5	442	40.9	1	1	0
Michael Essien		11	11	0	4	899	83.2	1	1	0
Laryea Kingston		7	5	2	3	390	36.1	2	2	0
Samuel Kyere		1	1	0	1	70	6.5	0	0	0
Sulley Muntari		8	8	0	5	679	62.9	2	2	0
Samuel Yeboah		1	1	0	0	90	8.3	0	0	0
Forwards										
Junior Agogo		7	5	2	3	435	40.3	4	1	0
Matthew Amoah		7	7	0	3	589	54.5	5	1	0
Kwadwo Asamoah		4	2	2	0	241	22.3	1	1	0
Eric Bekoe		4	1	3	1	75	6.9	0	0	0
Haminu Draman		10	2	8	0	279	25.8	0	0	0
Asamoah Gyan		4	2	2	0	201	18.6	0	0	0
Quincy Owusu-Abeyie		3	0	3	0	78	7.2	0	0	0
Prince Tagoe		8	7	1	3	625	57.9	3	0	0

FINAL PROSPECTS

One of the more highly rated of an impressive group of African teams at the World Cup, Ghana will fancy their chances of making the last 16 in South Africa.

Despite being one of the powerhouses of African football for many years, Ghana failed to qualify for a single World Cup until 2006. They made amends for their long-term absence by being the only African side to make it out of the group stage, losing to Brazil in the last 16.

The world-class Michael Essien is ably supported by Sulley Muntari and Stephen Appiah in a formidably strong midfield. It is this central unit that means Ghana will be a decent match for every side in Group D and are certainly worth a wager to progress.

However, a slightly suspect defence and a lack of genuine top-class options up front mean that the Black Stars lack the quality needed to become the first African World Cup final winners. It will be a surprise if they improve on their second-round best – particularly given that one of the tournament favourites, England, are the likely opponents in the second round if they do manage to make it through the group phase.

DREAM TEAM TOP 15 RANKING 17

THE MANAGER

A surprise choice when appointed Ghana coach in 2008. Never having played or managed outside of his home country of Serbia, Milovan Rajevac proved his doubters wrong leading the Black Stars to the 2010 finals with an impressive qualification campaign, losing just once in 12 games.

Success with club side Borac Cacak earned Rajevac international recognition. He has shown enough in the last two years to suggest he has the ability to guide Ghana into the last 16 – although he will need luck on his side to take a squad short on match-winning players any further than that.

GROUP FIXTURES

SERBIA	Sun 13 June 1500 BST
AUSTRALIA	Sat 19 June 1500 BST
GERMANY	Wed 23 June 1930 BST

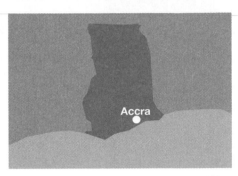

Accra

Zone	Africa
Population	22.2m
Language	English
Top league	Ghana Premiere League
Playing season	November - July

Major clubs and capacities
Hearts of Oak (40,000), Asante Kotoko (40,000),
Goldfields (30,000)

Where probable squad players play:

Premier League	4	Ligue 1	2
Serie A	3	Eredivisie	2
La Liga	-	Other Europe	7
Bundesliga	2	Outside Europe	3

Number of Ghanaian players playing:

Premier League	4	Bundesliga	3
Serie A	2	Ligue 1	6
La Liga	1	Eredivisie	7

World Cup record   ** best performance*

1930 - Did not enter	1974 - Did not qualify
1934 - Did not enter	1978 - Did not qualify
1938 - Did not enter	1982 - Withdrew
1950 - * Quarter finals	1986 - Did not qualify
1954 - Did not enter	1990 - Did not qualify
1958 - Did not enter	1994 - Did not qualify
1962 - Did not qualify	1998 - Did not qualify
1966 - Withdrew	2002 - Did not qualify
1970 - Did not qualify	2006 - Last 16

THE SQUAD

Goalkeepers	Club side	Age	QG
Richard Kingson	Wigan	31	12
Defenders			
Harrison Afful	Sportive de Tunis	23	10
Samuel Inkoom	Basel	20	4
Gabriel Issah	Asante Kotoko	28	1
John Mensah	Sunderland	27	8
John Paintsil	Fulham	28	11
Jonathan Quartey	Nice	22	4
Midfielders			
Eric Addo	Roda JC Kerk	31	11
Emm Agyemang-Badu	Udinese	19	3
Anthony Annan	Rosenborg BK	23	12
Stephen Appiah	Fenerbahce	29	6
John Boye	Rennes	23	1
Michael Kojo Essien	Chelsea	27	11
Laryea Kingston	Lokomotiv Moscow	29	7
Samuel Kyere	El Shorta	27	1
Sulley Muntari	Inter Milan	25	8
Isaac Vorsah	TSG Hoffenheim	21	4
Samuel Yeboah	Genk	23	1
Forwards			
Junior Agogo	Apollon Limassol	30	7
Matthew Amoah	NAC Breda	29	7
Kwadwo Asamoah	Udinese	21	4
Eric Bekoe	Petrojet	21	4
Haminu Draman	Lokomotiv Moscow	24	10
Asamoah Gyan	Rennes	24	4
Quincy Owusu-Abeyie	Spartak Moscow	24	3
Prince Tagoe	TSG Hoffenheim	23	8

■ Probable ■ Possible **QG** Qualification Games

KEY PLAYER

MICHAEL ESSIEN CHELSEA

One of the world's best central midfielders, Michael Essien is a crucial member of the Ghana side and a huge presence in the centre of midfield.

Equally adept in a defensive or more attacking role, the Chelsea man's versatility has seen him used in a variety of positions for the Premier League club. Ghana are a solid side, and Essien has world-class ability.

Playing record	12 months lge	wcq
Appearances:	23	11
Minutes played:	1784	899
Percentage played:	50.8%	83.2%
Goals scored:	4	1
Clean sheets:	14	8
Cards:	Y2, R0	Y1, R0
Strike rate:	446mins	899mins
Midfielder ranking:	83rd	75th

AGE 27	MIDFIELDER	DREAM TEAM RANKING 210

WORLD CUP SCHEDULE SOUTH AFRICA 2010

GROUP STAGE

MATCH 1 – JOHANNESBURG JSC 1500 BST (1600 SAST)
A SOUTH AFRICA V MEXICO

MATCH 2 – CAPE TOWN 1930 BST (2030 SAST)
A URUGUAY V FRANCE

MATCH 4 – PORT ELIZABETH 1230 BST (1330 SAST)
B SOUTH KOREA V GREECE

MATCH 3 – JOHANNESBURG JEP 1500 BST (1600 SAST)
B ARGENTINA V NIGERIA

MATCH 6 – POLOKWANE 1230 BST (1330 SAST)
C ALGERIA V SLOVENIA

MATCH 8 – PRETORIA 1500 BST (1600 SAST)
D SERBIA V GHANA

MATCH 9 – JOHANNESBURG JSC 1230 BST (1330 SAST)
E NETHERLANDS V DENMARK

MATCH 10 – BLOEMFONTEIN 1500 BST (1600 SAST)
E JAPAN V CAMEROON

MATCH 12 – RUSTENBURG 1230 BST (1330 SAST)
F NEW ZEALAND V SLOVAKIA

MATCH 13 – PORT ELIZABETH 1500 BST (1600 SAST)
G IVORY COAST V PORTUGAL

MATCH 15 – NELSPRUIT 1230 BST (1330 SAST)
H HONDURAS V CHILE

MATCH 16 – DURBAN 1500 BST (1600 SAST)
H SPAIN V SWITZERLAND

MATCH 20 – JOHANNESBURG JSC 1230 BST (1330 SAST)
B ARGENTINA V SOUTH KOREA

MATCH 19 – BLOEMFONTEIN 1500 BST (1600 SAST)
B GREECE V NIGERIA

MATCH 21 – PORT ELIZABETH 1230 BST (1330 SAST)
D GERMANY V SERBIA

MATCH 22 – JOHANNESBURG JEP 1500 BST (1600 SAST)
C SLOVENIA V USA

MATCH 25 – DURBAN 1230 BST (1330 SAST)
E NETHERLANDS V JAPAN

MATCH 24 – RUSTENBURG 1500 BST (1600 SAST)
D GHANA V AUSTRALIA

MATCH 27 – BLOEMFONTEIN 1230 BST (1330 SAST)
F SLOVAKIA V PARAGUAY

MATCH 28 – NELSPRUIT 1500 BST (1600 SAST)
F ITALY V NEW ZEALAND

MATCH 30 – CAPE TOWN 1230 BST (1330 SAST)
G PORTUGAL V NORTH KOREA

MATCH 31 – PORT ELIZABETH 1500 BST (1600 SAST)
H CHILE V SWITZERLAND

MATCH 33 – RUSTENBURG 1500 BST (1600 SAST)
A MEXICO V URUGUAY

MATCH 34 – BLOEMFONTEIN 1500 BST (1600 SAST)
A FRANCE V SOUTH AFRICA

MATCH 37 – PORT ELIZABETH 1500 BST (1600 SAST)
C SLOVENIA V ENGLAND

MATCH 38 – PRETORIA 1500 BST (1600 SAST)
C USA V ALGERIA

MATCH 41 – JOHANNESBURG JEP 1500 BST (1600 SAST)
F SLOVAKIA V ITALY

MATCH 42 – POLOKWANE 1500 BST (1600 SAST)
F PARAGUAY V NEW ZEALAND

MATCH 45 – DURBAN 1500 BST (1600 SAST)
G PORTUGAL V BRAZIL

MATCH 46 – NELSPRUIT 1500 BST (1600 SAST)
G NORTH KOREA V IVORY COAST

SECOND ROUND

MATCH 49 – PORT ELIZABETH 1500 BST (1600 SAST)
49 1ST A V 2ND B

JUNE 26TH

MATCH 50 – RUSTENBURG 1930 BST (2030 SAST)
50 1ST C V 2ND D

MATCH 51 – BLOEMFONTEIN 1500 BST (1600 SAST)
51 1ST D V 2ND C

JUNE 27TH

MATCH 52 – JOHANNESBURG JSC 1930 BST (2030 SAST)
52 1ST B V 2ND A

MATCH 53 – DURBAN 1500 BST (1600 SAST)
53 1ST E V 2ND F

JUNE 28TH

MATCH 54 – JOHANNESBURG JEP 1930 BST (2030 SAST)
54 1ST G V 2ND H

MATCH 55 – PRETORIA 1500 BST (1600 SAST)
55 1ST F V 2ND E

JUNE 29TH

MATCH 56 – CAPE TOWN 1930 BST (2030 SAST)
56 1ST H V 2ND G

MATCH 5 – RUSTENBURG 1930 BST (2030 SAST)

C | ENGLAND | V | USA

MATCH 7 – DURBAN 1930 BST (2030 SAST)

D | GERMANY | V | AUSTRALIA

MATCH 11 – CAPE TOWN 1930 BST (2030 SAST)

F | ITALY | V | PARAGUAY

MATCH 14 – JOHANNESBURG JEP 1930 BST (2030 SAST)

G | BRAZIL | V | NORTH KOREA

MATCH 17 – PRETORIA 1930 BST (2030 SAST)

A | SOUTH AFRICA | V | URUGUAY

MATCH 18 – POLOKWANE 1930 BST (2030 SAST)

A | FRANCE | V | MEXICO

MATCH 23 – CAPE TOWN 1930 BST (2030 SAST)

C | ENGLAND | V | ALGERIA

MATCH 26 – PRETORIA 1930 BST (2030 SAST)

E | CAMEROON | V | DENMARK

MATCH 29 – JOHANNESBURG JSC 1930 BST (2030 SAST)

G | BRAZIL | V | IVORY COAST

MATCH 32 – JOHANNESBURG JEP 1930 BST (2030 SAST)

H | SPAIN | V | HONDURAS

MATCH 35 – DURBAN 1930 BST (2030 SAST)

B | NIGERIA | V | SOUTH KOREA

MATCH 36 – POLOKWANE 1930 BST (2030 SAST)

B | GREECE | V | ARGENTINA

MATCH 39 – JOHANNESBURG JSC 1930 BST (2030 SAST)

D | GHANA | V | GERMANY

MATCH 40 – NELSPRUIT 1930 BST (2030 SAST)

D | AUSTRALIA | V | SERBIA

MATCH 43 – RUSTENBURG 1930 BST (2030 SAST)

E | DENMARK | V | JAPAN

MATCH 44 – CAPE TOWN 1930 BST (2030 SAST)

E | CAMEROON | V | NETHERLANDS

MATCH 47 – PRETORIA 1930 BST (2030 SAST)

H | CHILE | V | SPAIN

MATCH 48 – BLOEMFONTEIN 1930 BST (2030 SAST)

H | SWITZERLAND | V | HONDURAS

JUNE 11TH
JUNE 12TH
JUNE 13TH
JUNE 14TH
JUNE 15TH
JUNE 16TH
JUNE 17TH
JUNE 18TH
JUNE 19TH
JUNE 20TH
JUNE 21ST
JUNE 22ND
JUNE 23RD
JUNE 24TH
JUNE 25TH

QUARTER FINALS

MATCH 57 – PORT ELIZABETH 1500 BST (1600 SAST)

57 | W53 | V | W54 — JULY 2ND

MATCH 58 – JOHANNESBURG JSC 1930 BST (2030 SAST)

58 | W49 | V | W50

MATCH 59 – CAPE TOWN 1500 BST (1600 SAST)

59 | W52 | V | W51 — JULY 3RD

MATCH 60 – JOHANNESBURG JEP 1930 BST (2030 SAST)

60 | W55 | V | W56

SEMI FINALS

MATCH 61 – CAPE TOWN 1930 BST (2030 SAST)

61 | W58 | V | W57 — JULY 6TH

MATCH 62 – DURBAN 1930 BST (2030 SAST)

62 | W59 | V | W60 — JULY 7TH

THIRD PLACE

MATCH 63 – PORT ELIZABETH 1930 BST (2030 SAST)

63 | L61 | V | L62 — JULY 10TH

FINAL

MATCH 64 – JOHANNESBURG JSC 1930 BST (2030 SAST)

64 | W61 | V | W62 — JULY 11TH

Your own unique record of the 2010 World Cup.

This is a new kind of book, where we help you create your own personal memento of the 2010 World Cup.

A new kind of book

My World Cup Year provides you with all the match reports, stats, player ratings and top quality images from every single game at the tournament – as well as from qualifying – and you change as much or as little as you like.

The end product is your own unique account of England's World Cup – with your name on the front.

With My World Cup Year you can:

— Write your own match reports
— Choose the images
— Select the stats and quotes
— Rate the players
— Pick your own man-of-the-match
— Load up your own photos
— Choose your own lay-out

Choose your favourite images, quotes and headlines from the World Cup

'Capello instils fear, like a severe dad.' (Wayne Rooney)
All the interesting stats, facts and quotes at your fingertips.

Find out more at:
www.myworldcupyear.com

MY WORLD CUP YEAR

YES! YES! YES!

BY YOUR NAME

A GENUINELY UNIQUE AND PERSONAL
ROUND-UP OF THE WORLD CUP

12th YOANN GOURCUFF
FRANCE & BORDEAUX

An attacking midfield playmaker, Yoann Gourcuff is perhaps the only one of the current crop of French internationals compared to the great Zinedine Zidane who matches him for style – if not yet impact or ability.

Still only 23, he has plenty of time to grow on the world stage but he is already showing signs it will be a smooth transition. French Player of the Year for 2009, he is unbelievably skilful, a dead-ball specialist who can cut through a defence singlehandedly.

Playing record	12 mths lge	wcq
Appearances:	35	10
Minutes played:	2838	756
Percentage played:	80.9%	68.1%
Goals scored:	14	1
Clean sheets:	20	4
Cards:	Y2, R0	Y1, R0
Strike rate:	203mins	756mins
Strike rate ranking:	19th	70th

AGE 23 | **DREAM TEAM** | **RANKING 72**

11th STEVEN GERRARD
ENGLAND & LIVERPOOL

One of the finest players of his generation, Steven Gerrard at his best is a talismanic figure for Liverpool and England and is not far from being the complete midfielder.

Able to play anywhere across midfield and also as a second striker, Gerrard is a dynamic presence – tireless, direct and powerful going forward.

He often comes up with the miraculous and sets up, and scores goals on a regular basis. Gerrard will be expected to pitch in with match-winning performances.

Playing record	12 mths lge	wcq
Appearances:	30	7
Minutes played:	2580	530
Percentage played:	73.5%	58.9%
Goals scored:	13	3
Clean sheets:	14	2
Cards:	Y5, R0	Y0, R0
Strike rate:	198mins	177mins
Strike rate ranking:	17th	6th

AGE 30 | **DREAM TEAM** | **RANKING 71**

10th DANIELE DE ROSSI
ITALY & AS ROMA

A highly influential midfield general, Daniel De Rossi is widely expected to succeed Fabio Cannavaro as Italy's next captain and will be a major part of the Azzurri's bid to retain the World Cup.

A dominant and vocal, all-action box-to-box midfielder, De Rossi is at the centre of things, both defensively and going forward and he often scores spectacular goals. Watching him in full flow, he is reminiscent of Roy Keane at his best and he will be at the heart of everything Italy accomplish in South Africa.

Playing record	12 mths lge	wcq
Appearances:	34	9
Minutes played:	2954	745
Percentage played:	80.1%	82.8%
Goals scored:	7	2
Clean sheets:	10	5
Cards:	Y11, R1	Y3, R0
Strike rate:	422mins	372mins
Strike rate ranking:	76th	39th

AGE 26 | **DREAM TEAM** | **RANKING 56**

9th BASTIAN SCHWEINSTEIGER
GERMANY & BAYERN MUNICH

A talented midfielder usually found on the left wing, Bastian Schweinsteiger is already a veteran of the German national side at the tender age of 25.

Tipped by many to get close to Lothar Matthaus' record of 150 caps, Schweinsteiger is a powerful, skilful midfielder and versatile enough to play in a number of positions. Offering great delivery from free-kicks and often scoring crucial goals – he averages a goal every four games for Germany. He is the creative heart of the German side.

Playing record	12 mths lge	wcq
Appearances:	33	9
Minutes played:	2744	778
Percentage played:	89.7%	86.4%
Goals scored:	3	3
Clean sheets:	11	7
Cards:	Y4, R0	Y0, R0
Strike rate:	915mins	259mins
Strike rate ranking:	149th	20th

AGE 25 | **DREAM TEAM** | **RANKING 48**

8th JAVIER MASCHERANO
ARGENTINA & LIVERPOOL

One of the finest defensive midfielders in today's game, Javier Mascherano is the captain of Argentina and will be determined to lead his country on a successful campaign in South Africa with expectations high back at home.

A tough tackling midfield general with great awareness, he is a big presence on the pitch. Despite his obvious leadership skills, he had to be persuaded to take the captain's armband by manager Diego Maradonna who stated his team would be "Mascherano and ten more".

Playing record	12 mths lge	wcq
Appearances:	33	16
Minutes played:	2672	1412
Percentage played:	76.1%	87.2%
Goals scored:	0	0
Clean sheets:	14	8
Cards:	Y8, R2	Y5, R0
Strike rate:	- mins	- mins
Strike rate ranking:	154th	112nd

AGE 26   **DREAM TEAM** **RANKING 45**

7th ANDRES INIESTA
SPAIN & BARCELONA

An integral part of Barcelona's ascent to the pinnacle of European football, Andres Iniesta is a versatile midfielder who does everything well and is something of a player's player, with Wayne Rooney amongst those who have heralded him the best in the world.

For Spain, too, he has been a major influence – featuring in every game in Spain's triumphant Euro 2008 campaign – and you can expect Spain's quiet man to feature heavily again in South Africa, alongside club colleague Xavi in the heart of midfield.

Playing record	12 mths lge	wcq
Appearances:	32	6
Minutes played:	2139	433
Percentage played:	60.9%	48.1%
Goals scored:	3	1
Clean sheets:	18	5
Cards:	Y3, R0	Y2, R0
Strike rate:	713mins	433mins
Strike rate ranking:	127th	47th

AGE 26   **DREAM TEAM** **RANKING 36**

6th ANDREA PIRLO
ITALY & AC MILAN

A mercurial playmaker who controls the game from a deep-lying midfield role, Andrea Pirlo is no stranger to World Cup success, having been an integral part of Italy's 2006 winning side and man-of-the-match in the final against France.

A superb passer of the ball and set-piece specialist, Pirlo is the creative hub of the Azzurri and if he plays well, then so, invariably, do Italy. He may be something of a surly figure, but do not underestimate Pirlo's desire to help his side successfully retain their world crown.

Playing record	12 mths lge	wcq
Appearances:	37	7
Minutes played:	3249	530
Percentage played:	90.3%	58.9%
Goals scored:	1	1
Clean sheets:	16	5
Cards:	Y8, R0	Y1, R0
Strike rate:	249mins	530mins
Strike rate ranking:	31st	56th

AGE 31   **DREAM TEAM** **RANKING 27**

5th FELIPE MELO
BRAZIL & JUVENTUS

It has been a meteoric rise for defensive midfielder Felipe Melo who in 2009 sealed a 25 million euro move to Juventus, made his debut for Brazil and subsequently cemented his place in the side.

An impressive force for Fiorentina in 2008/09, he was called up by Brazil coach Dunga and starred in the Confederations Cup, in the 'volante' role alongside Gilberto Silva. His start at Juve was not ideal and he suffered much criticism as the team struggled but expect Dunga to retain faith in a player after his own heart.

Playing record	12 mths lge	wcq
Appearances:	30	6
Minutes played:	2537	499
Percentage played:	70.5%	30.8%
Goals scored:	3	1
Clean sheets:	7	2
Cards:	Y11, R2	Y1, R1
Strike rate:	846mins	499mins
Strike rate ranking:	142nd	55th

AGE 26   **DREAM TEAM** **RANKING 21**

4th

FRANK LAMPARD

ENGLAND & CHELSEA

The archetypal box-to-box midfielder with fantastic technique, Frank Lampard has been one of the best players in world football for over five years.

A hard worker on and off the pitch, Lampard's exquisite timing and eye for goal make him a genuine threat and he is one of England's top-20 all-time goal-scorers. Playing better than ever under Fabio Capello, Lampard's influence – and goals – could be instrumental if England are to do well.

Playing record	12 mths lge	wcq
Appearances:	36	10
Minutes played:	3193	889
Percentage played:	91.0%	98.8%
Goals scored:	10	4
Clean sheets:	19	4
Cards:	Y2, R0	Y0, R0
Strike rate:	319mins	222mins
Strike rate ranking:	48th	15th

AGE 31	DREAM TEAM	RANKING 9

3rd

XABI ALONSO

SPAIN & REAL MADRID

An inventive midfielder who always appears to have time on the ball, Xabi Alonso is not only one of the best midfielders in world football – he also brings out the best in those around him.

Preferring a deeper role in midfield, Alonso can pick a pass in an instant and his speed of thought and creativity are often the catalyst for his side's attacking intent. Part of a brilliant Spain midfield, he might not be the most eye-catching but will be one of the most effective.

Playing record	12 mths lge	wcq
Appearances:	27	8
Minutes played:	2249	537
Percentage played:	64.1%	59.7%
Goals scored:	1	1
Clean sheets:	14	6
Cards:	Y7, R0	Y0, R0
Strike rate:	249mins	537mins
Strike rate ranking:	30th	57th

AGE 28	DREAM TEAM	RANKING 8

2nd

KAKA

BRAZIL & REAL MADRID

One of the finest attacking midfielders in world football, Kaka needs only a World Cup triumph to seal his place in the pantheon of Brazilian greats.

With incredible skill, pace and vision – Kaka can do it all. He scores goals, creates goals and looks good doing it – no wonder Real Madrid were willing to pay almost 70 million euros for him. He is vital for Brazil, and if the side's attacking game clicks then he could be the player of the tournament.

Playing record	12 mths lge	wcq
Appearances:	30	11
Minutes played:	2303	954
Percentage played:	65.6%	58.9%
Goals scored:	12	5
Clean sheets:	17	7
Cards:	Y2, R0	Y2, R0
Strike rate:	192mins	191mins
Strike rate ranking:	16th	11th

AGE 28	DREAM TEAM	RANKING 6

THE TOP MIDFIELDER

SPAIN | XAVI HERNANDEZ

A truly sublime playmaker, Xavi can pick a pass like few others in the modern game and – for club and country – is a man very much in form.

A lifelong Barcelona fan, Xavi has been instrumental in his club's recent successes and, together with midfield partner Andres Iniesta, has helped bring the same success to the Spanish national side.

Playing record	12 mths lge	wcq
Appearances:	37	9
Minutes played:	3072	771
Percentage played:	87.5%	85.7%
Goals scored:	3	0
Clean sheets:	17	0
Cards:	Y5, R0	Y1, R0
Strike rate:	24mins	- mins
Strike rate ranking:	4th	83rd

| AGE 30 | BARCELONA | DREAM TEAM | RANKING 1 |

1st

TOTAL OF THE AVERAGE FIFA RANKINGS OF THE FOUR COUNTRIES 88

Position	1st	2nd	3rd	4th	5th	6th	7th	8th
Group	E	D	B	H	A	G	C	F
Total FIFA ranking	89	93	95	96	101	109	117	138

NETHERLANDS v DENMARK — Johannesburg JSC, Monday 14 June 1230 BST

The opener in Group E looks like being a close call between two of the tightest defences in European qualifying. The Danes missed out on the World Cup in Germany and will be extra keen to make an impression this time round. They may struggle to get their campaign off to a strong start against a Dutch side that has quality in virtually every area of the pitch. Daniel Agger and Simon Kjaer of Palermo will have to be at their best to hold off a talented Holland attack, while two Arsenal strikers go head-to-head, with Robin van Persie lining up against Nicklas Bendtner. A win here would put either side in pole position to make the second round.

JAPAN v CAMEROON — Bloemfontein, Monday 14 June 1500 BST

A defining game in Group E. Japan against Cameroon is a tough one to predict. The organised Asian side have high hopes of making it into the knockout stages, while Cameroon are probably the best placed African team to make a splash in the continent's first World Cup. Samuel Eto'o will be on a different level to the strikers that Japan's defenders face in their domestic J-League, while a solid looking Cameroon side will be difficult to break down.

NETHERLANDS v JAPAN — Durban, Saturday 19 June 1230 BST

These two sides met in a friendly back in September 2009, with Netherlands running out comfortable 3-0 winners. While their encounter in Durban will be on a totally different level to that game, it would be no surprise if the Dutch similarly ran out winners again. Japan have a solid defensive record, but may struggle to contain Holland's star-studded attacking line-up, and a lack of quality up-front themselves could see Shunsuke Nakamura's set-piece deliveries as the main threat to the European side's defence.

Denmark's Nicklas Bendtner

CAMEROON v DENMARK — Pretoria, Saturday 19 June 1930 BST

Qualification for the second round or an early exit may well be hanging in the balance for these two sides going into the clash in Pretoria, so expect the atmosphere to be electric as the African fans get behind one of the continent's best teams. Denmark are solid at the back and could be hard to break down, but if Cameroon manage to create chances then Samuel Eto'o will be a real test for an inexperienced Denmark back two. Christian Poulsen will need a good game to protect those centre-backs. The Lions haven't been strong at the back for a few years either, but Denmark are hit and miss going forward. This could be a tight encounter.

DENMARK v JAPAN — Rustenburg, Thursday 24 June 1930 BST

While this isn't the most entertaining of matches on paper, if either side still have a chance of going through then it could actually turn out to be a great one for the neutrals. Both Denmark and Japan are solid at the back, but will need to throw bodies forward in search of a win. Shunsuke Nakamura could thrive if given enough space to allow his creative game to come to the fore but Japan's main strength is their defensive work-rate. If they can starve Arsenal striker Nicklas Bendtner of possession, then they have a great chance of getting a positive result. Though this is unlikely to see them progress to the last 16.

CAMEROON v NETHERLANDS — Cape Town, Thursday 24 June 1930 BST

A potentially huge game to round off Group E in style, Cameroon v Netherlands will be even better to watch if both teams still have something to play for. The Dutch attack in numbers and will be a real test for a defence that has only recently become settled under new manager Paul Le Guen. The battle in midfield will be key, with Alexandre Song and Jean Makoun facing off against Mark van Bommel and Nigel de Jong. Whichever team gets the upper hand here will be favourites to the win, as both teams' strikers will fancy their chances against back lines that can be shaky at times. If either of these crash out at this stage of the competition then it will be a major shock.

VIEW FROM THE EXPERTS

NETHERLANDS: A fantastic football nation and a threat at any World Cup. Robin van Persie is a class act but has been dogged by injury. Should emerge from this group in good shape though and fairly comfortably.
HARRY'S VERDICT: Quarters.

DENMARK: The Danes have dipped below the radar recently. Were thrashed 3-0 by England in Japan eight years ago. Now back with Morten Olsen in charge they are rejuvenated. I can't see them sticking around long but could make a run for second place in the group.
HARRY'S VERDICT: Group stage only.

JAPAN: I can't really see them causing much of an impact. This is not the toughest group but I still think it will be beyond them to make any headway other than a flying visit for the first stage. Their 15 minutes of fame was co-hosting the tournament in 2002.
HARRY'S VERDICT: Group stage only.

CAMEROON: Inter Milan's Samuel Eto'o is clearly a top international striker and will enjoy star billing. The Indomitable Lions have some decent players and could be dangerous. I look forward to seeing Tottenham defenders Bassong and Assou-Ekotto play in South Africa.
HARRY'S VERDICT: Last 16.

NETHERLANDS: Bert van Marwijk's boys were the first European team to qualify for South Africa as they breezed through Group 9 with a 100 per cent record from eight games, conceding just twice in the process. This has raised expectations that this may finally be the Dutch's year. They certainly have enough quality on the pitch.
TEL'S VERDICT: Looking good for the last four.

DENMARK: They came through arguably the hardest European qualifying group, finishing top ahead of Portugal, Sweden and Hungary, to reach their first major tournament since Euro 2004. But I do not know if they have enough quality to make it through to the latter stages.
TEL'S VERDICT: No Dane-ger.

JAPAN: Appearing at their fourth successive finals there is no doubt the Japanese are a force in the Asian game. They made it to round two when they co-hosted the tournament in 2002 and they will do well to emulate that this time.
TEL'S VERDICT: Sayonara.

CAMEROON: Made hard work of qualification, but former Rangers boss Paul

Le Guen has licked them into shape and guided them to their sixth appearance at the finals a record for an African team. And they have enough quality in their line-up, such as Inter Milan's Samuel Eto'o, Arsenal's Alex Song and Tottenham's Sebastien Bassong to make an impact.

TEL'S VERDICT: Possible surprise package.

NETHERLANDS: A faultless qualifying campaign, having won all eight of their group games and conceding just twice in the process. But the Dutch are the World Cup's perennial underachievers and there is bound to be some controversy or dispute that blights their summer.

WRIGHTY'S VERDICT: Waiting for things to go wrong.

DENMARK: The Danes qualified as winners of one of the hardest European groups, beating Portugal home and away along the way. But despite possessing a sprinkling of talented players, such as Bendtner and Poulsen, it is unlikely they will come close to repeating their triumph at Euro 1992.

WRIGHTY'S VERDICT: Not so great Danes.

JAPAN: The Japanese reached round two when they co-hosted the tournament in 2002, but they will do well to reach that stage again. Well drilled and disciplined, it will be up to ex-Celtic midfielder Shunsuke Nakamura, now with Espanyol, to provide the spark.

WRIGHTY'S VERDICT: Rising Sun eclipsed in South Africa.

CAMEROON: Playing in the finals for a sixth time, the Indomitable Lions have enough experience to go far in South Africa and in striker Samuel Eto'o they have a player I believe could win the Golden Boot and become one of the stars of Africa's first World Cup.

WRIGHTY'S VERDICT: Must get their heads right.

"Robin van Persie is a class act but has been dogged by injury"

THE LIKELY ROUTES FOR THE TOP TWO TEAMS FROM THE GROUP

For the full draw please see page 80

GROUP STAGE

FIRST GROUP E

NETHERLANDS

LAST SIXTEEN

v SECOND GROUP F

NETHERLANDS v SLOVAKIA

QUARTER-FINALS

v FIRST GROUP G or SECOND GROUP H

NETHERLANDS v BRAZIL

SECOND GROUP E

CAMEROON

v FIRST GROUP F

CAMEROON v ITALY

v FIRST GROUP H or SECOND GROUP G

ITALY v SPAIN

GROUP E
NETHERLANDS, DENMARK, JAPAN, CAMEROON

GROUP F
ITALY, PARAGUAY, NEW ZEALAND, SLOVAKIA

GROUP G
BRAZIL, NORTH KOREA (KOREA DPR), IVORY COAST, PORTUGAL

GROUP H
SPAIN, SWITZERLAND, HONDURAS, CHILE

ROUTE TO THE FINALS

Netherlands coasted through qualifying with consummate ease, winning all eight games, scoring 17 goals and conceding just two.

Drawn in one of the more straightforward European qualification groups, second-half goals from Johnny Heitinga and Rafael van der Vaart secured an opening 2-1 win against Macedonia. The Dutch did not concede again in international football for another ten months.

Wins home and away against Norway confirmed Holland's dominance. They ended up 14 points clear, as the Norwegians and Scotland both failed to pick up enough points to secure even a place in the play-offs. Holland were coasting by the time they met the Scots in their final game, and a first international goal from 22-year-old sub Eljero Elia finished the campaign in style and secured their impressive 100% record.

Manager Bert van Marwijk used 25 players in the eight games, of which seven players only featured once qualification was secured, and the Dutch squad are rightly one of the favourites for the title in South Africa.

Goals come from all areas of the pitch, with 11 players contributing in qualifying. Strikers Klaas-Jan Huntelaar and Dirk Kuyt were joint top-scorers with three apiece.

Tougher tests await in South Africa, but Holland will be confident of making a big impression on the tournament.

FINAL QUALIFYING TABLE
EUROPE GROUP 9

	P	W	D	L	F	A	Pts
Netherlands	8	8	0	0	17	2	24
Norway	8	2	4	2	9	7	10
Scotland	8	3	1	4	6	11	10
FYR Macedonia	8	2	1	5	5	11	7
Iceland	8	1	2	5	7	13	5

FIFA ranking

1	10 Sep 08	Away	Macedonia	93	W	1	2	Heitinga 46, Van der Vaart 60
2	11 Oct 08	Home	Iceland	90	W	2	0	Mathijsen 15, Huntelaar 65
3	15 Oct 08	Away	Norway	43	W	0	1	van Bommel 63
4	28 Mar 09	Home	Scotland	26	W	3	0	Huntelaar 30, Van Persie 45, Kuyt 77pen
5	01 Apr 09	Home	Macedonia	93	W	4	0	Kuyt 16, 41, Huntelaar 25, Van der Vaart 88
6	06 Jun 09	Away	Iceland	90	W	1	2	De Jong 9, Van Bommel 16
7	10 Jun 09	Home	Norway	43	W	2	0	Ooijer 33, Robben 51
8	09 Sep 09	Away	Scotland	26	W	0	1	Elia 82

Average FIFA ranking of opposition	63

MAIN PLAYER PERFORMANCES IN QUALIFICATION

Key: ■ played 90 mins ◄◄ subbed off ►► subbed on ▢ on bench

Match	1 2 3 4 5 6 7 8	Appearances	Started	Subbed on	Subbed off	Mins played	% played	Goals	Yellow	Red
Venue	A H A H H A H A									
Result	W W W W W W W W									
Goalkeepers										
Maarten Stekelenburg		5	5	0	0	450	62.5	0	0	0
Edwin van der Sar		2	2	0	0	180	25.0	0	0	0
Michel Vorm		1	1	0	0	90	12.5	0	0	0
Defenders										
Khalid Boulahrouz		1	0	1	0	63	8.8	0	0	0
Edson Braafheid		1	0	1	0	45	6.3	0	0	0
John Heitinga		3	3	0	0	270	37.5	1	0	0
Dirk Marcellis		2	2	0	0	180	25.0	0	0	0
Joris Mathijsen		8	8	0	0	720	100.0	1	0	0
Andre Ooijer		8	8	0	1	657	91.3	1	0	0
Giovanni van Bronckhorst		8	8	0	1	675	93.8	0	0	0
Gregory van der Wiel		3	3	0	0	270	37.5	0	0	0
Midfielders										
Ibrahim Afellay		5	0	5	0	117	16.3	0	0	0
Nigel de Jong		6	6	0	3	441	61.3	1	2	0
Demy de Zeeuw		3	2	1	0	257	35.7	0	0	0
David Mendes da Silva		1	0	1	0	11	1.5	0	0	0
Stijn Schaars		2	1	1	0	101	14.0	0	0	0
Wesley Sneijder		5	2	3	2	202	28.1	0	0	0
Mark van Bommel		7	7	0	0	630	87.5	2	0	0
Rafael van der Vaart		7	5	2	3	439	61.0	2	1	0
Forwards										
Ryan Babel		5	2	3	2	166	23.1	0	0	0
Eljero Elia		1	0	1	0	18	2.5	1	0	0
Klaas-Jan Huntelaar		8	5	3	2	443	61.5	3	2	0
Dirk Kuyt		8	7	1	2	617	85.7	3	1	0
Arjen Robben		6	6	0	4	455	63.2	1	1	0
Robin van Persie		6	5	1	4	423	58.8	1	2	0

FINAL PROSPECTS

One of the form teams going into the tournament, Netherlands will expect to qualify from this group.

Anything less than a semi-final appearance would be a major disappointment for the side ranked third in the world.

The Dutch have a reputation of imploding at major tournaments. A possible quarter-final clash against the winners of Group G – likely to be one of Brazil, Ivory Coast or Portugal – will be a huge test of their credentials. Twice losing finalists, in 1974 and 1978, they have never won a World Cup. They have only a 1988 European Championship to show for decades of being one of the most talented teams in world football.

Bert van Marwijk will be hoping that Arsenal's Robin van Persie is fit.

Phenomenal in the group stages in Euro 2008, a quarter-final exit to Russia was a shock, but continued the nation's history of underachievement at major finals.

Scintillating going forward, the Dutch also tightened up at the back in qualifying, conceding just two goals in eight games, but in truth were rarely tested by their out-of-form opponents. The lack of an experienced goalkeeper is a weakness, while a first-choice of back-four of Giovanni van Bronckhorst, Andre Ooijer, Joris Mathijsen and Johnny Heitinga has plenty of experience but lacks the quality of some of the other defences.

Arjen Robben, Dirk Kuyt and Klaas-Jan Huntelaar are dangerous attacking options, but manager Bert van Marwijk will be hoping that Arsenal striker Robin van Persie is fit and in form to spearhead the front three.

A typically talented midfield has been strengthened by the return of the manager's son-in-law, Mark van Bommel, to the national set-up.

The holding midfielder will need to be at his commanding best if and when the Oranje come up against the better attacking teams in the knockout stages. Manchester City's Nigel de Jong partners Van Bommel in a terrific defensive midfield, while Rafael van der Vaart is likely to be the attacking player in the Netherlands three-man midfield.

Hugely talented, with plenty of goals in them and a settled side, the Dutch will be highly-fancied to challenge Brazil and Spain for the World Cup title.

DREAM TEAM TOP 15 RANKING 7

GROUP FIXTURES

DENMARK	Mon 14 June 1230 BST
JAPAN	Sat 19 June 1230 BST
CAMEROON	Thur 24 June 1930 BST

KEY PLAYER

WESLEY SNEIJDER INTER MILAN

A player whose three career clubs have been Ajax, Real Madrid and Inter Milan must be something special – Wesley Sneijder is exactly that.

Sneijder will turn 26 just before the start of South Africa 2010 and is certain to play a crucial role in Holland's campaign. Sneijder is renowned for scoring spectacular goals, particularly set-pieces.

Playing record	12 months lge	wcq
Appearances:	24	5
Minutes played:	1723	202
Percentage played:	47.9%	28.1%
Goals scored:	4	0
Clean Sheets:	18	5
Cards:	Y8, R1	Y0, R0
Strike rate:	431mins	-
Strike rate ranking:	78th	91st

AGE 26   **MIDFIELDER**   **DREAM TEAM RANKING** 92

Amsterdam

Zone	Europe
Population	16.4m
Language	Dutch
Top league	Eredivisie
Playing season	August - May

Major clubs and capacities
Ajax (51,638), Feyenoord (51,577), PSV Eindhoven (45,186), AZ Alkmaar (17,150)

Where probable squad players play:

Premier League	5	Ligue 1	-
Serie A	2	Eredivisie	10
La Liga	1	Other Europe	-
Bundesliga	5	Outside Europe	-

Number of Dutch players playing:

Premier League	18	Bundesliga	9
Serie A	3	Ligue 1	-
La Liga	5	Eredivisie	296

World Cup record * best performance

1930 - Did not enter		1974 -	* Runners up
1934 - Round 1		1978 -	* Runners up
1938 - Round !		1982 -	Did not qualify
1950 - Did not enter		1986 -	Did not qualify
1954 - Did not enter		1990 -	Round 2
1958 - Did not qualify		1994 -	Quarter finals
1962 - Did not qualify		1998 -	4th place
1966 - Did not qualify		2002 -	Did not qualify
1970 - Did not qualify		2006 -	Round 2

THE SQUAD

	Club side	Age	QG
Goalkeepers			
Maarten Stekelenburg	Ajax	27	5
Michel Vorm	Utrecht	26	1
Defenders			
Khalid Boulahrouz	Stuttgart	28	1
Edson Braafheid	Bayern Munich	27	1
John Heitinga	Everton	26	3
Dirk Marcellis	PSV Eindhoven	22	2
Joris Mathijsen	Hamburg	30	8
Andre Ooijer	PSV Eindhoven	35	8
Gio van Bronckhorst	Feyenoord	35	8
Gregory van der Wiel	Ajax	22	3
Midfielders			
Ibrahim Afellay	PSV Eindhoven	24	5
Nigel de Jong	Man City	25	6
Demy de Zeeuw	Ajax	27	3
David Mendes da Silva	AZ Alkmaar	27	1
Stijn Schaars	AZ Alkmaar	26	2
Wesley Sneijder	Inter Milan	26	5
Mark van Bommel	Bayern Munich	33	7
Rafael van der Vaart	Real Madrid	27	7
Forwards			
Ryan Babel	Liverpool	23	5
Eljero Elia	Hamburg	23	1
Klaas-Jan Huntelaar	AC Milan	26	8
Dirk Kuyt	Liverpool	29	8
Arjen Robben	Bayern Munich	26	6
Robin van Persie	Arsenal	26	6

■ Probable ■ Possible **QG** Qualification Games

KEY GOALKEEPERS

MAARTEN STEKELENBURG
AJAX

Playing record	12 months lge	wcq
Appearances:	25	5
Minutes played:	2250	450
Percentage played:	71.4%	62.5%
Goals conceded:	26	2
Clean sheets:	10	3
Cards:	Y2, R0	Y0, R0
Minutes between goals:	87mins	225mins
Goalkeeper ranking:	-	13th

AGE 27	DREAM TEAM	RANKING 165

MICHEL VORM
UTRECHT

Playing record	12 months lge	wcq
Appearances:	26	1
Minutes played:	2295	90
Percentage played:	72.9%	12.5%
Goals conceded:	25	0
Clean sheets:	13	1
Cards:	Y1, R0	Y0, R0
Minutes between goals:	92mins	-
Goalkeeper ranking:	8th	-

AGE 26	DREAM TEAM	RANKING 530

KEY DEFENDERS

JORIS MATHIJSEN
HAMBURG

A mainstay in the centre of the Dutch defence.

Joris Mathijsen played more minutes than any other player in the squad during qualifying and is a certainty to start if fit.

Mathijsen is a Top 12 defender

KHALID BOULAHROUZ
STUTTGART

For a player once tipped to fill Jaap Stam's considerable boots, Khalid Boulahrouz hasn't quite lived up to expectations in recent seasons.

The former Chelsea defender, now playing for Stuttgart, has fallen out of favour with Bert van Marwijk but should still see some action in South Africa due to his ability to play anywhere across the back line.

He'll also be keen to erase memories of a World Cup 2006 red card against Portugal.

Playing record	12 months lge	wcq
Appearances:	13	1
Minutes played:	1063	63
Percentage played:	34.7%	8.8%
Goals conceded:	20	1
Clean sheets:	4	0
Cards:	Y2, R0	Y0, R0
Minutes between goals:	53mins	-
Defender ranking:	159th	-

AGE 28	DREAM TEAM	RANKING 1475

GIOVANNI VAN BRONCKHORST
FEYENOORD

Despite approaching the twilight of his career, Giovanni van Bronckhurst is still very much an important part of the Dutch defence.

The 35-year-old has enjoyed an illustrious career, which flourished at Feyenoord in the 1990s and then led him to Rangers, Arsenal and Barcelona. After winning domestic title honours at all three of those clubs, Van Bronckhurst's club career peaked with a Champions League winners' medal for Barcelona's victory over former team Arsenal in 2006. Van Bronckhurst then returned to Feynoord where he was appointed captain and continued his consistently high level of defensive performances. For Holland, he has been selected for two World Cups and three European Championships, proving equally adept at left back, left midfield or central midfield. His pace may have slowed a yard or two over the years, but Van Bronckhurst's impeccable positioning, perfectly-timed tackles and wide range of passing has seen him become a valuable member of the squad.

Playing record	12 months lge	wcq
Appearances:	27	8
Minutes played:	2415	675
Percentage played:	76.7%	93.8%
Goals conceded:	30	2
Clean sheets:	12	6
Cards:	Y8, R1	Y0, R0
Minutes between goals:	80mins	337mins
Defender ranking:	79th	12th

AGE 35	DREAM TEAM	RANKING 261

THE MANAGER

An experienced club coach, Lamberus 'Bert' van Marwijk was a surprise appointment as the Netherlands boss when he took over from Marco van Basten in 2008.

In a clear switch from the policy of naming big-name former players as manager of Holland, Van Marwijk has so far succeeded in uniting a squad packed full of sizeable egos.

A handy creative player, he was capped just once by Holland in a 20-year career that failed to really take off at international level.

Two spells in charge of Feyenoord earned Van Marwijk a reputation as a clever coach, leading the club to UEFA Cup glory in 2002, before impressing enough on his return to De Kuip to get the Holland job.

Playing to the strengths of a talented squad, Van Marwijk has kept his tactics simple and his side settled, sticking with the classic Dutch 4-3-3 system, with two solid defensive midfielders shielding the defence.

The retirement of Edwin van der Saar and Ruud van Nistelrooy from international football was a blow, but Van Marwijk has shown faith in the likes of Klaas-Jan Huntelaar and Rafael van der Vaart, who have both struggled in club football over the past few seasons.

Plenty of options on the bench give the manger scope for change and he will need to be at his best if Holland are to reach the final.

JOHNNY HEITINGA
EVERTON

He may be famed for his versatility, but it seems Johnny Heitinga has finally matured into a first-choice centre back for Holland.

The Everton defender is expected to partner Joris Mathijsen in the Dutch's assault on South Africa 2010 and may well have his work cut out. Holland's attacking abilities have never been in doubt but defensive mistakes have so often let them down in years gone by. However Heitinga, formerly of Ajax and Atletico Madrid, possesses all the attributes required to shore up their back line. He has now racked up over 50 caps for Holland and is set to be a regular fixture in orange for many years to come.

Playing record	12 months lge	wcq
Appearances:	32	3
Minutes played:	2643	270
Percentage played:	75.3%	37.5%
Goals conceded:	44	2
Clean sheets:	6	1
Cards:	Y12, R0	Y0, R0
Minutes between goals:	60mins	135mins
Defender ranking:	143rd	61st

AGE 26	DREAM TEAM	RANKING 158

KEY PLAYER

MARK VAN BOMMEL BAYERN MUNICH

Mark van Bommel is back in the Dutch side after a very public fall-out with previous manager Marco van Basten in 2006.

Since then the midfielder, who can act as enforcer or playmaker, has rebuilt his career; first as the club captain of Bayern Munich and now as the form midfield cog in the Dutch side. Van Bommel will be vital.

Playing record	12 months lge	wcq
Appearances:	25	7
Minutes played:	2220	630
Percentage played:	72.5%	87.5%
Goals scored:	1	2
Clean sheets:	9	5
Cards:	Y12, R0	Y0, R0
Strike rate:	220mins	315mins
Strike rate ranking:	23rd	28th

AGE 33	MIDFIELDER	DREAM TEAM	RANKING 97

KEY MIDFIELDERS

ARJEN ROBBEN
BAYERN MUNICH

In a Dutch team full of creative outlets, Arjen Robben is surely the most spectacular to watch when in full flow.

Like Robin van Persie, injuries have disrupted his progress, but the Bayern Munich winger has the capacity to win any football match single-handedly, such are the abilities at his disposal. A huge talent from a very young age, Robben was courted by the best sides in Europe before Chelsea snapped him up in 2004. After a hugely successful spell at Stamford Bridge, Real Madrid came calling and now Robben plies his trade in Germany. He was excellent for Holland at the 2006 World Cup.

Playing record	12 months lge	wcq
Appearances:	28	6
Minutes played:	1988	455
Percentage played:	65.0%	63.2%
Goals scored:	10	1
Clean sheets:	14	4
Cards:	Y2, R0	Y1, R0
Strike rate:	199mins	455mins
Midfielder ranking:	18th	51st

AGE 26	DREAM TEAM RANKING 268

RAFAEL VAN DER VAART
REAL MADRID

Being compared to the likes of Johan Cryuff, Ruud Gullit and Phillip Cocu could be a burden for some but Holland's chief playmaker in 2010, Rafael van der Vaart, looks up to the job.

Another player to come through Ajax's academy. Van der Vaart has developed into an essential cog in Holland's midfield. At the age of 27 he has already amassed over 70 caps and at this rate will hit the magical century mark before he's 30. The left-footed midfielder, who has been known to operate on either flank, spent five years in Ajax's first team before moving to Hamburg. There he was handed the captaincy and enjoyed three fruitful seasons before moving to Real Madrid in 2008. For Holland, Van der Vaart made his senior debut aged just 18 and went on to feature at Euro 2004 and 2008, although injury restricted him to a bit-part role in the 2006 World Cup. He has captained the Dutch side and it seems Van der Vaart is maturing into one of the wise old heads of the squad. Creating goals is his specialty but he knows where the net is too, having scored 15 international goals in total. It's in attack where Holland's strength lies and if Van der Vaart can orchestrate the likes of Robin van Persie and Arjen Robben, the Dutch have the potential to go all the way this summer.

Playing record	12 months lge	wcq
Appearances:	29	7
Minutes played:	1166	439
Percentage played:	33.2%	61.0%
Goals scored:	3	2
Clean sheets:	20	6
Cards:	Y4, R0	Y1, R0
Strike rate:	389mins	219mins
Midfielder ranking:	65th	14th

AGE 27	DREAM TEAM RANKING 1093

NIGEL DE JONG
MAN CITY

Playing record	12 months lge	wcq
Appearances:	32	6
Minutes played:	2510	441
Percentage played:	69.7%	61.3%
Goals scored:	0	1
Clean sheets:	10	5
Cards:	Y7, R0	Y2, R0
Strike rate:	-	441mins
Midfielder ranking:	162nd	48th

AGE 25	DREAM TEAM RANKING 319

KEY STRIKERS

DIRK KUYT
LIVERPOOL

Dirk Kuyt could be considered a rarity in modern football – an unselfish striker whose outstanding work rate puts many of his team mates to shame.

Kuyt, who more often than not is utilised on the right wing for his club side Liverpool, has been a valuable member of Holland's squad for over six years. Now 29, he was an outstanding prospect as a fledgling striker at Feyenoord, netting 83 goals in 122 games. That prompted Liverpool to shell out £10 million for Kuyt's services, but a barren spell in front of goal saw him converted into a winger. For Holland he plays in either position and was used in every game in qualifying, netting three goals along the way. What he lacks in pace, Kuyt makes up for when straining every sinew to chase down lost causes and help out team mates.

Playing record	12 months lge	wcq
Appearances:	38	8
Minutes played:	3082	617
Percentage played:	87.8%	85.7%
Goals scored:	12	3
Percentage share:	15.19%	17.65%
Cards:	Y1, R0	Y1, R0
Strike rate:	257mins	206mins
Strike rate ranking:	78th	39th

AGE 29	DREAM TEAM RANKING 68

KLASS-JAN HUNTELAAR
AC MILAN

The latest in a long line of prolific Dutch strikers, Klaas-Jan Huntelaar has a point to prove in this summer's World Cup.

Sensational goal records at Heerenveen and Ajax earned Huntelaar a dream move to Real Madrid but, as at subsequent club AC Milan, things just didn't click for the 26-year-old. However, his undoubted ability has never forsaken him at international level where Huntelaar, Holland's all-time record under 21 goalscorer, has continued his Dutch club form. With a senior Holland record just shy of one goal every two games, Huntelaar could find himself thrust into the spotlight in South Africa.

Playing record	12 months lge	wcq
Appearances:	31	8
Minutes played:	1558	443
Percentage played:	43.3%	61.5%
Goals scored:	11	3
Percentage share:	15.07%	17.65%
Cards:	Y3, R1	Y2, R0
Strike rate:	142mins	148mins
Strike rate ranking:	20th	20th

AGE 26	DREAM TEAM RANKING 806

ONE TO WATCH

ROBIN VAN PERSIE ARSENAL

Pace, power, creativity, skill, technique - Robin van Persie has got it all.

The left-footed Arsenal striker has excelled in the Premier League where he has consistently, often extravagantly, found the net if it weren't for numerous injuries Van Persie would surely have propelled himself into the pantheon of world strikers for, when fit, he is practically unstoppable.

Playing record	12 months lge	wcq
Appearances:	23	6
Minutes played:	1910	423
Percentage played:	53.1%	58.8%
Goals scored:	10	1
Percentage share:	11.36%	5.88%
Cards:	Y4, R0	Y2, R0
Strike rate:	191mins	423mins
Strike rate ranking:	45th	73rd

AGE 26	STRIKER	DREAM TEAM RANKING 122

ROUTE TO THE FINALS

Cameroon's star man Samuel Eto'o scored nine goals to help The Indomitable Lions ease through the lengthy African qualification process.

Five wins out of five helped Cameroon through their first stage of qualifying, but they had a shaky start to the final group stage, losing to an Emmanuel Adebayor inspired Togo side in their opening game. With pressure mounting, a goalless draw at home to Morocco in their second match was enough to see off manager Otto Pfister.

In came new boss Paul Le Guen and the highly-rated coach had the desired effect, managing his side to back-to-back wins over group leaders Gabon, before victories over

Togo and Morocco wrapped up top spot in their group and bagged a thoroughly deserved spot in South Africa. Without Eto'o's goal-scoring heroics, the Lions may have been struggling to make the World Cup, but no defender will relish facing the clinical Inter Milan striker at the tournament.

FINAL QUALIFYING TABLE
AFRICA ROUND 3 GROUP A

	P	W	D	L	F	A	Pts
Cameroon	6	4	1	1	9	2	13
Gabon	6	3	0	3	9	7	9
Togo	6	2	2	2	3	7	8
Morocco	6	0	3	3	3	8	3

	Date		Opponent	Avge FIFA ranking	Result			Scorers
1	31 May 08	Home	Cape Verde Islands	103	W	2	0	R.Song 8, Eto'o 57pen
2	08 Jun 08	Away	Mauritius	172	W	0	3	Bikey 11, Eto'o 27, Bebbe 87
3	14 Jun 08	Away	Tanzania	104	D	0	0	
4	21 Jun 08	Home	Tanzania	104	W	2	1	Eto'o 65, 89
5	06 Sep 08	Away	Cape Verde Islands	103	W	1	2	Emana 51, Somen 65
6	11 Oct 08	Home	Mauritius	172	W	5	0	Eto'o 26, 46pen, Meyong Ze 56, 72, Makoun 70
7	28 Mar 09	Away	Togo	78	L	1	0	
8	07 Jun 09	Home	Morocco	46	D	0	0	
9	05 Sep 09	Away	Gabon	59	W	0	2	Emana 66, Eto'o 68
10	09 Sep 09	Home	Gabon	59	W	2	1	Makoun 25, Eto'o 64
11	10 Oct 09	Home	Togo	78	W	3	0	Geremi 32, Makoun 47, Emana 52
12	14 Nov 09	Away	Morocco	46	W	0	2	Webo 19, Eto'o 52
	Average FIFA ranking of opposition			**94**				

MAIN PLAYER PERFORMANCES IN QUALIFICATION

Match	1 2 3 4 5 6 7 8 9 10 11 12	Appearances	Started	Subbed on	Subbed off	Mins played	% played	Goals	Yellow	Red
Venue	H A A H A H A H A H H A									
Result	W W D W W W L D W W W W									
Goalkeepers										
Idriss Carlos Kameni		12	12	0	0	1080	100.0	0	0	0
Defenders										
Benoit Assou-Ekotto		4	4	0	0	360	33.3	0	2	0
Timothee Atouba		5	5	0	1	434	40.2	0	1	0
Henri Bedimo Nsame		1	1	0	0	90	8.3	0	0	0
Andre Bikey		6	6	0	0	540	50.0	1	2	0
Geremi Njitap		11	11	0	1	977	90.5	1	1	0
Nicolas Nkoulou		5	5	0	0	450	41.7	0	0	0
Alexandre Song		8	8	0	0	719	66.6	0	2	1
Rigobert Song		12	11	1	0	1057	97.9	1	1	0
Pierre Nlend Wome		1	1	0	0	90	8.3	0	0	0
Midfielders										
Giles Augustin Binya		3	2	1	0	190	17.6	0	0	0
Eric Djemba-Djemba		2	0	2	0	77	7.1	0	0	0
Achille Emana		10	6	4	4	536	49.6	3	1	0
Enoh Eyong		4	1	3	0	127	11.8	0	0	0
Stephane M'bia		10	6	4	3	535	49.5	0	1	0
Jean Makoun		12	12	0	4	1000	92.6	3	0	0
Modeste Mbami		7	7	0	4	522	48.3	0	0	0
Landry Nguemo		3	3	0	1	248	23.0	0	1	0
Daniel Ngom Kome		4	2	2	1	178	16.5	0	1	0
Alain Mosely Nkong		3	1	2	1	112	10.4	0	0	0
Atchoyi Somen		6	3	3	2	275	25.5	1	0	0
Forwards										
Paul Alo'o Efoulou		4	1	3	1	182	16.9	0	0	0
Samuel Eto'o		11	11	0	1	967	89.5	9	2	0
Albert Meyong		2	1	1	0	135	12.5	2	0	0
Achille Webo		10	10	0	9	714	66.1	1	2	0

FINAL PROSPECTS

The Indomitable Lions are the most successful African World Cup nation and will aim to put in a good showing in the first tournament on their continent.

They are the highest-ranked African country at the finals, and can put out a first XI of players based in top European clubs. Of the six African sides, they appear to be one of the best-placed to reach the quarters – with Ghana and Ivory Coast in tough qualification groups.

2010 will be the country's sixth appearance at a World Cup, with the Lions only missing one tournament since 1990, when the put in their best ever showing, winning three games and reaching the quarter-finals.

This may be the best World Cup for the peerless Samuel Eto'o

Manager Paul Le Guen took over mid-way through qualifying and quickly worked out the best formation to recover a qualification campaign that was beginning to stutter. Keeper Carlos Kameni is only 25 but has been one of the top keepers in Spain's La Liga for five years, while the colourful Rigobert Song – now 33 – leads a defensive line-up that can call on Benoit Assou-Ekotto and Sebastien Bassong of Spurs.

In midfield the talented Jean Makoun partners Arsenal's Alexandre Song – nephew of Rigobert – in a solid defensive partnership, while Geremi brings quality on the ball either in the centre of the park or out on the right.

This may be the best World Cup for the peerless Samuel Eto'o, who brings genuine world-class quality up front, and his form for Inter Milan in his first season suggests he could be a major star in South Africa. Certainly if the Lions are to make it far in the tournament then Eto'o will need to continue his phenomenal scoring record from qualifying.

In addition to the star names, there is plenty of quality elsewhere in the Cameroon squad. Monaco's 19-year-old Nicolas Nkoulou started the last five games in qualifying and is a hot prospect in France's Ligue 1 and Burnley's Andre Bikey is having a fine season.

A last-eight exit to eventual winners Egypt in the 2010 African Cup of Nations was a disappointment for one of the pre-tournament favourites, but they will undoubtedly up their game against the best of the world in South Africa.

DREAM TEAM   **TOP 15 RANKING**   13

GROUP FIXTURES

JAPAN	Mon 14 June 1500 BST
DENMARK	Sat 19 June 1930 BST
NETHERLANDS	Thur 24 June 1930 BST

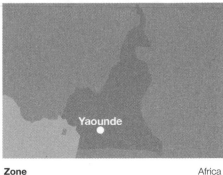

Yaounde

Zone	Africa
Population	18.5m
Language	French, English
Top league	MTN Elite One
Playing season	October - June

Major clubs and capacities
Contosport Garoua (35,043), Tiko United (8,067),
Canon Yaounde (48,720)

Where probable squad players play:

Premier League	3	Ligue 1	5
Serie A	2	Eredivisie	2
La Liga	4	Other Europe	6
Bundesliga	-	Outside Europe	1

Number of Cameroonian players playing:

Premier League	4	Bundesliga	4
Serie A	2	Ligue 1	9
La Liga	2	Eredivisie	3

World Cup record * best performance

1930 - Did not enter		1974 -	Did not qualify
1934 - Did not enter		1978 -	Did not qualify
1938 - Did not enter		1982 -	Round 1
1950 - Did not enter		1986 -	Did not qualify
1954 - Did not enter		1990 -	* Quater finals
1958 - Did not enter		1994 -	Round 1
1962 - Did not enter		1998 -	Round 2
1966 - Withdrew		2002 -	Round 3
1970 - Did not qualify		2006 -	Did not qualify

THE SQUAD

Goalkeepers	Club side	Age	QG
Carlos Kameni	Espanyol	26	12
Defenders			
Benoit Assou-Ekotto	Tottenham	26	4
Timothee Atouba	Ajax	28	5
Henri Bedimo Nsame	Lens	26	1
Andre Bikey	Burnley	25	6
Geremi Njitap	Ankaraguku	31	11
Nicolas Nkoulou	AS Monaco	20	5
Alexandre Song	Arsenal	22	8
Rigobert Song	Trabzonspor	33	12
Pierre Nlend Wome	Cologne	31	1
Midfielders			
Giles Augustin Binya	Neuchatel	25	3
Aurelien Chedjou	Lille	24	2
Eric Djemba-Djemba	Odense	29	2
Achille Emana	Real Betis	28	10
Enoh Eyong	Ajax	23	4
Stephane M'bia	Marseille	24	10
Jean Makoun	Lyon	27	12
Modeste Mbami	Almeria	27	7
Landry Nguemo	Celtic	24	3
Daniel Ngom Kome	Tenerife	30	4
Alain Mosely Nkong	Indios	31	3
Atchoyi Somen	Salzburg	27	6
Forwards			
Paul Alo'o Efoulou	Nancy	26	4
Samuel Eto'o	Inter Milan	29	11
Albert Meyong	Braga	29	2
Achille Webo	Mallorca	28	10

■ Probable ■ Possible **QG** Qualification Games

KEY PLAYER

RIGOBERT SONG TRABZONSPOR

One of the most experienced players at South Africa 2010, Rigobert Song has been the heartbeat of Cameroon's side for many years.

He featured in the 1994 USA World Cup, and has gone on to become his country's record cap holder with over 130 appearances to his name. Now 33, this is surely the defender's last hurrah.

Playing record	12 months lge	wcq
Appearances:	-	12
Minutes played:	-	1057
Percentage played:	-	97.9%
Goals conceded:	-	3
Clean sheets:	-	8
Cards:	-	Y1, R0
Minutes between goals:	-	352mins
Defender ranking:	-	10th

AGE 33 **DEFENDER** **DREAM TEAM RANKING** 925

KEY GOALKEEPER

CARLOS KAMENI
ESPANYOL

Firmly established as Cameroon's number one keeper, Carlos Kameni now has the chance to prove his worth on the biggest stage of them all. Since making his international debut aged just 17, Kameni has matured into one of the finest shot-stoppers in Africa.

Plying his trade with Espanyol in Spain has given Kameni the platform to play against some of the finest strikers in world football, which should stand him in good stead in South Africa. He has over 50 caps.

Playing record	12 months lge	wcq
Appearances:	37	12
Minutes played:	3329	1080
Percentage played:	94.8%	100%
Goals conceded:	44	4
Clean sheets:	13	8
Cards:	Y2, R1	Y0, R0
Minutes between goals:	76mins	270mins
Goalkeeper ranking:	19th	6th

AGE 26	DREAM TEAM	RANKING 103

KEY DEFENDERS

ALEXANDRE SONG
ARSENAL

Nephew of Cameroon team mate Rigobet Song, Alex Song burst onto the international scene at the 2008 African Cup of Nations. Despite only making his national debut in the group stages, Song was named in the Team of the Tournament.

Playing record	12 months lge	wcq
Appearances:	32	8
Minutes played:	2494	719
Percentage played:	69.3%	66.6%
Goals conceded:	-	-
Clean sheets:	14	5
Cards:	Y7, R0	Y2, R1
Minutes between goals:	-	-
Defender ranking:	-	-

GEREMI NJITAP
ANKARAGUKU

A veteran of Champions League finals, Premier League titles and African Cup of Nations triumphs, Geremi has done it all in world football. The former Real Madrid and Chelsea midfielder, still only 31, has won over 100 caps for the Indomitable Lions.

Playing record	12 months lge	wcq
Appearances:	-	11
Minutes played:	-	977
Percentage played:	-	90.5%
Goals conceded:	-	2
Clean sheets:	-	8
Cards:	-	Y1, R0
Minutes between goals:	-	-
Defender ranking:	-	-

AGE 31	DREAM TEAM	RANKING 2610

KEY MIDFIELDERS

JEAN MAKOUN
LYON

Already a dominant force in the French Ligue 1, Jean Makoun has the ability to leave an indelible mark on South Africa 2010. The Lyon midfielder played in every qualifying game for the Indomitable Lions.

A typical box-to-box player, Makoun has a scoring record of roughly one in four for Cameroon but doesn't mind doing the dirty work either. Strong in the tackle, he specialises in breaking up opposition attacks with his boundless energy and willingness to sacrifice personal gain for the good of the team. Having been a regular at three Africa Cup of Nations tournaments, it's now time for Makoun to prove himself on the world stage.

Playing record	12 months lge	wcq
Appearances:	33	12
Minutes played:	2709	1000
Percentage played:	79.2%	92.6%
Goals scored:	5	3
Clean sheets:	11	10
Cards:	Y5, R0	Y0, R0
Strike rate:	542mins	333mins
Midfielder ranking:	100th	33rd

ACHILLE EMANA
REAL BETIS

Playing record	12 months lge	wcq
Appearances:	-	10
Minutes played:	-	536
Percentage played:	-	49.6%
Goals scored:	-	3
Clean sheets:	-	-
Cards:	-	Y1, R0
Strike rate:	-	178mins
Midfielder ranking:	-	-

AGE 28	DREAM TEAM	RANKING 2001

THE MANAGER

A former France international defender, Paul Le Guen has had an inconsistent start to his management career.

Massive success with Lyon in France earned Le Guen a reputation as one of the best young coaches in the game, but he struggled on leaving Ligue 1 and lasted less than a season as manager of Rangers in the 2006/07 season. More disappointment was to follow with Paris Saint Germain - for whom he had made over 200 appearances as a player - and he was let go by the club in 2009.

Le Guen took over from Otto Pfister as Cameroon manager that summer, with the Lions languishing in their qualification group after picking up just one point from their opening two games. However, he turned the campaign around, and his decision to give Samuel Eto'o the responsibility of captain was key, as the Inter Milan striker's inspired form helped Le Guen's side to four wins from four in the remainder of qualifying, sealing a place in South Africa.

KEY STRIKER

ACHILLE WEBO
MALLORCA

An unsung hero of the Cameroon side, Pierre Webo has been a loyal servant to The Indomitable Lions for over seven years. Never a prolific scorer, Webo is more likely to be found setting goals up on a plate for Samuel Eto'o.

The 28-year-old, currently following in Eto'o's footsteps at Spanish club Mallorca, uses his unparalleled work rate and unselfish play to create space for his attacking team-mates. He certainly knows where the back of the net is, though, as proved in 2005 when he netted a famous hat trick against the Ivory Coast in a World Cup qualifier.

Playing record	12 months lge	wcq
Appearances:	29	10
Minutes played:	952	714
Percentage played:	27.1%	66.1%
Goals scored:	4	1
Percentage share:	6.06%	4.35%
Cards:	Y2, R0	Y2, R0
Strike rate:	238mins	714mins
Strike rate ranking:	74th	80th

AGE 28   **DREAM TEAM RANKING** 1777

ONE TO WATCH

SAMUEL ETOO INTER MILAN

Surely no other team at South Africa 2010 relies so heavily on one player than Cameroon do on their superstar striker Samuel Eto'o.

The Inter Milan player has scored goals at a phenomenal rate throughout his career, averaging one every two games despite playing at the very highest level. He first came to prominence with Spanish side Mallorca, but it was a big-money move to Barcelona which was the making of the 29-year-old. Eto'o scored 130 goals in 200 appearances for Barca to establish himself as one of the world's most prolific goalscorers. His passionate nature can often be the driving force behind Cameroon's play.

Eto'o is a Top 12 striker

AGE 29   **STRIKER**   **DREAM TEAM RANKING** 3

ROUTE TO THE FINALS

A defeat to Australia was Japan's only disappointment as they breezed through qualification.

Japan and Australia played out a 0-0 draw in Yokohama, and a Tim Cahill brace in the dead rubber at the end of qualification was the difference when they met in Melbourne.

The first stage was comfortable for a side who racked up seven goals in two games against Thailand. A 1-0 defeat in Bahrain was a surprise, but little more than a stumble.

Japan got their revenge in the final group stage, beating Bahrain both home and away.

Three wins and two draws was enough to secure a place in South Africa with ease, and Japan will be confident of making an impression on the tournament after an impressive showing back in 2002.

Japan's biggest problem was a lack of a reliable option up front, with manager Takeshi Odaka using ten forwards in 14 qualifying games – who only managed six goals between them. Shunsuke Nakamura weighed in with three from midfield, while defenders Marcus Tulio and Yuki Nakazawa scored three apiece from the back, as they cemented their places in a settled back four.

For final qualification table see Australia.

Avge FIFA ranking

1	06 Feb 08	Home	Thailand	113	W	**4**	**1**	Endo 21, Okubo 54, Nakazawa 66, Maki 90
2	26 Mar 08	Away	Bahrain	71	L	**1**	**0**	
3	02 Jun 08	Home	Oman	85	W	**3**	**0**	Nakazawa 10, Okubo 22, S.Nakamura 49
4	07 Jun 08	Away	Oman	85	D	**1**	**1**	Endo 53pen
5	14 Jun 08	Away	Thailand	113	W	**0**	**3**	Tanaka 23, Nakazawa 38, K.Nakamura 88
6	22 Jun 08	Home	Bahrain	71	W	**1**	**0**	Uchida 90
7	06 Sep 08	Away	Bahrain	71	W	**2**	**3**	S.Nakamura 18, Endo 44pen, K.Nakamura 85
8	15 Oct 08	Home	Uzbekistan	71	D	**1**	**1**	Tamada 40
9	19 Nov 08	Away	Qatar	85	W	**0**	**3**	T.Tanaka 19, Tamada 47, MT.Tanaka 68
10	11 Feb 09	Home	Australia	30	D	**0**	**0**	
11	28 Mar 09	Home	Bahrain	71	W	**1**	**0**	S.Nakamura 47
12	06 Jun 09	Away	Uzbekistan	71	W	**0**	**1**	Okazaki 9
13	10 Jun 09	Home	Qatar	85	D	**1**	**1**	Al Binali 3og
14	17 Jun 09	Away	Australia	30	L	**2**	**1**	MT.Tanaka 39
	Average FIFA ranking of opposition			75				

MAIN PLAYER PERFORMANCES IN QUALIFICATION

Match	1 2 3 4 5 6 7 8 9 10 11 12 13 14	Appearances	Started	Subbed on	Subbed off	Mins played	% played	Goals	Yellow	Red
Venue	H A H A A H A H A H H H A H									
Result	W L W D W W W D W D W W W L									
Goalkeepers										
Yoshikatsu Kawaguchi		3	3	0	0	270	21.4	0	0	0
Seigo Narazaki		10	10	0	0	900	71.4	0	0	0
Ryota Tsuzuki		1	1	0	0	90	7.1	0	0	0
Defenders										
Yuki Abe		7	6	1	2	498	39.5	0	1	0
Yuichi Komano		6	6	0	0	540	42.9	0	1	0
Yasuyuki Konno		8	3	5	0	313	24.8	0	0	0
Yuto Nagatomo		6	6	0	1	532	42.2	0	1	0
Yuji Nakazawa		12	12	0	0	1080	85.7	3	1	0
Marcus Tulio Tanaka		12	12	0	0	1080	85.7	3	0	0
Shuhei Terada		1	1	0	0	90	7.1	0	0	0
Atsuto Uchida		11	11	0	1	989	78.5	1	0	0
Michihiro Yasuda		2	2	0	2	142	11.3	0	0	0
Midfielders										
Yasuhito Endo		12	11	1	0	1026	81.4	3	1	0
Makoto Hasebe		9	9	0	2	786	62.4	0	1	1
Hideo Hashimoto		3	2	1	1	188	14.9	0	0	0
Keisuke Honda		3	1	2	1	114	9.0	0	0	0
Shinji Kagawa		3	2	1	2	175	13.9	0	1	0
Daisuka Matsui		9	6	3	5	492	39.0	0	2	0
Kengo Nakamura		8	6	2	1	557	44.2	2	0	0
Shunsuke Nakamura		11	11	0	3	958	76.0	3	1	0
Keita Suzuki		2	2	0	0	180	14.3	0	0	0
Forwards										
Seiichiro Maki		4	1	3	0	136	10.8	1	0	0
Shinji Okazaki		7	3	4	0	317	25.2	1	0	0
Yoshito Okubo		9	8	1	5	657	52.1	2	0	1
Keiji Tamada		12	11	1	7	927	73.6	2	0	0
Tatsuya Tanaka		4	4	0	3	327	26.0	1	1	0
Koji Yamase		4	2	2	2	161	12.8	0	0	0

FINAL PROSPECTS

Underdogs of the group, Japan have high hopes of defying expectations and making it into the knockout stages in South Africa.

Organised at the back, with quality in midfield, they do struggle to score from open play – although 23-year-old Shinji Okazaki has forced his way into the reckoning with three starts at the end of qualifying and a hat-trick in a 5-0 friendly win over Togo in October hinted at a bright future.

Most of the squad play in Japan's own J-League, with only Shunsuke Nakamura – now with Espanyol – and Wolfsburg's Makoto Hasebe based with top European sides. If Japan can keep Samuel Eto'o quiet – which would be no mean feat – then an opening game against Cameroon offers a chance to get points on the board. A 3-0 defeat to the Netherlands in September 2009 suggests that the game against the Dutch might be too tough an ask. But if qualification for the second round is still up for grabs, then they will fancy being able to take points off an unspectacular Denmark.

Takeshi Odaka's team will need luck on their side, but they have an opportunity of at least making the last 16.

DREAM TEAM	TOP 15 RANKING	22

THE MANAGER

Former Japan international defender Takeshi Okada took charge of Japan for the second time in 2007 when coach Ivica Osim suffered a stroke.

An experienced manager in the J-League, he has made the most of a limited pool of players available to lead Japan to a World Cup for the second time - he also steered the national side to France 1998. Okada has confidently targeted a semi-final spot in South Africa, but a lack of genuine quality up front means that he will need to be at his tactical best to even steer Japan out of the group stage.

GROUP FIXTURES

CAMEROON	Mon 14 June 1500 BST
NETHERLANDS	Sat 19 June 1230 BST
DENMARK	Thur 24 June 1930 BST

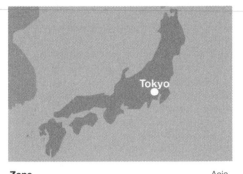

Zone	Asia
Population	127m
Language	Japanese
Top league	League 1
Playing season	March - December

Major clubs and capacities
Furukawa Electric, JEF United Chiba (19,781),
Toyo Industries, Sanfrecce Hiroshima (50,761),
Mitsubishi Motors, Urawa Red Diamonds (63,702)

Where probable squad players play:

Premier League	-	Ligue 1	1
Serie A	-	Eredivisie	-
La Liga	1	Other Europe	-
Bundesliga	1	Outside Europe	20

Number of Japanese players playing:

Premier League	-	Bundesliga	2
Serie A	1	Ligue 1	2
La Liga	1	Eredivisie	1

World Cup record   * best performance

1930 - Did not enter	1974 -	Did not qualify
1934 - Did not enter	1978 -	Did not qualify
1938 - Withdrew	1982 -	Did not qualify
1950 - Banned	1986 -	Did not qualify
1954 - Did not qualify	1990 -	Did not qualify
1958 - Did not enter	1994 -	Did not qualify
1962 - Did not qualify	1998 -	Round 1
1966 - Did not enter	2002 -	* Last 16
1970 - Did not qualify	2006 -	Round 1

THE SQUAD

Goalkeepers	Club side	Age	QG
Yoshikatsu Kawaguchi	Jubilo Iwata	34	3
Seigo Narazaki	Nagoya Grampus	34	10
Ryota Tsuzuki	Urawa Reds	32	1
Defenders			
Yuki Abe	Urawa Reds	28	7
Yuichi Komano	Jubilo Iwata	28	6
Yasuyuki Konno	FC Tokyo	27	8
Yuto Nagatomo	FC Tokyo	23	6
Yuji Nakazawa	Yokohama F Marinos	32	12
Marcus Tulio Tanaka	Urawa Reds	29	12
Atsuto Uchida	Kashima Antlers	22	11
Michihiro Yasuda	Gamba Osaka	22	2
Midfielders			
Yasuhito Endo	Gamba Osaka	30	12
Makoto Hasebe	Wolfsburg	26	9
Hideo Hashimoto	Gamba Osaka	31	3
Keisuke Honda	CSKA Moscow	23	3
Shinji Kagawa	Cerezo Osaka	21	3
Daisuka Matsui	Grenoble	29	9
Kengo Nakamura	Kawasaki Frontale	29	8
Shunsuke Nakamura	Espanyol	31	11
Keita Suzuki	Urawa Reds	29	2
Forwards			
Seiichiro Maki	JEF United Chiba	29	4
Shinji Okazaki	Shimizu S-Pulse	24	7
Yoshito Okubo	Vissel Kobe	28	9
Keiji Tamada	Nagoya Grampus	30	12
Tatsuya Tanaka	Urawa Reds	27	4
Koji Yamase	Yokohama F Marinos	28	4

■ Probable ■ Possible **QG** Qualification Games

KEY PLAYER

SHUNSUKE NAKAMURA ESPANYOL

Following the retirement of Hidetoshi Nakata after the 2006 World Cup, Shunsuke Nakamura became the new darling of Japanese football.

Already a dominant force at Celtic, Nakamura was the new focal point of the national side and has since gone on to earn over 90 caps. His wand of a left foot has dazzled many a defence.

Playing record	12 months lge	wcq
Appearances:	29	11
Minutes played:	2014	958
Percentage played:	57.4%	76.0%
Goals scored:	3	3
Clean Sheets:	14	7
Cards:	Y2, R0	Y1, R0
Strike rate:	671mins	319mins
Strike rate ranking:	120th	29th

AGE 31   **MIDFIELDER**   DREAM TEAM **RANKING** 717

ROUTE TO THE FINALS

Denmark topped a tricky qualification group containing Portugal, Sweden and Hungary to reach the World Cup. Despite a lack of star names and a squad of lesser quality than their group opponents, the Danes were consistently the strongest side and fully deserved to finish ahead of their more illustrious opponents.

After a 0-0 draw away in Hungary in their opening game, a thrilling win in Lisbon kick-started the successful campaign.

Nicklas Bendtner's 82nd minute equaliser looked to have earned the visitors a point, only for Deco to put Portugal ahead again from the spot with five minutes left on the clock.

However, late, late goals from Christian Poulsen and Daniel Jensen wrapped up all three points and left the underperforming Portuguese in real trouble.

A 1-0 win away in Sweden and a point against Portugal put Morten Olsen's side in pole position for the automatic qualification spot with three games remaining.

A draw away against minnows Albania threatened to derail the campaign and let one of Sweden and Portugal leapfrog into top spot, but Jakob Poulsen's strike against Sweden secured a crucial 1-0 win in their penultimate match to wrap up first place.

Despite their qualification success, Denmark will still be one of the less-fancied sides in South Africa, and will attempt to use that to their advantage to make it out of one of the easier groups.

For final qualification table see Portugal.

				Avge FIFA ranking				
1	06 Sep 08	Away	Hungary	49	D	0 0	
2	10 Sep 08	Away	Portugal	11	W	2 3	Bendtner 84, D.Jensen 90, Chistian.Poulsen 90
3	11 Oct 08	Home	Malta	144	W	3 0	Larsen 10, 47, Agger 29pen
4	28 Mar 09	Away	Malta	144	W	0 3	Larsen 12, 23, Nordstrand 89
5	01 Apr 09	Home	Albania	89	W	3 0	Andreasen 31, Larsen 37, Chistian.Poulsen 80
6	06 Jun 09	Away	Sweden	32	W	0 1	Kahlenberg 22
7	05 Sep 09	Home	Portugal	11	D	1 1	Bendtner 42
8	09 Sep 09	Away	Albania	89	D	1 1	Bendtner 40
9	10 Oct 09	Home	Sweden	32	W	1 0	Jakob.Poulsen 79
10	14 Oct 09	Home	Hungary	49	L	0 1	
	Average FIFA ranking of opposition			65			

MAIN PLAYER PERFORMANCES IN QUALIFICATION

Match	1 2 3 4 5 6 7 8 9 10	Appearances	Started	Subbed on	Subbed off	Mins played	% played	Goals	Yellow	Red
Venue	A A H A H A H A H H									
Result	D W W W W W D D W L									
Goalkeepers										
Stephan Andersen		3	3	0	0	270	30.0	0	1	0
Thomas Sorensen		7	7	0	0	630	70.0	0	2	0
Defenders										
Daniel Agger		8	8	0	0	720	80.0	1	0	0
Kasper Bogelund		1	1	0	0	90	10.0	0	0	0
Anders Christensen		3	3	0	0	270	30.0	0	1	0
Lars Christian Jacobsen		9	9	0	1	764	84.9	0	1	0
Michael Jakobsen		4	4	0	0	360	40.0	0	1	0
Simon Kjaer		4	4	0	0	360	40.0	0	1	0
Per Billeskov Kroldrup		1	1	0	0	90	10.0	0	0	0
William Kvist Jorgensen		3	2	1	0	205	22.8	0	0	0
Martin Laursen		3	3	0	0	270	30.0	0	1	0
Christopher Poulsen		1	1	0	0	90	10.0	0	1	0
Thomas Rasmussen		1	1	0	0	90	10.0	0	0	0
Midfielders										
Leon Andreasen		3	2	1	1	205	22.8	1	0	0
Daniel Monberg Jensen		6	5	1	3	384	42.7	1	1	0
Thomas Kahlenberg		3	3	0	1	239	26.6	1	0	0
Christian Bager Poulsen		10	10	0	0	900	100.0	2	1	0
Jakob Poulsen		6	5	1	3	437	48.6	1	0	0
Michael Silberbauer		4	1	3	1	176	19.6	0	0	0
Forwards										
Nicklas Bendtner		9	8	1	3	705	78.3	3	0	0
Jonas Borring		4	0	4	0	131	14.6	0	0	0
Lars Martin Jorgensen		6	6	0	5	363	40.3	0	0	0
Soren Larsen		5	3	2	2	307	34.1	5	1	0
Morten Nordstrand		2	1	1	0	99	11.0	1	0	0
Dennis Rommedahl		10	10	0	2	860	95.6	0	1	0
Jon Dahl Tomasson		6	6	0	3	472	52.4	0	1	0

FINAL PROSPECTS

Denmark will have high hopes of at least making it into the last 16 after being drawn in one of the less daunting groups.

The Netherlands are the stand out team in Group E, but Morten Olsen's side will fancy their chances against an inconsistent Cameroon and a Japan team which lacks any sort of cutting edge.

Well-organised defensively, only the Netherlands conceded less goals in all of the European qualifying groups, while a strong spine of Thomas Sorensen, Daniel Agger, Christian Poulsen and Nicklas Bendtner means there is quality throughout all of the team.

A lack of strength in depth could prove their undoing if they suffer any injury or suspension problems, but if the main players are available then don't bet against Denmark as surprise quarter-finalists.

The second group game against Cameroon will be key to their chances of making the last 16.

The winner of that game will be huge favourites to make it out of the group along with the Netherlands.

DREAM TEAM TOP 15 RANKING 10

THE MANAGER

With over 100 caps Morten Olsen was a permanent fixture in the Danish defence for 19 years.

He seemed a natural to succeed at management and started with top Danish Superliga side Brondby as soon as his playing career ended.

He was fired after short spells with both Cologne and Ajax before moving to the Danish national team in 2000.

He has mixed and matched brilliantly around a handful of class players to qualify ahead of Portugal and Sweden and he could spring a surprise on heavyweights Cameroon and the Netherlands.

GROUP FIXTURES

NETHERLANDS	Mon 14 June 1230 BST
CAMEROON	Sat 19 June 1930 BST
JAPAN	Thur 24 June 1930 BST

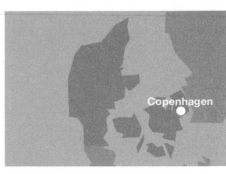

Copenhagen

Zone	Europe
Population	5.5m
Language	Danish
Top league	Superligaen (SAS Ligaen)
Playing season	August - May

Major clubs and capacities
FC Copenhagen (38,050), Brondby IF (29,955),
AaB (16,342)

Where probable squad players play:

Premier League	4	Ligue 1	-
Serie A	3	Eredivisie	3
La Liga	-	Other Europe	10
Bundesliga	3	Outside Europe	-

Number of Danish players playing:

Premier League	5	Bundesliga	4
Serie A	6	Ligue 1	-
La Liga	1	Eredivisie	14

World Cup record *best performance*

1930 - Did not enter	1974 -	Did not qualify
1934 - Did not enter	1978 -	Did not qualify
1938 - Did not enter	1982 -	Did not qualify
1950 - Did not enter	1986 -	Round 2
1954 - Did not enter	1990 -	Did not qualify
1958 - Did not qualify	1994 -	Did not qualify
1962 - Did not enter	1998 -	* Quarter finals
1966 - Did not qualify	2002 -	Round 2
1970 - Did not qualify	2006 -	Did not qualify

KEY PLAYER

DANIEL AGGER LIVERPOOL

Having already established himself in the Premier League and the Champions League, Daniel Agger is set to make his mark on the international stage in his first major championships.

Still only 25, the left-footed Liverpool centre half will play an integral role in Denmark's 2010 World Cup side. He is a quick, strong defender who is good in the air.

Playing record	12 months lge	wcq
Appearances:	20	8
Minutes played:	1468	720
Percentage played:	41.8%	80.0%
Goals conceded:	15	3
Clean sheets:	12	6
Cards:	Y1, R0	Y0, R0
Minutes between goals:	98mins	240mins
Defender ranking:	36th	22nd

AGE 25   **DEFENDER**   **DREAM TEAM**   **RANKING** 569

THE SQUAD

Goalkeepers	Club side	Age	QG
Stephan Andersen	Brondby	28	3
Thomas Sorensen	Stoke	33	7
Defenders			
Daniel Agger	Liverpool	25	8
Kasper Bogelund	Aalborg BK	29	1
Anders Christensen	Odense	32	3
Lars Christian Jacobsen	Blackburn	30	9
Michael Jakobsen	Aalborg BK	24	4
Simon Kjaer	Palermo	21	4
Per Kroldrup	Fiorentina	30	1
William Kvist	FC Copenhagen	25	3
Christopher Poulsen	Silkeborg	28	1
Thomas Rasmussen	Brondby	33	1
Midfielders			
Leon Andreasen	Hannover 96	27	3
Daniel Jensen	W Bremen	30	6
Thomas Kahlenberg	Wolfsburg	27	3
Christian Poulsen	Juventus	30	10
Jakob Poulsen	AGF Aarhus	26	6
Michael Silberbauer	Utrecht	28	4
Forwards			
Nicklas Bendtner	Arsenal	22	9
Jonas Borring	Midtjylland	25	4
Jesper Gronkjaer	FC Copenhagen	32	3
Lars Martin Jorgensen	Fiorentina	34	6
Soren Larsen	Duisburg	28	5
Morten Nordstrand	Groningen	27	2
Dennis Rommedahl	Ajax	31	10
Jon Dahl Tomasson	Feyenoord	33	6

■ Probable ■ Possible **QG** Qualification Games

Position	1st	2nd	3rd	4th	5th	6th	7th	8th
Group	E	D	B	H	A	G	C	F
Total FIFA ranking	88	89	98	104	130	147	160	161

KEY MATCH

ITALY V PARAGUAY

Cape Town, Monday 14 June 1930 BST

The reigning champions take the first step towards attempting to retain their trophy in what could be the stand out match of the group. Paraguay are in the best shape in their history having defeated South American heavyweights Brazil and Argentina in qualifying and could be a genuine force in the tournament, while the Italians made South Africa at a mild canter, never really getting out of second gear. Marcello Lippi's side were underwhelming in the group stages in 2006 and despite the fact Italy should qualify regardless of whether they win this game or not, they will need to be very careful to set the right tone first up. Roque Santa Cruz and co. will be gunning for them and this game is highly likely to decide if one of these sides can top the group.

NEW ZEALAND V SLOVAKIA

Rustenburg, Tuesday 15 June 1230 BST

It goes without saying that this is a massive game for both sides with each knowing that – on paper at least – this fixture offers the best chance to pick up invaluable points in a tough group. It also offers New Zealand the chance to prove that they will not be the whipping boys of Group F, with captain Ryan Nelsen no doubt desperate to prove to the naysayers that the All Whites will not prove a whitewash.

For Slovakia, goals are likely to be the key, with Bochum's Stanislav Sestak the most likely source.

SLOVAKIA V PARAGUAY

Bloemfontein, Sunday 20 June 1230 BST

If the odds are to be believed, this game should decide which of these teams make the last 16 alongside Italy and that alone should guarantee an action packed affair. The big games bring forth the big players and for Slovakia, that means their young captain Marek Hamsik. The 22-year old attacking midfielder has been making waves in Italy for Napoli and he won't have a better chance to make his mark on the biggest stage in world soccer.

Italy's Alberto Gilardino

ITALY V NEW ZEALAND

Nelspruit, Sunday 20 June 1500 BST

This game should be a banker for Marcello Lippi's Italian side but they will have to make sure that complacency does not creep in against possibly the weakest side in the whole tournament. The defending champions will hope this ends up being shooting practice for Alberto Gilardino and co. but for New Zealand, Plymouth Argyle's Rory Fallon – only recently qualified to play for the All Whites – will be looking for the chance to leave the Azzurri faithful choking on their pasta.

SLOVAKIA V ITALY

Johannesburg JEP, Thur 24 June 1500 BST

If Italy have already qualified for the last 16, this might not be a thriller but it won't be for the want of trying on Slovakia's part, with Vladimir Weiss' side almost certainly needing at least a point to progress further in this tournament. It might also be a chance for Italy to rest some of their leading players ahead of the knockout stages with many of the expected first team the wrong side of 30.

PARAGUAY V NEW ZEALAND

Polokwane, Thursday 24 June 1500 BST

Paraguay could not have hoped for a better fixture if winning this game means they have a chance of making the last 16. No matter how New Zealand have done so far, you only have to look back to Spain's 5-0 demolition of the All Whites in the 2009 Confederations Cup to know that they are a side capable of taking a beating. The Paraguayan strike force will be relishing the opportunity to dish out just that, especially if goal difference is important.

VIEW FROM THE EXPERTS

ITALY: Defending champions and always good in competition, but the current squad is not their strongest. But Marcello Lippi is a top manager and the Azzurri will be well organised and difficult to beat.
HARRY'S VERDICT: Quarters.
PARAGUAY: Roque Santa Cruz has dominated the team sheet but has had more than his fair share of injury problems. If he makes it for the finals then he can prove a bit of a handful although the rest of the squad is not of the same quality.
HARRY'S VERDICT: Group stage only.
NEW ZEALAND: Ryan Nelsen is their most famous name. The Kiwis should perhaps stick to rugby because I can't see this lot doing much. Soccer is not nearly as high on the agenda as it is in England or even in Australia. It is hard to see them doing anything except enjoying the experience and then going home early.
HARRY'S VERDICT: Group stage only.
SLOVAKIA: Not a team sheet which trips off the tongue. Nevertheless the country borne out of the old Czechoslovakia still possesses the same attitude to football as its predecessors - good passing and technical skill. Skrtel is a solid defender and I can see them sneaking into second place and into the knockout stages.
HARRY'S VERDICT: Last 16.

ITALY: The reigning champions will be determined to retain their crown. The Azzurri did not have it all their own way in qualifying, but they remained unbeaten and with Lippi, his talented group of players and their World Cup pedigree, I would be surprised if they do not reach the latter stages.
TEL'S VERDICT: Will not give up trophy without fight.
PARAGUAY: Finished one point behind Brazil in qualifying for their fourth successive finals. Gerardo Martino's side are renowned for their counter-attacking and in Nelson Haedo Valdez, Oscar Cardozo and Roque Santa Cruz they have the firepower to cause damage.
TEL'S VERDICT: Could reach second phase.
NEW ZEALAND: New Zealand have already bagged the tag of "whipping boys" as they prepare for only their second appearance at the World Cup finals. In Spain in 1982 they did not get further than the first round and I cannot see them doing any better this time.
TEL'S VERDICT: Kiwi fruitless.

SLOVAKIA: Did well to top their qualifying group ahead of Slovenia, Czech Republic and Northern Ireland, but their 4-0 defeat by England in a friendly in March 2009 may be a more accurate reflection on their chances in South Africa. In midfielder and captain Marek Hamsik they have a true star in the making, but there is a lack of quality elsewhere.

TEL'S VERDICT: Will be a feat if they make it through group.

ITALY: Marcelo Lippi's men will be worthy reigning champions and they will not give up their trophy without a fight. The World Cup is what the Italians live for. Everything The Azzurri does is geared towards this. Nothing else matters. They will put in strong a challenge as they did four years ago.

WRIGHTY'S VERDICT: Need a goalscorer.

PARAGUAY: Appearing at their fourth successive finals, Paraguay will be looking to improve on Germany 2006 when they failed to make it through the group stages. Whether they can better it this time depends on the displays and goal-scoring of Manchester City's Roque Santa Cruz.

WRIGHTY'S VERDICT: Santa must deliver.

NEW ZEALAND: What a shame they are not in England's group! Yes they have done well to reach their first finals since 1982. Yes they will be happy to be there, sharing the stage with the world's best. But I reckon they could be the tournament's whipping boys.

WRIGHTY'S VERDICT: Good luck to them...because they'll need it.

SLOVAKIA: Qualified for their first World Cup by winning their group, ahead of Poland and the fancied Czech Republic. But I do not expect them to record many more shocks in South Africa. England beat them 4-0 in a friendly last year.

WRIGHTY'S VERDICT: Happy just to be there.

"In Nelson Haedo Valdez, Oscar Cardozo and Roque Santa Cruz they have the firepower to cause damage"

THE LIKELY ROUTES FOR THE TOP TWO TEAMS FROM THE GROUP

For the full draw please see page 80

GROUP STAGE	LAST SIXTEEN	QUARTER-FINALS
FIRST GROUP F	v SECOND GROUP E	v FIRST GROUP H or SECOND GROUP G
ITALY	**ITALY v CAMEROON**	**ITALY v SPAIN**
SECOND GROUP F	v FIRST GROUP E	v FIRST GROUP G or SECOND GROUP H
SLOVAKIA	**SLOVAKIA v NETHERLANDS**	**NETHERLANDS v BRAZIL**
GROUP G ITALY, PARAGUAY, NEW ZEALAND, SLOVAKIA	**GROUP E** NETHERLANDS, DENMARK, JAPAN, CAMEROON	**GROUP G** BRAZIL, NORTH KOREA (KOREA DPR), IVORY COAST, PORTUGAL **GROUP H** SPAIN, SWITZERLAND, HONDURAS, CHILE

ROUTE TO THE FINALS

The Azzurri were effective in qualifying as they strolled their way to the finals without really breaking sweat. They won seven and drew three of their ten games - but it was very much substance over style.

Following a relatively disappointing Euro 2008, Italy dispensed with manager Roberto Donadoni and returned to Marcello Lippi who brought them the World Cup in 2006.

Much in the way that Lippi's side of 2006 did the bare minimum for periods of those World Cup finals, so too did his team here.

They made a habit of sealing matters late, but only twice did it really influence the result - in the final two games when they claimed a draw and a win against Republic of Ireland and Cyprus respectively.

They only once scored more than two goals in a game and it was Alberto Gilardino who scored all three against Cyprus, and a crucial equaliser against Ireland, but it was Daniele De Rossi who was the star of the campaign. They will need to improve in South Africa if they want to retain their title.

FINAL QUALIFYING TABLE
EUROPE GROUP 8

	P	W	D	L	F	A	Pts
Italy	10	7	3	0	18	7	24
Rep of Ireland	10	4	6	0	12	8	18
Bulgaria	10	3	5	2	17	13	14
Cyprus	10	2	3	5	14	16	9
Montenegro	10	1	6	3	9	14	9
Georgia	10	0	3	7	7	19	3

Avge FIFA ranking

1	06 Sep 08	Away	Cyprus	77	W	1 2	Di Natale 8, 90
2	10 Sep 08	Home	Georgia	100	W	2 0	De Rossi 17, 89
3	11 Oct 08	Away	Bulgaria	21	D	0 0	
4	15 Oct 08	Home	Montenegro	117	W	2 1	Aquilani 8, 29
5	28 Mar 09	Away	Montenegro	117	W	0 2	Pirlo 11pen, Pazzini 74
6	01 Apr 09	Home	Rep of Ireland	36	D	1 1	Iaquinta 10
7	05 Sep 09	Away	Georgia	100	W	0 2	Kaladze 57og, 67og
8	09 Sep 09	Home	Bulgaria	21	W	2 0	Grosso 11, Iaquinta 40
9	10 Oct 09	Away	Rep of Ireland	36	D	2 2	Camoranesi 26, Gilardino 90
10	14 Oct 09	Home	Cyprus	77	W	3 2	Gilardino 78, 81, 90
Average FIFA ranking of opposition				70			

MAIN PLAYER PERFORMANCES IN QUALIFICATION

Key: ■ played 90 mins ◀◀ subbed off ▶▶ subbed on ▨ on bench

Match	Appearances	Started	Subbed on	Subbed off	Mins played	% played	Goals	Yellow	Red
Venue	A H A H A H A H A H								
Result	W W D W W D W W D W								
Goalkeepers									
Marco Amelia	2	2	0	0	180	20.0	0	1	0
Gianluigi Buffon	7	7	0	0	630	70.0	0	0	0
Federico Marchetti	1	1	0	0	90	10.0	0	0	0
Defenders									
Salvatore Bocchetti	2	1	1	0	105	11.7	0	0	0
Fabio Cannavaro	9	9	0	0	810	90.0	0	2	0
Giorgio Chiellini	7	7	0	0	630	70.0	0	1	0
Domenico Criscito	1	1	0	0	90	10.0	0	1	0
Andrea Dossena	4	3	1	1	275	30.6	0	0	0
Alessandro Gamberini	2	2	0	1	93	10.3	0	0	0
Fabio Grosso	5	5	0	2	362	40.2	1	1	0
Nicola Legrottaglie	2	2	0	0	180	20.0	0	0	0
Davide Santon	2	1	1	0	109	12.1	0	0	0
Gianluca Zambrotta	9	9	0	0	810	90.0	0	0	0
Midfielders									
Alberto Aquilani	2	2	0	1	155	17.2	2	1	0
Matteo Brighi	2	1	1	0	100	11.1	0	0	0
Mauro Camoranesi	6	5	1	1	476	52.9	1	1	0
Gaetano D'Agostino	3	1	2	1	105	11.7	0	0	0
Daniele De Rossi	9	8	1	0	745	82.8	2	3	0
Gennaro Ivan Gattuso	4	3	1	0	315	35.0	0	2	0
Angelo Palombo	5	3	2	1	358	39.8	0	1	0
Simone Pepe	7	4	3	2	380	42.2	0	0	0
Andrea Pirlo	7	7	0	3	530	58.9	1	1	0
Forwards									
Antonio Di Natale	7	6	1	5	416	46.2	2	0	0
Alberto Gilardino	6	5	1	2	414	46.0	4	0	0
Vincenzo Iaquinta	6	5	1	3	429	47.7	2	1	0
Fabio Quagliarella	5	2	3	0	230	25.6	0	0	0
Giuseppe Rossi	4	2	2	2	158	17.6	0	0	0
Luca Toni	3	2	1	2	133	14.8	0	2	0

FINAL PROSPECTS

It is difficult to find any compelling reasons why Italy should be ruled out of World Cup contention in South Africa.

Results-wise they have done what has been necessary and many of the calm heads that were a key part of their 2006 triumph remain an important part of the side.

Fabio Cannavaro still marshals the defence and captains the side, Gianluigi Buffon is still an imperious presence between the posts, Gianluca Zambrotta and Fabio Grosso remain the versatile full-backs, while Andrea Pirlo pulls the strings as he did in 2006, with Gennaro Gattuso his midfield enforcer. Up front, Alberto Gilardino and Vincenzo Iaquinta still offer the best source of goals. So, why not expect the same result as 2006?

The main protagonists are four years older and hardly setting the world on fire – yet the same could be said in the 2006 finals when Italy were lukewarm for much of the tournament. The key could be the players who have come into the equation since Italy were crowned world champions.

De Rossi is a leader, dominates midfield and the team unify around him.

Daniele De Rossi was in the 2006 squad but an elbow to Brian McBride meant he missed much of it. He is now the heartbeat of the side and is set to inherit the captaincy from Cannavaro. He is a leader, dominates midfield and the team unify around him.

In defence, Giorgio Chiellini has taken over from the retired Alessandro Nesta and looks every bit the part, while going forward Antonio Di Natale and Alberto Aquilani, despite the latter's injury woes, are working to fill the gap left by Francesco Totti.

So where do the question marks appear in Italian's quest to reclaim the trophy?

In 2006, unbelievably, Italy played no South American sides. That run will end when they face Paraguay in their opening match. They also played no side in any particular form and should they make it into the quarter-finals and beyond, that will all end with Spain and Brazil lurking in their part of the draw.

In terms of Group F, however, they will huff and puff and at some stage they will blow the door down but don't expect it to be pretty or straightforward. After that sterner tests and greater challenges await.

Italy are definitely in the hunt and stand as good a chance as a handful of sides of making the latter stages.

DREAM TEAM TOP 15 RANKING 2

GROUP FIXTURES

PARAGUAY	Mon 14 June 1930 BST
NEW ZEALAND	Sun 20 June 1500 BST
SLOVAKIA	Thur 24 June 1500 BST

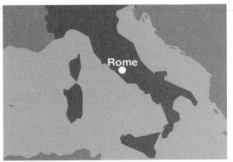

Zone	Europe
Population	58.1m
Language	Italian
Top league	Serie A
Playing season	August - May

Major clubs and capacities
AC Milan (80,074), Inter Milan (80,074), Juventus (65,895), AS Roma (72,698)

Where probable squad players play:

Premier League	1	Ligue 1	-
Serie A	21	Eredivisie	-
La Liga	1	Other Europe	-
Bundesliga	-	Outside Europe	-

Number of Italian players playing:

Premier League	7	Bundesliga	4
Serie A	342	Ligue 1	2
La Liga	5	Eredivisie	1

World Cup record   * best performance

1930 - Did not enter	1974 -	Round 1
1934 - * Champions	1978 -	4th place
1938 - * Champions	1982 -	* Champions
1950 - Round 1	1986 -	Last 16
1954 - Round 1	1990 -	3rd place
1958 - Did not qualify	1994 -	Runners up
1962 - Round 1	1998 -	Quater finals
1966 - Round 1	2002 -	Last 16
1970 - Runners up	2006 -	* Champions

THE SQUAD

Goalkeepers	Club side	Age	QG
Marco Amelia	Genoa	28	2
Gianluigi Buffon	Juventus	32	7
Defenders			
Salvatore Bocchetti	Genoa	23	2
Fabio Cannavaro	Juventus	36	9
Giorgio Chiellini	Juventus	25	7
Andrea Dossena	Napoli	28	4
Alessandro Gamberini	Fiorentina	28	2
Fabio Grosso	Juventus	32	5
Nicola Legrottaglie	Juventus	33	2
Davide Santon	Inter Milan	19	2
Gianluca Zambrotta	AC Milan	33	9
Midfielders			
Alberto Aquilani	Liverpool	25	2
Matteo Brighi	Roma	29	2
Mauro Camoranesi	Juventus	33	6
Gaetano D'Agostino	Udinese	28	3
Daniele De Rossi	Roma	26	9
Gennaro Ivan Gattuso	AC Milan	32	4
Angelo Palombo	Sampdoria	28	5
Simone Pepe	Udinese	26	7
Andrea Pirlo	AC Milan	31	7
Forwards			
Antonio Di Natale	Udinese	32	7
Alberto Gilardino	Fiorentina	27	6
Vincenzo Iaquinta	Juventus	30	6
Fabio Quagliarella	Napoli	27	5
Giuseppe Rossi	Villarreal	23	4
Luca Toni	Roma	33	3

■ Probable ■ Possible **QG** Qualification Games

KEY PLAYER

DANIELE DE ROSSI ROMA

For years Daniele De Rossi has been an unsung hero at international level, with Andrea Pirlo and Gennaro Gattuso earning Italy's midfield plaudits, while at Roma he has constantly played second fiddle to Francesco Totti.

Finally, at the age of 26, it seems the midfield lynchpin has emerged from the shadows to become an outstanding player in his own right. Essentially the heartbeat of Italy's team, his work-rate is phenomenal. Playing with the kind of commitment and passion which has made him hugely popular with the Azzurri faithful, De Rossi scores, prevents and creates goals on a regular basis. The midfielder is set to play an integral role in South Africa.

De Rossi is a Top 12 Midfielder

AGE 26   **MIDFIELDER**   **DREAM TEAM RANKING** 56

KEY GOALKEEPERS

GIANLUIGI BUFFON
JUVENTUS

Buffon is a Top 4 goalkeeper

AGE 32	DREAM TEAM	RANKING 20

MARCO AMELIA
GENOA

Playing record	12 months lge	wcq
Appearances:	35	2
Minutes played:	3123	180
Percentage played:	86.8%	20.0%
Goals conceded:	56	1
Clean sheets:	8	1
Cards:	Y2, R0	Y1, R0
Minutes between goals:	56mins	-
Goalkeeper ranking:	31st	-

AGE 28	DREAM TEAM	RANKING 241

KEY DEFENDERS

GIORGIO CHIELLINI
JUVENTUS

No-nonsense defender Giorgio Chiellini, equally adept at left-back or centre-half, has become an Italy regular over the last two years.

Impressive displays at Euro 2008 brought him to prominence and the 25-year-old hasn't looked back since. Compared favourably with Paolo Maldini, the Juventus man is very much regarded as a classic Italian defender.

Playing record	12 months lge	wcq
Appearances:	29	7
Minutes played:	2590	630
Percentage played:	71.9%	70.0%
Goals conceded:	32	4
Clean sheets:	10	4
Cards:	Y4, R0	Y1, R0
Minutes between goals:	81mins	157mins
Defender ranking:	77th	47th

AGE 25	DREAM TEAM	RANKING 54

FABIO GROSSO
JUVENTUS

Since playing a starring role in Italy's successful 2006 World Cup, Fabio Grosso's club career hasn't quite taken off as expected, but the 32-year-old has been a mainstay down Italy's left flank.

A tall, accomplished defender, Grosso can bomb forward to great effect, as showcased when he famously scored Italy's extra time opener in their semi-final win over Germany four

GIANLUCA ZAMBROTTA
AC MILAN

Italy's 'Mr Dependable', Gianluca Zambrotta is set to appear at his third World Cup. When he first burst onto the international scene, the then-Juventus player was an established right midfielder before he was moulded into an attacking full-back.

Now at Milan, after a two-year spell with Barcelona, Zambrotta's experience could prove priceless for the Azzurri in South Africa. At 33 his pace may have slowed a yard or two, but Zambrotta's positioning, technique and smart footballing brain continue to see him get the better of some of the world's best wingers. His flexibility remains his greatest asset, though, with Zambrotta able to play on both the right and left flanks. He will play an integral part if Italy are going to retain their title.

Zambrotta is a Top 12 defender

AGE 33	DREAM TEAM	RANKING 38

years ago. Grosso should start every game.

Playing record	12 months lge	wcq
Appearances:	27	5
Minutes played:	2259	362
Percentage played:	62.8%	40.2%
Goals conceded:	32	2
Clean sheets:	7	3
Cards:	Y5, R0	Y1, R0
Minutes between goals:	71mins	181mins
Defender ranking:	115th	32nd

AGE 32	DREAM TEAM	RANKING 77

THE MANAGER

A charismatic leader and scholar of the game, Marcello Lippi has very definite ideas on how a football team should be managed - and with the record of achievement he can boast, who could argue with him.

Following a ten-year career as a centre-half with Sampdoria, Lippi turned his hand to management and success at Napoli led to him taking the helm at Juventus where, apart from an ill-fated season in charge of Inter Milan, he spent nine seasons between 1994 and 2004, winning Serie A five times and the Champions league in 1996. He left Juve to become national team boss in 2004 and despite an at times turgid and stuttering campaign, Lippi inspired the Azzurri to lift the 2006 World Cup in Germany. He promptly resigned but after a poor showing by Italy in Euro 2008 was lured back to the helm and under his guidance, Italy comfortably qualified for South Africa. His belief in team spirit and the system fitting the personnel have always inspired great loyalty in the dressing room - and this loyalty has made its way into his selections, with the bulk of this squad remnants of their 2006 side - including captain Fabio Cannavaro. It is a risk for Lippi who has faced criticism from the media for relying on the old guard but he is not fazed by adversity nor does it hinder his chances at success.

FABIO CANNAVARO
JUVENTUS

The man who lifted the 2006 World Cup returns for his fourth and surely final outing in the tournament.

Italy's captain, most accomplished defender and highest-capped player in history, Fabio Cannavaro has enjoyed a glittering career at the very top. In recent seasons the 36-year-old has taken his talents to Spain, winning La Liga twice with Real Madrid, but is now back at Juventus and forming a formidable partnership with Giorgio Chiellini. On his day, this strong, intelligent, stylish defender is practically unbeatable. However, his height will always be a disadvantage to the Azzurri captain.

Playing record	12 months lge	wcq
Appearances:	31	9
Minutes played:	2605	810
Percentage played:	72.4%	90.0%
Goals conceded:	38	5
Clean sheets:	12	5
Cards:	Y6, R0	Y2, R0
Minutes between goals:	69mins	162mins
Defender ranking:	121st	44th

AGE 36   **DREAM TEAM** **RANKING** 70

KEY PLAYER

ANDREA PIRLO AC MILAN

The phrase 'playmaker' could well have been invented for Andrea Pirlo, such is his association with the role for both Italy and AC Milan over the last ten years.

Pirlo leads by example, particularly at international level where his influence on the Azzurri has been undeniable. Winning three Man of the Match awards at the last World Cup, including in the final, Pirlo played a pivotal role in Italy's success, forming an almost telepathic partnership with team mate Gennaro Gattuso. Now 30, the AC Milan legend has added experience to his considerable list of assets, which also includes pinpoint passing, deadly set-pieces and exceptional positional sense.

Pirlo is a Top 12 midfielder

AGE 31   **MIDFIELDER**   **DREAM TEAM** **RANKING** 26

KEY MIDFIELDERS

GENNARO GATTUSO
AC MILAN

A tough-tackling midfield terrier if ever there was one, Gennaro Gattuso has been the brawn to Andrea Pirlo's brain during the last ten years for Italy.

The 32-year-old, a veteran of two World Cups, has long been the undoing of many a flamboyant attacking midfielder. Gattuso hasn't found his place in the national side a certainty since Euro 2008, mostly due to a serious knee injury restricting his appearances. But his combative, uncompromising style at the fulcrum of midfield should see him play an important role once again this summer if he manages to keep his fitness up.

Playing record	12 months lge	wcq
Appearances:	10	4
Minutes played:	611	315
Percentage played:	17.0%	35.0%
Goals scored:	0	0
Clean sheets:	5	2
Cards:	Y3, R1	Y2, R0
Strike rate:	-	-
Midfielder ranking:	216th	95th

AGE 32	DREAM TEAM	RANKING 2191

MAURO CAMORANASI
JUVENTUS

Despite being one of the more unheralded members of the victorious 2006 World Cup winning side, Mauro Camoranesi has been a regular for Italy since making his debut back in 2003.

The Argentine-born midfielder is often mistaken for being too over-confident, but is actually one of the hardest-working players at Marcello Lippi's disposal.

His crossing abilities are second to none and his work-rate is a great asset to the Italy squad. These qualities have helped Camoranesi earn 50 caps for his country, making him the most-capped naturalised player in Italy's history.

At club level, he's been at Juventus since 2002, staying loyal to the Old Lady despite enforced relegation to Serie B and several advances from some of Europe's top clubs.

Never one to shirk a challenge, the versatile Camoranesi can also play centrally or wide on the left and is likely to be a valuable commodity in Italy's defence of their World Cup crown.

On what could well be his swansong at international level, Camoranesi will be looking to leave his mark on football's greatest tournament and he could well do this if he manages to play the way we know he can.

Playing record	12 months lge	wcq
Appearances:	27	6
Minutes played:	1711	476
Percentage played:	47.5%	52.9%
Goals scored:	3	1
Clean sheets:	13	3
Cards:	Y4, R1	Y1, R0
Strike rate:	570mins	476mins
Midfielder ranking:	103rd	54th

AGE 33	DREAM TEAM	RANKING 262

SIMONE PEPE
UDINESE

Playing record	12 months lge	wcq
Appearances:	31	7
Minutes played:	2158	380
Percentage played:	59.9%	42.2%
Goals scored:	3	0
Clean sheets:	-	-
Cards:	Y6, R0	Y0, R0
Strike rate:	719mins	-
Midfielder ranking:	127th	-

AGE 26	DREAM TEAM	RANKING 403

KEY STRIKERS

ALBERTO GILARDINO
FIORENTINA

Gilardino is a Top 12 striker

With Franceso Totti and Christian Vieri retired from football altogether and Alessandro Del Piero and Luca Toni well into their 30s, it seems the baton of Italy's main striking berth has passed to Alberto Gilardino.

Aged 27, the Fiorentina striker's career has blossomed in recent years as he finally realises the enormous potential shown at Under 21 level, where he became Italy's all-time record scorer.

At senior level, despite enjoying a decent goal record, he has often been on the fringes and indeed was left out of Roberto Donadoni's Euro 2008 squad.

But Gilardino possesses all the attributes needed to be a top striker and it was only a matter of time before the speedy, adaptable, clinical six-footer established himself in Marcello Lippi's side.

Italy's top scorer in qualifying with four goals from six appearances, Gilardino's prolific form at club level for La Viola should ensure he reaches South Africa with the world at his feet.

If the Azzurri are going to reach the latter stages, Gilardino may be their top-scorer.

AGE 27	DREAM TEAM	RANKING 49

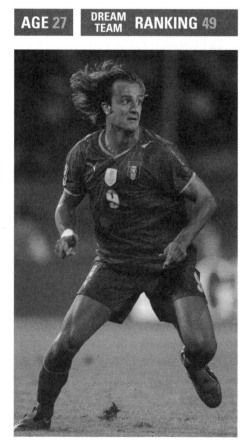

VINCENZO IAQUINTA
JUVENTUS

A tall, hard-working striker with an eye for goal, Vincenzo Iaquinta has been a useful option for Italy since debuting in 2005.

A Juventus regular for the last three years since moving from Udinese, his impressive domestic form has kept him in the Italy squad.

Never prolific for his country, the powerful striker represents an ideal focal point up front, but can also be utilised on either flank.

He made five substitute appearances at Germany 2006 and this is probably the last chance that Iaquinta will get to play at the World Cup finals so he will be desperate to make an impression for the Azzurri.

Playing record	12 months lge	wcq
Appearances:	25	6
Minutes played:	1730	429
Percentage played:	50.1%	47.7%
Goals scored:	13	2
Percentage share:	27%	11.1%
Cards:	Y2, R1	Y1, R0
Strike rate:	133mins	214mins
Strike rate ranking:	17th	43rd

AGE 30 | **DREAM TEAM** **RANKING 844**

ONE TO WATCH

GIUSEPPE ROSSI VILLARREAL

A rarity in the Italy squad in that he plies his trade abroad, Rossi represents the next generation of Azzurri talent.

At 23 the Villarreal striker is inexperienced compared to many of his Italy team-mates, but Rossi's abilities could see him star at South Africa 2010. Blessed with a wicked left foot, the former Manchester United youngster can score goals from nothing.

Playing record	12 months lge	wcq
Appearances:	36	4
Minutes played:	2634	158
Percentage played:	75.0%	17.6%
Goals scored:	10	0
Percentage share:	16.67%	0.00%
Cards:	Y2, R0	Y0, R0
Strike rate:	263mins	-
Strike rate ranking:	82nd	-

AGE 23 | **STRIKER** | **DREAM TEAM** **RANKING 108**

ROUTE TO THE FINALS

When FIFA decided to move Australia into the Asian Federation's World Cup qualification arena, life got a lot easier for New Zealand.

The All Whites are top dogs in the Oceania Federation. When your main rivals turn out to be the tiny New Caledonian islands, then the play-offs beckon. Ryan Nelsen and his team duly obliged, the only hiccup being a weakened side's 2-0 defeat to Fiji, after they had already confirmed top spot.

Bahrain offered a real test though, having come through a rigorous three stage qualification process. They had finished third behind Australia and Japan in Asian Qualifying Round Four, before beating Saudi Arabia over two legs to reach this point. Bahrain were also ranked 61st by FIFA, compared to New Zealand's 83rd, and had narrowly missed out on Germany 2006.

The first leg finished 0-0 in Manama so New Zealand couldn't concede in the return in Wellington's 'Cake Tin'. It was nerve-wracking stuff as Plymouth's Rory Fallon put the All Whites through, after Celtic striker Chris Killen had hit the bar in the first half. Bahrain hit back, earning a penalty that Mark Paston famously saved in the 50th minute. They also had the ball in the net only to see it disallowed.

FINAL QUALIFYING TABLE
OCEANA GROUP

	P	W	D	L	F	A	Pts
New Zealand *	6	5	0	1	14	5	15
New Caledonia	6	2	2	2	12	10	8
Fiji	6	2	1	3	8	11	7
Vanuatu	6	1	1	4	5	13	4

* New Zealand beat Bahrain in a play off.

					Avge FIFA ranking			
1	17 Oct 07	Away	Fiji	119	W	0 2	Vicelich 37, Smeltz 86
2	17 Nov 07	Away	Vanuatu	145	W	1 2	Smeltz 52, Mulligan 90
3	21 Nov 07	Home	Vanuatu	145	W	4 1	Mulligan 14, 81, Smeltz 29pen, 34
4	06 Sep 08	Away	New Caledonia	128	W	1 3	Nelsen 15, Smeltz 66, 76
5	10 Sep 08	Home	New Caledonia	128	W	3 0	Smeltz 50, 76, Christie 69
6	19 Nov 08	Home	Fiji	119	L	0 2	
7	10 Oct 09	Away	Bahrain	71	D	0 0	
8	14 Nov 09	Home	Bahrain	71	W	1 0	Fallon 45

Average FIFA ranking of opposition	116

MAIN PLAYER PERFORMANCES IN QUALIFICATION

Match	1 2 3 4 5 6 7 8	Appearances	Started	Subbed on	Subbed off	Mins played	% played	Goals	Yellow	Red
Venue	A A H A H H A H									
Result	W W W W W L D W									

		Appearances	Started	Subbed on	Subbed off	Mins played	% played	Goals	Yellow	Red
Goalkeepers										
Glen Moss		2	2	0	0	148	20.6	0	0	1
Mark Paston		6	6	0	0	540	75.0	0	1	0
Jacob Spoonley		1	0	1	0	32	4.4	0	0	0
Defenders										
Andrew Boyens		5	3	2	1	270	37.5	0	0	0
Tony Lochhead		7	7	0	0	630	87.5	0	0	0
David Mulligan		6	5	1	2	433	60.1	3	1	0
Ryan Nelsen		4	4	0	1	333	46.3	1	1	0
Steven Old		2	1	1	0	97	13.5	0	0	0
James Pritchett		3	2	1	0	195	27.1	0	0	0
Ben Sigmund		8	7	1	0	658	91.4	0	1	0
Ivan Vicelich		5	5	0	1	430	59.7	1	0	0
Midfielders										
Leo Bertos		6	6	0	0	540	75.0	0	0	0
Tim Brown		6	6	0	2	516	71.7	0	4	0
Jeff Campbell		2	0	2	0	37	5.1	0	1	0
Jeremy Christie		5	3	2	1	313	43.5	1	1	0
Simon Elliott		3	3	0	0	270	37.5	0	0	0
Chris James		3	2	1	0	182	25.3	0	0	0
Michael McGlinchey		2	1	1	1	86	11.9	0	0	0
Duncan Oughton		5	5	0	1	426	59.2	0	0	0
Cole Peverley		1	1	0	0	90	12.5	0	0	0
Forwards										
Costa Barbarouses		1	1	0	1	67	9.3	0	0	0
Jeremy Brockie		2	2	0	0	180	25.0	0	0	0
Greg Draper		1	1	0	1	58	8.1	0	0	0
Rory Fallon		2	2	0	1	155	21.5	1	0	0
Christopher Killen		3	3	0	2	257	35.7	0	1	0
Allan Pearce		1	1	0	1	56	7.8	0	0	0
Shane Smeltz		7	7	0	3	598	83.1	8	0	0
Jarrod Smith		4	2	2	1	200	27.8	0	0	0
Christopher Wood		2	0	2	0	34	4.7	0	0	0

FINAL PROSPECTS

The only time New Zealand previously reached the World Cup finals, in 1982, they lost all three group games, conceding 12 goals.

International football has changed since then and New Zealand will go to South Africa with a decent defence. It is therefore unlikely that they will be whipping boys of Group F, but saying that, they will have to punch above their weight to pick up points.

With qualifying so uncompetitive, the only recent yardstick was the 2009 Confederations Cup and the All Whites hardly distinguished themselves.

They were thrashed 5-0 by Spain, lost 2-0 to hosts South Africa and managed only a solitary point in their group in a 0-0 draw with Iraq.

The key to New Zealand's tournament might be their opening game against Slovakia - the third best side in the group according to the FIFA rankings. If they can secure some kind of result in that game, then they will be looking to do the same against Italy or Paraguay. However, the chances of them picking up any points is small, and barring a miracle, they will not make the last 16.

DREAM TEAM	TOP 15 RANKING	31

THE MANAGER

Ricki Herbert was one of the New Zealand defenders during the 1982 World Cup and he will be determined that none of the current side have to go through the same humiliation he did.

In the All Whites' only World Cup outing to date, they were hopelessly out-classed, losing all three games and shipping twelve goals in the process. Herbert knows his chances of steering New Zealand out of Group F are small, but he has had some good results since his appointment in 2005, some decent players at his disposal and an inviting opening game in the form of the third ranked side in the group, Slovakia.

GROUP FIXTURES

SLOVAKIA	Tue 15 June 1230 BST
ITALY	Sun 20 June 1500 BST
PARAGUAY	Thur 24 June 1500 BST

KEY PLAYER

RYAN NELSEN BLACKBURN

The Blackburn captain is a tenacious centre-back and one of the Premier League's most underrated players.

He was one of Mark Hughes' super signings in 2005 and instantly made a relegation threatened Rovers side into one of the tightest defensive units around. He has 38 caps for New Zealand and is definitely their most vital player.

Playing record	12 months lge	wcq
Appearances:	34	2
Minutes played:	2848	153
Percentage played:	77.2%	21.3%
Goals conceded:	48	1
Clean sheets:	9	1
Cards:	Y5, R0	Y0, R0
Minutes between goals:	59mins	-
Defender ranking:	144th	-

AGE 32	DEFENDER	DREAM TEAM	RANKING 310

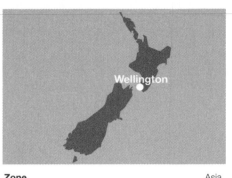

Wellington

Zone	Asia
Population	4.2m
Language	English, Maori
Top league	N.Z.F. Championship
Playing season	October - March

Major clubs and capacities
Waitakere United (5,563), Auckland City (3,000)
YoungHeart Manawatu (18,759)

Where probable squad players play:

Premier League	1	Ligue 1	-
Serie A	-	Eredivisie	-
La Liga	-	Other Europe	4
Bundesliga	-	Outside Europe	18

Number of New Zealander players playing:

Premier League	1	Bundesliga	-
Serie A	-	Ligue 1	-
La Liga	-	Eredivisie	-

World Cup record   * best performance

1930 - Did not enter		1974 -	Did not enter
1934 - Did not enter		1978 -	Did not enter
1938 - Did not enter		1982 -	Did not qualify
1950 - Did not enter		1986 -	Did not enter
1954 - Did not enter		1990 -	Did not enter
1958 - Did not enter		1994 -	Did not enter
1962 - Did not enter		1998 -	Did not enter
1966 - Did not enter		2002 -	Did not enter
1970 - Did not enter		2006 -	Did not enter

THE SQUAD

Goalkeepers	Club side	Age	QG
Glen Moss	Melbourne Victory	27	2
Mark Paston	Wellington Phoenix	33	6
Jacob Spoonley	Auckland City	23	1
Defenders			
Andrew Boyens	New York Red Bulls	26	5
Tony Lochhead	Wellington Phoenix	28	7
David Mulligan	Wellington Phoenix	28	6
Ryan Nelsen	Blackburn	32	4
Steven Old	Kilmarnock	24	2
James Pritchett	Auckland City	27	3
Ben Sigmund	Wellington Phoenix	29	8
Ivan Vicelich	Auckland City	33	5
Midfielders			
Leo Bertos	Wellington Phoenix	28	6
Tim Brown	Wollington Phoonix	29	6
Jeremy Christie	Waitakere Utd	27	5
Simon Elliott	Sn Jose Earthquakes	36	3
Chris James	Floating	22	3
Michael McGlinchey	Centl Coast Mariners	26	2
Duncan Oughton	Columbus Crew	32	5
Forwards			
Jeremy Brockie	N Queensland Fury	22	2
Greg Draper	Team Wellington	20	1
Rory Fallon	Plymouth	28	2
Christopher Killen	Celtic	28	3
Allan Pearce	Waitakere Utd	27	1
Shane Smeltz	Gold Coast United	28	7
Jarrod Smith	Floating	25	4
Christopher Wood	West Brom	18	2

■ Probable ■ Possible **QG** Qualification Games

ROUTE TO THE FINALS

Paraguay took four points off Argentina and beat Brazil early in the qualifying campaign to claim their place in South Africa.

They flew off the blocks with 13 points from the first five games. These included wins over key rivals Chile away, Uruguay and Ecuador. The fifth game against Brazil announced them. Roque Santa Cruz only started three out of 18 qualifying games but came in for this match, opening the scoring on 26 minutes. Mexico-based Salvador Cabanas netted a second and a full-strength Brazil couldn't reply.

FINAL QUALIFYING TABLE
SOUTH AMERICA GROUP

	P	W	D	L	F	A	Pts
Brazil	18	9	7	2	33	11	34
Chile	18	10	3	5	32	22	33
Paraguay	18	10	3	5	24	16	33
Argentina	18	8	4	6	23	20	28
Uruguay	18	6	6	6	28	20	24
Ecuador	18	6	5	7	22	26	23
Colombia	18	6	5	7	14	18	23
Venezuela	18	6	4	8	23	29	22
Bolivia	18	4	3	11	22	36	15
Peru	18	3	4	11	11	34	13

	Date	Venue	Opponent	Avge FIFA ranking	Result	Score	Scorers
1	14 Oct 07	Away	Peru	76	D	0 0	
2	17 Oct 07	Home	Uruguay	22	W	1 0	Valdez 15
3	18 Nov 07	Home	Ecuador	44	W	5 1	Valdez 9, Riveros 27, 88, Santa Cruz 51, N.Ayala 83
4	22 Nov 07	Away	Chile	32	W	0 3	Cabanas 24, Da Silva 45, 57
5	15 Jun 08	Home	Brazil	4	W	2 0	Santa Cruz 26, Cabanas 49
6	18 Jun 08	Away	Bolivia	66	L	4 2	Santa Cruz 66, Valdez 82
7	06 Sep 08	Away	Argentina	6	D	1 1	Heinze 13og
8	10 Sep 08	Home	Venezuela	60	W	2 0	Riveros 28, Valdez 45
9	12 Oct 08	Away	Colombia	38	W	0 1	Cabanas 9
10	15 Oct 08	Home	Peru	76	W	1 0	Benitez 82
11	28 Mar 09	Away	Uruguay	22	L	2 0	
12	01 Apr 09	Away	Ecuador	44	D	1 1	Benitez 90
13	06 Jun 09	Home	Chile	32	L	0 2	
14	11 Jun 09	Away	Brazil	4	L	2 1	Cabanas 25
15	05 Sep 09	Home	Bolivia	66	W	1 0	Cabanas 45pen
16	10 Sep 09	Home	Argentina	6	W	1 0	Valdez 27
17	10 Oct 09	Away	Venezuela	60	W	1 2	Cabanas 55, O.Cardozo 79
18	15 Oct 09	Home	Colombia	38	L	0 2	
	Average FIFA ranking of opposition			39			

MAIN PLAYER PERFORMANCES IN QUALIFICATION

Match	Appearances	Started	Subbed on	Subbed off	Mins played	% played	Goals	Yellow	Red
Venue — A H H A H A A H A H A A H A H H A H									
Result — D W W W L D W W W L D L L W W W L									
Goalkeepers									
Aldo Bobadilla	1	1	0	0	90	5.6	0	0	0
Justo Villar	17	17	0	0	1530	94.4	0	1	0
Defenders									
Antolin Alcaraz	1	1	0	0	90	5.6	0	0	0
Marcos Caceres	1	1	0	0	90	5.6	0	1	0
Julio Cesar Caceres	14	14	0	0	1260	77.8	0	5	0
Denis Caniza	8	7	1	0	648	40.0	0	0	0
Paulo Da Silva	17	17	0	0	1524	94.1	2	1	1
Julio Manzur	3	3	0	0	270	16.7	0	2	0
Claudio Morel Rodriguez	9	9	0	2	753	46.5	0	3	0
Dario Veron	11	10	1	0	868	53.6	0	4	1
Midfielders									
Sergio Aquino	3	1	2	1	144	8.9	0	0	0
Edgar Barreto	14	12	2	7	986	60.9	0	2	0
Carlos Bonet	10	7	3	1	665	41.0	0	0	0
Victor Caceres	13	11	2	0	1038	64.1	0	3	0
Eduardo Ledesma	5	2	3	2	219	13.5	0	0	0
Osvaldo Martinez	7	3	4	2	365	22.5	0	1	0
Nestor Ortigoza	1	1	0	0	90	5.6	0	0	0
Cristian Riveros	17	17	0	1	1519	93.8	3	3	0
Jonathan Santana	9	8	1	3	659	40.7	0	4	0
Aureliano Torres	6	3	3	1	311	19.2	0	1	0
Enrique Vera	13	13	0	4	1054	65.1	0	3	0
Forwards									
Jorge Achucarro	4	1	3	1	106	6.5	0	1	0
Edgar Benitez	5	0	5	0	95	5.9	0	0	0
Salvador Cabanas	15	15	0	8	1220	75.3	6	2	0
Oscar Cardozo	12	3	9	3	345	21.3	1	2	0
Nelson Haedo Valdez	17	16	1	12	1192	73.6	5	2	0
Roque Santa Cruz	5	3	2	2	308	19.0	3	0	0

FINAL PROSPECTS

The media focus will be on favourites Italy in Group F, but Marcello Lippi's team aside, the bookies are backing Paraguay to make it into the last 16 ahead of Slovakia and they have good reason to do so.

Paraguay overcame mountains to reach South Africa and the results Gerardo Martino's side secured against the likes of fellow qualifiers Argentina, Brazil, Uruguay and Chile - as well as some impressive performances away from home - point to an extremely effective side who can be a genuine force in this competition.

They have a tight and experienced defensive unit, marshalled by goalkeeper and captain Justo Villar - only Brazil conceded fewer goals in qualifying - and a solid midfield, but it is up front they look particularly juicy, with Nelson Valdeez and Manchester City's Roque Santa Cruz providing the firepower up top.

When they beat Argentina 1-0 to seal qualification, the country declared a national holiday - and they will not get a better chance to prove their worth than in the Group F opener against reigning champions Italy.

DREAM TEAM TOP 15 RANKING   27

THE MANAGER

A decent player in his time, Gerardo Martino was an attacking midfielder and played most of his career in his native Argentina, with two brief stints in Spain.

When he retired from playing, he earned his managerial spurs at a number of lower league Argentinian sides before going on to make his name in Paraguay with First Division sides Cerro Porteno and Club Libertad, winning the title in 2004. He was awarded for his achievements by being handed a stab at the national job and he has done a superb job, quietly guiding Paraguay to their best ever South America zone qualifying campaign.

GROUP FIXTURES

ITALY	Mon 14 June 1930 BST
SLOVAKIA	Sun 20 June 1230 BST
NEW ZEALAND	Thur 24 June 1500 BST

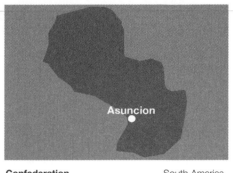

Asuncion

Confederation	South America
Population	7m
Language	Spanish and Guarani
Top league	Primera Division
Playing season	January - May

Major clubs and capacities
Club Nacional (5,124), Libertad (10,000), Guarani (8,290)

Where probable squad players play:

Premier League	2	Ligue 1	-
Serie A	-	Eredivisie	2
La Liga	2	Other Europe	2
Bundesliga	2	Outside Europe	15

Number of Paraguayan players playing:

Premier League	2	Bundesliga	1
Serie A	1	Ligue 1	1
La Liga	3	Eredivisie	1

World Cup record   * best performance

1930 - Round 1	1974 - Did not qualify
1934 - Did not enter	1978 - Did not qualify
1938 - Did not enter	1982 - Did not qualify
1950 - Round 1	1986 - * Last 16
1954 - Did not qualify	1990 - Did not qualify
1958 - Round 1	1994 - Did not qualify
1962 - Did not qualify	1998 - * Last 16
1966 - Did not qualify	2002 - * Last 16
1970 - Did not qualify	2006 - Round 1

THE SQUAD

Goalkeepers	Club side	Age	QG
Aldo Bobadilla	Boca Juniors	34	1
Justo Villar	Valladolid	32	17
Defenders			
Antolin Alcaraz	Club Brugge	27	1
Marcos Caceres	Racing Club	24	1
Julio Cesar Caceres	Boca Juniors	30	14
Denis Caniza	Olimpia	35	8
Paulo Da Silva	Sunderland	30	17
Julio Manzur	Tigre	29	3
Cla Morel Rodriguez	Boca Juniors	32	9
Dario Veron	Universidad	30	11
Midfielders			
Sergio Aquino	Libertad	30	3
Edgar Barreto	Atalanta	25	14
Carlos Bonet	Olimpia	32	10
Victor Caceres	Libertad	25	13
Eduardo Ledesma	Lanus	24	5
Osvaldo Martinez	Monterrey	24	7
Cristian Riveros	Cruz Azul	27	17
Jonathan Santana	Wolfsburg	28	9
Aureliano Torres	San Lorenzo	27	6
Enrique Vera	LDU Quito	31	13
Forwards			
Jorge Achucarro	Newells Old Boys	28	4
Edgar Benitez	Pachuca	22	5
Cristian Bogado	Colo Colo	23	1
Oscar Cardozo	Benfica	27	12
Nelson Haedo Valdez	B Dortmund	26	17
Roque Santa Cruz	Man City	28	5

■ Probable ■ Possible **QG** Qualification Games

KEY PLAYER

ROQUE SANTA CRUZ MAN CITY

A striking star for his local club Olimpia from an early age, Roque Santa Cruz was brought to Europe by Bayern Munich, but injury and a strong squad limited his chances.

That changed when Mark Hughes snapped him up for Blackburn where 23 goals in 53 games earned a £17.5m transfer to Manchester City. On his day he is lethal.

Playing record	12 months lge	wcq
Appearances:	16	5
Minutes played:	696	308
Percentage played:	19.3%	19.0%
Goals scored:	3	3
Percentage share:	4.84%	12.50%
Cards:	Y1, R0	Y0, R0
Strike rate:	-	-
Strike rate ranking:	-	-

AGE 28   **STRIKER**   **DREAM TEAM**   **RANKING** 1893

SLOVAKIA

ROUTE TO THE FINALS

Qualification brought Slovakia together with three of its closest neighbours and few would have backed Vladimir Weiss' side to make it over the line ahead of the Czech Republic and Poland.

That they - on paper at least - cruised through qualifying to top the group ahead of their third close neighbour Slovenia, was one of the biggest upsets in the European zone. However, qualification is testament to a side that - like many of the 'smaller' international teams - adds up to more than the sum of its parts.

They opened up with a 2-1 win against Northern Ireland but four days later slumped to a 2-0 reverse in Slovenia and at that stage, few would have expected the run they were about to embark on. Despite the fact they were

beaten by Slovenia again in their penultimate game, that would be their only other loss of the campaign.

Having edged out lowly San Marino 3-1, they won back-to-back games against two of the favourites to win the group, sealing a late win at home to Poland and then sensationally earning a 2-1 victory over the Czech Republic in their own back yard - again sealing the win with a goal in the last ten minutes.

By this stage, they were top of their group and looking real contenders, and sealed a place in South Africa with a 7-0 thrashing of San Marino, a draw with the Czech Republic and victories over Poland and Northern Ireland.

For final qualification table see Slovenia.

#	Date	Venue	Opponent	Avge FIFA ranking	Result		Scorers
1	06 Sep 08	Home	N Ireland	109	W	2 1	Skrtel 46, Hamsik 70
2	10 Sep 08	Away	Slovenia	64	L	2 1	Jakubko 83
3	11 Oct 08	Away	San Marino	201	W	1 3	Sestak 33, Kozak 38, Karhan 50
4	15 Oct 08	Home	Poland	35	W	2 1	Sestak 85, 86
5	01 Apr 09	Away	Czech Republic	12	W	1 2	Sestak 23, Jendrisek 83
6	06 Jun 09	Home	San Marino	201	W	7 0	Cech 3, 32, Pekarik 12, Stoch 35, Kozak 42, Jakubko 63, Hanzel 68
7	05 Sep 09	Home	Czech Republic	12	D	2 2	Sestak 60, Hamsik 73pen
8	09 Sep 09	Away	N Ireland	109	W	0 2	Sestak 15, Holosko 67
9	10 Oct 09	Home	Slovenia	64	L	0 2	
10	14 Oct 09	Away	Poland	35	W	0 1	Gancarczyk 3og
			Average FIFA ranking of opposition	**84**			

MAIN PLAYER PERFORMANCES IN QUALIFICATION

Match	1 2 3 4 5 6 7 8 9 10	Appearances	Started	Subbed on	Subbed off	Mins played	% played	Goals	Yellow	Red
Venue	H A A H A H H A H A									
Result	W L W W W W D W L W									
Goalkeepers										
Lubos Kamenar		1	1	0	0	90	10.0	0	0	0
Jan Mucha		6	6	0	0	540	60.0	0	0	0
Stefan Senecky		3	3	0	0	270	30.0	0	1	0
Defenders										
Marek Cech		4	3	1	0	279	31.0	2	0	0
Jan Durica		8	8	0	2	663	73.7	0	2	0
Lubos Hanzel		1	1	0	0	90	10.0	1	1	0
Matej Krajcik		1	1	0	0	90	10.0	0	0	0
Roman Kratochvil		1	1	0	0	71	7.9	0	1	1
Peter Pekarik		9	9	0	0	810	90.0	1	0	0
Martin Petras		4	4	0	0	360	40.0	0	0	0
Peter Petras		2	1	1	0	96	10.7	0	1	0
Kornel Salata		1	1	0	0	90	10.0	0	0	0
Martin Skrtel		6	6	0	0	540	60.0	1	2	0
Radoslav Zabavnik		6	5	1	1	458	50.9	0	2	0
Midfielders										
Balazs Borbely		2	1	1	1	74	8.2	0	0	0
Marek Hamsik		8	8	0	2	656	72.9	2	2	1
Miroslav Karhan		7	4	3	2	405	45.0	1	0	0
Kamil Kopunek		2	2	0	0	180	20.0	0	0	0
Jan Kozak		6	4	2	1	374	41.6	2	0	0
Marek Sapara		7	3	4	1	319	35.4	0	0	0
Zdeno Strba		6	6	0	1	533	59.2	0	1	0
Dusan Svento		3	0	3	0	93	10.3	0	0	0
Vladimir Weiss		4	4	0	2	342	38.0	0	2	0
Forwards										
Filip Holosko		4	3	1	2	247	27.4	1	0	0
Martin Jakubko		6	3	3	2	272	30.2	2	0	0
Erik Jendrisek		7	4	3	2	375	41.7	1	0	0
Marek Mintal		2	1	1	1	69	7.7	0	0	0
Stanislav Sestak		6	6	0	5	466	51.8	6	2	0
Miroslav Stoch		4	3	1	2	248	27.6	1	2	0
Robert Vittek		9	8	1	2	703	78.1	0	0	0

FINAL PROSPECTS

The surprise package in the European Zone, Slovakia defied the odds – and the history books – to knock out prestigious neighbours Poland and the Czech Republic to top Group 3.

They have not qualified for a World Cup since their independence in 1993 and – hardly bristling with big-name talent – few would have expected them to do so this time around. They will be more than likely largely unfancied to make it out of Group F, and but for the presence of New Zealand would have been the minnows of the group.

However, playing underdogs again will no doubt suit Vladimir Weiss and co. down to the ground. In terms of personnel, they have Liverpool's Martin Skrtel at the heart of defence and Bochum's Stanislav Sestak – who netted six goals in qualifying – up front, but it is young captain Marek Hamsik of Napoli who could make the biggest impact from midfield. They face lowly New Zealand in their low-key opener and then – favourites to finish second in the group – Paraguay next, and that could give them the perfect platform to mount a challenge to reach the last 16 – it would certainly be rash to bet against them doing just that.

DREAM TEAM	TOP 15 RANKING	26

THE MANAGER

Vladimir Weiss has taken his young side to an unexpected first World Cup finals and from 65 to 34 in the FIFA world rankings.

He took Artmedia Bratislava to the Slovakian League title and into the Champions League in 2005/06 and managed briefly in Russia before returning to make Artmedia champions again.

On the back of that he took over the national side for the qualifying tournament. He has pulled his side together out of scraps, enticing good contributions from players who rarely feature for their club sides and could shock the teams in Group F.

GROUP FIXTURES

NEW ZEALAND	Ddd 15 June 1230 BST
PARAGUAY	Sun 20 June 1230 BST
iTALY	Thur 24 June 1500 BST

KEY PLAYER

MARTIN SKRTEL LIVERPOOL

Pacy, strong in the air, aggressive and a tough-tackler, Slovakia's most recognised player has all the qualities required to become a world class central defender.

He moved from Zenit St Petersburg to Liverpool in January 2008. A lot rests on his shoulders but Slovakia can rest assured that Skrtel can handle the pressure.

Playing record 12 months lge		wcq
Appearances:	26	6
Minutes played:	2108	540
Percentage played:	60.1%	60.0%
Goals conceded:	26	8
Clean sheets:	9	1
Cards:	Y6, R0	Y2, R0
Minutes between goals:	81mins	67mins
Defender ranking:	76th	122nd

AGE 25	DEFENDER	DREAM TEAM	RANKING 182

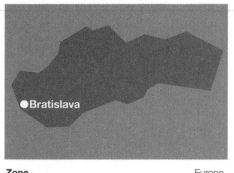
●Bratislava

Zone	Europe
Population	5.5m
Language	Slovak
Top league	Corgo Liga
Playing season	July - April

Major clubs and capacities
MSK Zilina (11,181), Slovan Bratislava (30,087), Dukla Banska Bystrica (11,505)

Where probable squad players play:

Premier League	2	Ligue 1	1
Serie A	1	Eredivisie	1
La Liga	-	Other Europe	14
Bundesliga	4	Outside Europe	-

Number of Slovakian players playing:

Premier League	3	Bundesliga	6
Serie A	2	Ligue 1	2
La Liga	-	Eredivisie	3

World Cup record   * best performance

1930 - Did not enter	1974 -	Did not qualify
1934 - * Final	1978 -	Did not qualify
1938 - Quarter finals	1982 -	Round 1
1950 - Did not enter	1986 -	Did not qualify
1954 - Round 1	1990 -	Quarter finals
1958 - Round 1	1994 -	Did not qualify
1962 - * Final	1998 -	Did not qualify
1966 - Did not qualify	2002 -	Did not qualify
1970 - Round 1	2006 -	Did not qualify

THE SQUAD

Goalkeepers	Club side	Age	QG
Lubos Kamenar	Cesena	30	1
Jan Mucha	Cesena	30	6
Stefan Senecky	Ankaraspor	30	3
Defenders			
Marek Cech	West Brom	27	4
Jan Durica	Hannover	28	8
Lubos Hanzel	Schalke	23	1
Matej Krajcik	Slavia Prague	32	1
Peter Pekarik	Wolfsburg	23	9
Martin Petras	Cesena	30	4
Peter Petras	Slovan Bratislava	31	2
Kornel Salata	Slovan Bratislava	25	1
Martin Skrtel	Liverpool	25	6
Radoslav Zabavnik	Terek Grozny	29	6
Midfielders			
Marek Hamsik	Napoli	22	8
Miroslav Karhan	Mainz	33	7
Jan Kozak	Slovan Bratislava	30	6
Marek Sapara	Rosenborg	27	7
Zdeno Strba	Xanthi	34	6
Dusan Svento	Salzburg	24	3
Vladimir Weiss	Man City	20	4
Forwards			
Filip Holosko	Besiktas	26	4
Martin Jakubko	FC Moscow	30	6
Erik Jendrisek	Kaiserslautern	23	7
Stanislav Sestak	Bochum	27	6
Miroslav Stoch	Twente	20	4
Robert Vittek	Lille	28	9

■ Probable ■ Possible **QG** Qualification Games

12th GIANLUCA ZAMBROTTA
ITALY & AC MILAN

A highly versatile and effective wing-back, Gianluca Zambrotta can operate on either flank and has done so at the very highest level for more than a decade with Juventus, Barcelona and AC Milan.

Now something of a veteran – he is close to 100 caps for Italy – he seems to be settled in the left-back berth for club and country and his experience will be a big asset. His versatility is also key and his ability to slot into the midfield on either flank could be useful if Italy go deep into the competition.

Playing record	12 mths lge	wcq
Appearances:	35	9
Minutes played:	2898	810
Percentage played:	80.5%	90.0%
Goals conceded:	32	5
Clean sheets:	15	5
Cards:	Y3, R0	Y0, R0
Minutes between goals:	91mins	162mins
Defender ranking:	51st	45th

AGE 33	DREAM TEAM	RANKING 38

11th GABRIEL HEINZE
ARGENTINA & MARSEILLE

A tough-tackling left-back with a stack of experience, Gabriel Heinze is a world-class operator as he has consistently proved for club and country.

A tenacious presence on the flank, his energy and directness make him effective – whether his side are in possession or not. Now playing well for Marseille, he will be in good form and looking forward to contributing to Argentina's push for a third World Cup success. One of the few automatic picks during qualifying, only three players played more.

Playing record	12 mths lge	wcq
Appearances:	31	14
Minutes played:	2672	1206
Percentage played:	78.1%	74.4%
Goals conceded:	35	16
Clean sheets:	15	5
Cards:	Y6, R0	Y2, R0
Minutes between goals:	76mins	75mins
Defender ranking:	98th	116th

AGE 32	DREAM TEAM	RANKING 37

10th DANI ALVES
BRAZIL & BARCELONA

Fast becoming known as one of the best full-backs in domestic European football, Dani Alves is excelling at right-back for Barcelona and has made his way into the reckoning for Brazil.

He became the most expensive defender in world football when Barcelona paid just shy of 30 million euros for him in the summer of 2008. Despite his defensive prowess and effectiveness going forward, he plays second fiddle to Maicon for Brazil, but will still be an important member of the squad.

Playing record	12 mths lge	wcq
Appearances:	33	1
Minutes played:	2788	5
Percentage played:	79.4%	0.3%
Goals conceded:	28	0
Clean sheets:	17	1
Cards:	Y8, R0	Y0, R0
Minutes between goals:	100mins	-
Defender ranking:	32nd	-

AGE 27	DREAM TEAM	RANKING 34

9th ALVARO ARBELOA
SPAIN & REAL MADRID

A product of Real Madrid's academy, Alvaro Arbeloa is now back at the club of his youth following an 18-month stint at Liverpool.

In England he played as a right-back – the position he is most known for – and impressed in bursts, although he was never as heralded as some of his team-mates. Now back at Madrid, he is being asked to play left-back due to the personnel available and having featured in only one qualifying game, he will have to impress to claim a place in the Spain side.

Playing record	12 mths lge	wcq
Appearances:	23	1
Minutes played:	2038	81
Percentage played:	58.1%	9.0%
Goals conceded:	18	0
Clean sheets:	13	1
Cards:	Y5, R0	Y0, R0
Minutes between goals:	113mins	-
Defender ranking:	14th	-

AGE 27	DREAM TEAM	RANKING 32

8th JORIS MATHIJSEN
NETHERLANDS & HAMBURG

A veteran of domestic football in the Netherlands and Germany, Joris Mathijsen is perhaps not a household name across Europe, but if the Netherlands realise the potential they have shown in the last 18 months, he might soon be.

Ever-present as the Dutch qualified impressively for South Africa, he is an uncompromising central defender – tough in the tackle and good in the air – and is a good foil for the more cultured Jonny Heitinga who is likely to partner him in the heart of defence.

Playing record	12 mths lge	wcq
Appearances:	33	8
Minutes played:	2970	720
Percentage played:	97.1%	100%
Goals conceded:	41	2
Clean sheets:	8	6
Cards:	Y8, R0	Y0, R0
Minutes between goals:	72mins	360mins
Defender ranking:	109th	11th

AGE 30 | **DREAM TEAM** | **RANKING 28**

7th JAVIER ZANETTI
ARGENTINA & INTER MILAN

As the most capped Argentina international of all time, Javier Zanetti is a living legend in his homeland and the current captain for his club, and formerly for his country.

With a world class all-round game, his flexibility means that he has no fixed position – able to play at full-back on either flank or equally comfortable in midfield – and is one of the first names on Diego Maradona's team sheet. Having been overlooked for Germany 2006, he will be desperate to play.

Playing record	12 mths lge	wcq
Appearances:	40	16
Minutes played:	3600	1395
Percentage played:	100%	86.1%
Goals conceded:	38	19
Clean sheets:	16	6
Cards:	Y2, R0	Y1, R0
Minutes between goals:	95mins	73mins
Defender ranking:	43rd	119th

AGE 36 | **DREAM TEAM** | **RANKING 26**

6th PATRICE EVRA
FRANCE & MAN UTD

Only two players played more minutes for France in qualifying than Patrice Evra and while Raymond Domenech might have many of his selections called into question, Evra has been a reliable performer at left-back.

The diminutive defender is hitting his peak as a player – he will be 29 by the time the tournament starts – and his ability to surge down the left flank and link play will be a vital outlet for France. He's no mug as a defender either, so expect Evra to play a starring role.

Playing record	12 mths lge	wcq
Appearances:	34	10
Minutes played:	2992	930
Percentage played:	81.1%	83.8%
Goals conceded:	32	8
Clean sheets:	14	5
Cards:	Y5, R0	Y1, R0
Minutes between goals:	93mins	116mins
Defender ranking:	47th	76th

AGE 29 | **DREAM TEAM** | **RANKING 22**

5th ASHLEY COLE
ENGLAND & CHELSEA

One of the most highly regarded left-backs in world football, Ashley Cole is also one of the most consistent performers and has a lot of experience at the highest level, with this his third World Cup finals.

Fast and direct, he is also a very balanced full-back – equally capable going forward as he is in defence. He will be Capello's first-choice for the tournament, as he was in qualifying where only Frank Lampard and Wayne Rooney played more minutes than him, he will be vital in South Africa.

Playing record	12 mths lge	wcq
Appearances:	35	8
Minutes played:	2990	693
Percentage played:	85.2%	77.0%
Goals conceded:	30	5
Clean sheets:	17	3
Cards:	Y6, R0	Y0, R0
Minutes between goals:	100mins	139mins
Defender ranking:	30th	57th

AGE 29 | **DREAM TEAM** | **RANKING 19**

4th
MAICON

BRAZIL & INTER MILAN

A dangerous attacking full-back, Maicon has stepped into the void left by former captain Cafu and will be an instrumental part of Brazil's push to win the title for a sixth time.

Fast, skilful and able to open up a game with his delivery from the right flank, Maicon is also defensively adept and plays in one of the tightest backlines in Europe with Inter Milan. An automatic pick in qualifying – only keeper Julio Cesar played more minutes for Brazil.

Playing record	12 mths lge	wcq
Appearances:	28	15
Minutes played:	2456	1278
Percentage played:	68.2%	78.9%
Goals conceded:	23	9
Clean sheets:	13	9
Cards:	Y4, R1	Y0, R0
Minutes between goals:	107mins	142mins
Defender ranking:	21st	54th

AGE 28	DREAM TEAM	RANKING 18

3rd
GERARD PIQUE

SPAIN & BARCELONA

A centre-back with bags of potential, Gerard Pique has made something of a meteoric rise in European football and will shortly be able to test himself on the very highest stage at just 23.

Now back at Barcelona having won the Champions League with Manchester United, he picked up another winners' medal against his former side in 2009. He made his debut for Spain in place of injured team-mate Carles Puyol and is now the first choice centre-back.

Playing record	12 mths lge	wcq
Appearances:	30	6
Minutes played:	2483	481
Percentage played:	70.7%	53.4%
Goals conceded:	23	2
Clean sheets:	15	4
Cards:	Y7, R1	Y0, R0
Minutes between goals:	108mins	240mins
Defender ranking:	17th	21st

AGE 23	DREAM TEAM	RANKING 10

2nd
JOHN TERRY

ENGLAND & CHELSEA

A throwback compared to some of the more cultured defenders on the world scene, John Terry is an old fashioned, blood and guts, no-nonsense defender and England's first choice centre-back.

An inspirational figure on the pitch, Terry possesses courage and determination in abundance; and these attributes, coupled with his inherent ability and positional awareness make him one of the giants of world football at centre-back.

Playing record	12 mths lge	wcq
Appearances:	37	8
Minutes played:	3327	718
Percentage played:	94.8%	79.8%
Goals conceded:	30	4
Clean sheets:	19	4
Cards:	Y7, R0	Y1, R0
Minutes between goals:	111mins	179mins
Defender ranking:	15th	38th

AGE 29	DREAM TEAM	RANKING 7

THE TOP DEFENDER

BRAZIL **LUCIO**

Brazil's captain Lucio is a dominant centre-back and one of the most experienced players currently playing in world football.

Approaching a century of caps for his country, Lucio played every single minute of Brazil's 2002 cup-winning campaign and then again in 2006 when they lost out in the quarter-finals to France.

Playing record	12 mths lge	wcq
Appearances:	34	14
Minutes played:	3005	1260
Percentage played:	83.5%	77.8%
Goals conceded:	28	6
Clean sheets:	13	9
Cards:	Y2, R0	Y4, R0
Minutes between goals:	107mins	210mins
Defender ranking:	19th	27th

AGE 32 **INTER MILAN** **DREAM TEAM** **RANKING 5**

1st

Position	1st	2nd	3rd	4th	5th	6th	7th	8th
Group	E	D	B	H	A	**G**	C	F
Total FIFA ranking	88	89	98	104	130	**147**	160	161

IVORY COAST V PORTUGAL
Port Elizabeth, Tuesday 15 June 1500 BST

A massive game, Ivory Coast against Portugal should kick-start the 'Group of Death' in style. Portugal may have limped through qualifying, but they have an extremely talented squad and are still a major threat, while the Ivory Coast side is probably the most highly-fancied African team ever at a World Cup. Even tipped by some as potential outsiders for the title, The

Elephants have talent all over the pitch and failure to make the last 16 would be a huge blow. A win for either nation in this one would give them a fantastic chance of qualifying – with games against North Korea still to come – while defeat would leave them knowing that they must get a result against Brazil to stand any chance of making it to the knockout stages.

BRAZIL V NORTH KOREA
Johannesburg JEP, Tuesday 15 June 1930 BST

Anything other than a comfortable win for Brazil in this one would come as a massive shock. A win for the North Koreans would be one of, if not the greatest World Cup shock of all time. The chances of them pulling off a positive result are obviously slim. With the make-up of the North Korean side shrouded in secrecy, the one thing that is known is that they will play an

extremely defensive game, hitting teams on the counter-attack when possible and generally defending deep in numbers – tactics that may frustrate Brazil, but are unlikely to keep them out for 90 minutes. If the unthinkable happens and the South Americans lose, then they will be in very serious danger of crashing out of the tournament at the first hurdle.

BRAZIL V IVORY COAST
Johannesburg JSC, Sunday 20 June 1930 BST

Probably the most anticipated game of the group stages, the highly-rated Ivory Coast take on one of the best teams in world football. If either or both of these sides won their first game then qualification could be secured today, but likewise, two defeats from two would likely guarantee an early exit from the competition. The atmosphere should be wonderful, with the

African crowd getting fully behind the continent's leading representatives. Both teams are decent going forward, but also have solid defences, meaning that this one is extremely tough to call. With North Korea to come next, a win for Ivory Coast here would leave one of Brazil and Portugal facing the likelihood of a shock exit.

Portugal's Ronaldo and Nani

PORTUGAL V NORTH KOREA
Cape Town, Monday 21 June 1230 BST

None of the three big sides in Group G will accept defeat to North Korea, but the minnows won't just roll over. Their defensive record in qualification was phenomenal, and despite a plethora of attacking talent, Portugal have struggled to score over recent years. Even so, North Korea are likely to be out of the competition after this game. Portugal will know that a win will either send them through, or leave them needing a result against Brazil.

PORTUGAL V BRAZIL
Durban, Friday 25 June 1500 BST

In the likely event that qualification is still not guaranteed for either of these sides, this is a massive match. While few would be surprised if Portugal failed to make it out of the group stage, an early exit for Brazil would be a huge

shock, with many tipping the South Americans for the title. Even if both teams are already through to the next round this should still be a great game to watch, with some of the world's best attacking players on display.

NORTH KOREA V IVORY COAST
Nelspruit, Friday 25 June 1500 BST

If the Ivory Coast are still in with a chance of qualifying for the knock-out stages at this point then a game against the weakest team at the tournament gives them a terrific opportunity to do so. However, North Korea will be keen to go put in a great performance in what is likely to be their last game at this World Cup. If the

Ivorians don't get an early goal then this has the potential to be an extremely nervy encounter. Suspensions and injuries also come into play, and if Didier Drogba is missing then that will be a huge blow to The Elephants. If the African side go through, then expect the atmosphere in Nelspruit to be fantastic.

VIEW FROM THE EXPERTS

BRAZIL: The Samba Kings are a big favourite with the neutrals and have fabulous players spread all round the world. They are a lot of people's choice to win the tournament outright but do face a tough group stage. Don't be too shocked if in the end they go home disappointed.
HARRY'S VERDICT: The Final ?????
NORTH KOREA: I have not been there lately to watch them play. I don't think even the North Korean people know much about their national football team. But I'm pretty convinced they will be heading back to their secretive homeland quite quickly.
HARRY'S VERDICT: Group stage only.
PORTUGAL: It's a toss-up between Portugal and the Ivory Coast to finish behind Brazil. But on their day the Portuguese are capable of shocking even the world's best team. They have an awesome line-up with great players such as Cristiano Ronaldo and Ricardo Carvalho.
HARRY'S VERDICT: Last 16.
IVORY COAST: Scary. Didier Drogba alone is enough to give any rival team sleepless nights. It's possible and plausible they could edge Brazil - this is a tough, tough group and one I shall be watching with enormous excitement.
HARRY'S VERDICT: Group stage only.

BRAZIL: You cannot talk about the World Cup without mentioning Brazil. They are the only country to have appeared at every finals and have lifted the trophy five times. With the likes of Kaka and Luis Fabiano in their squad they have every chance of making it six.
TEL'S VERDICT: Possible, some would say probable, champs.
NORTH KOREA: South Africa's genuine unknown quantity after reaching their first finals since 1966. Back then, they famously defeated Italy 1-0 before being beaten 5-3 in the quarter-finals by Portugal - having taken a 3-0 lead. They are unlikely to reach that stage this time, but who knows?
TEL'S VERDICT: The most unpredictable team in tournament.
PORTUGAL: You can never rule out any team which contains a player like Cristiano Ronaldo. But they will have to improve on their displays in qualification in which they only secured their place at the finals with a hard-fought play-off win over Bosnia.
TEL'S VERDICT: Must do better or will be out in Africa.

IVORY COAST: Regardless of their performance in the 2010 Africa Cup of Nations they are the strongest African nation at the finals. With Kolo Toure at the back, Didier Zokora in midfield and Didier Drogba up front, the Elephants will be a test for any team. They just need to make sure they keep their discipline.

TEL'S VERDICT: One to watch.

BRAZIL: One of the favourites to lift the trophy and rightly so, their World Cup record is simply awesome. Defensively, they might appear lackadaisical at times but there is no doubting their attacking threat, particularly with Seville's prolific striker Luis Fabiano leading the line.

WRIGHTY'S VERDICT: There or thereabouts.

NORTH KOREA: South Africa's mystery men. The majority of players in the North Korean squad are based domestically. In the recent 0-0 draw against Congo in France - their first match on European soil since 1966 – they gave little away despite the side missing six key players.

WRIGHTY'S VERDICT: Who knows?

PORTUGAL: Another strongly tipped nation who stuttered through qualification. Coach Carlos Queiroz, the former Manchester United No. 2, has been heavily criticised in his homeland and that means the likes of Cristiano Ronaldo and Deco will hardly be in the best of spirits as they head to South Africa.

WRIGHTY'S VERDICT: Under pressure already.

IVORY COAST: Reckoned to be one of Africa's strongest challengers and their striker Didier Drogba can definitely enhance his reputation and become the tournament's highest scorer, provided he gets the service he does at Chelsea and, of course, his country remain in the competition long enough.

WRIGHTY'S VERDICT: Force to be reckoned with.

"Scary. Didier Drogba alone is enough to give any rival team sleepless nights"

THE LIKELY ROUTES FOR THE TOP TWO TEAMS FROM THE GROUP

For the full draw please see page 80

GROUP STAGE	LAST SIXTEEN	QUARTER-FINALS
FIRST GROUP G	v SECOND GROUP H	v FIRST GROUP E or SECOND GROUP F
BRAZIL	**BRAZIL v CHILE**	**BRAZIL v NETHERLANDS**
SECOND GROUP G	v FIRST GROUP H	v FIRST GROUP F or SECOND GROUP E
PORTUGAL	**PORTUGAL v SPAIN**	**SPAIN v ITALY**

GROUP G
BRAZIL, NORTH KOREA (KOREA DPR), IVORY COAST, PORTUGAL

GROUP H
SPAIN, SWITZERLAND, HONDURAS, CHILE

GROUP E
NETHERLANDS, DENMARK, JAPAN, CAMEROON

GROUP F
ITALY, PARAGUAY, NEW ZEALAND, SLOVAKIA

ROUTE TO THE FINALS

Unlike fellow South Americans Argentina, qualification was a breeze for Brazil, as Dunga's side recovered from a slow start to top the ten-nation group.

Two wins from their opening six games put the manager under pressure, with fans and pundits critical of the European-based players' commitment to the cause, but seven victories in the next ten saw Brazil reach the World Cup with ease. With Sevilla's Luis Fabiano

spearheading a fearsome attacking unit, Dunga's main achievement as Brazil boss has been to add defensive solidity to a side that has never struggled to score goals. This more conservative style has won the manager few friends in Brazil, but it was the cornerstone of the team's successful run in qualification and saw a place at the finals secured with three games to spare.

For final qualification table see Paraguay.

Avge FIFA ranking

#	Date	Venue	Opponent	Rank	Result	Score	Scorers
1	14 Oct 07	Away	Colombia	38	D	0 0	
2	18 Oct 07	Home	Ecuador	44	W	5 0	Love 18, Ronaldinho 71, Kaka 76, 84, Elano 82
3	18 Nov 07	Away	Peru	76	D	1 1	Kaka 40
4	21 Nov 07	Home	Uruguay	22	W	2 1	Fabiano 44, 64
5	15 Jun 08	Away	Paraguay	20	L	2 0	
6	19 Jun 08	Home	Argentina	6	D	0 0	
7	08 Sep 08	Away	Chile	32	W	0 3	Fabiano 21, 83, Robinho 45
8	11 Sep 08	Home	Bolivia	66	D	0 0	
9	12 Oct 08	Away	Venezuela	60	W	0 4	Kaka 6, Robinho 9, 66, Leite Ribeiro 19
10	16 Oct 08	Home	Colombia	38	D	0 0	
11	29 Mar 09	Away	Ecuador	44	D	1 1	Baptista 72
12	02 Apr 09	Home	Peru	76	W	3 0	Fabiano 18pen, 27, Melo de Carvalho 64
13	06 Jun 09	Away	Uruguay	22	W	0 4	D.Alves 12, dos Santos 36, Fabiano 52, Kaka 75pen
14	11 Jun 09	Home	Paraguay	20	W	2 1	De Souza 40, Honorato da Silva 50
15	06 Sep 09	Away	Argentina	6	W	1 3	Da Silva 23, Fabiano Clemente 30, 68
16	10 Sep 09	Home	Chile	32	W	4 2	Honorato da Silva 31, 74, 76, Baptista 40
17	11 Oct 09	Away	Bolivia	66	L	2 1	Nilmar 70
18	14 Oct 09	Home	Venezuela	60	D	0 0	
	Average FIFA ranking of opposition			**40**			

MAIN PLAYER PERFORMANCES IN QUALIFICATION

Key: ■ played 90 mins ◄◄ subbed off ►► subbed on ▨ on bench

Match	1 2 3 4 5 6 7 8 9 10 11 12 13 14 15 16 17 18	Appearances	Started	Subbed on	Subbed off	Mins played	% played	Goals	Yellow	Red
Venue	A H A H A H A H A H A H A H A H A H									
Result	D W D W L D W D W D D W W W W W L D									
Goalkeepers										
Julio Cesar		18	18	0	0	1620	100.0	0	1	0
Defenders										
Daniel Alves		9	5	4	0	625	38.6	1	2	0
Andre Santos		3	3	0	2	225	13.9	0	1	0
Adriano		3	2	1	2	126	7.8	0	0	0
Gilberto		8	8	0	0	720	44.4	0	1	0
Kleber		6	6	0	0	496	30.6	0	1	1
Miranda		4	3	1	0	316	19.5	0	0	1
Maicon		15	15	0	2	1278	78.9	0	0	0
Lucio		14	14	0	0	1260	77.8	0	4	0
Luisao		8	8	0	1	641	39.6	1	4	0
Juan Maldonado		2	1	1	0	128	7.9	0	1	0
Juan		10	10	0	2	830	51.2	1	2	0
Marcelo		1	1	0	0	90	5.6	0	1	0
Midfielders										
Alex Costa		1	1	0	0	90	5.6	0	0	0
Josue		10	6	4	2	570	35.2	0	2	0
Gilberto Silva		14	14	0	0	1260	77.8	0	2	0
Julio Baptista		7	2	5	1	264	16.3	2	1	0
Elano		14	7	7	6	594	36.7	1	1	0
Mineiro		6	6	0	1	509	31.4	0	0	0
Ronaldinho		8	7	1	4	540	33.3	1	0	0
Diego		5	3	2	4	268	16.5	0	2	0
Kaka		11	11	0	4	954	58.9	5	2	0
Lucas Leiva		2	2	0	1	150	9.3	0	0	0
Felipe Melo		6	6	0	0	499	30.8	1	1	1
Ramires		5	2	3	1	245	15.1	0	3	0
Forwards										
Jo		2	1	1	0	94	5.8	0	0	0
Robinho		15	15	0	8	1201	74.1	4	0	0
Luis Fabiano		11	9	2	3	801	49.4	9	4	1
Nilmar		5	4	1	1	358	22.1	5	0	0
Adriano		3	2	1	0	191	11.8	1	2	0
Vagner Love		4	3	1	3	229	14.1	1	0	0

FINAL PROSPECTS

The most successful national side in football history and the only nation to have appeared at every single World Cup, Brazil are once again one of the tournament favourites.

Winners of the tournament in 1994, losing finalists at France '98 and champions again in 2002 – despite having one of the weakest line-ups for many years, Brazil's recent World Cup pedigree is more than a match for their glittering past.

A quarter-final defeat to France in 2006 came as a huge disappointment, and saw coach Carlos Alberto Parreira replaced by Dunga, even though the former World Cup winning captain had no previous managerial experience.

Over the course of his four years in charge Dunga has transformed Brazil into an uncharacteristically well-drilled outfit, often opting for two defensively minded central midfielders to shield the back four, allowing the full-backs to roam forward and a hugely talented attacking unit freedom to play.

Don't be surprised if Fabiano is challenging for the Golden Boot at the end of the tournament.

The coach's decision to move away from the policy of just picking players from the major European sides was greeted with scepticism at first. The likes of Luis Fabiano, Nilmar and Vagner Love played a large part in the team's improvement and the introduction of many home-based players to the set-up was also a welcome change to the usually European dominated squads.

Triumphs in the 2007 Copa America and the 2009 FIFA Confederations Cup signalled Brazil's return to form, and with their new-found defensive solidity added to the usual attacking flair, the Samba stars are considered to be one of the leading candidates for the title.

The most likely stumbling block for the Brazilians could be in this year's 'Group of Death', with the mercurial Portugal and a hugely talented Ivory Coast side presenting a serious threat to Dunga's hopes of leading the squad to the knock out stages.

If Kaka and co. do play to their potential then they could go to the final and with Luis Fabiano leading the frontline for the Samba stars, anything is possible.

Don't be surprised if Fabiano is challenging for the Golden Boot at the end of the tournament.

DREAM TEAM TOP 15 RANKING   6

GROUP FIXTURES

NORTH KOREA	Tue 15 June 1930 BST
IVORY COAST	Sun 20 June 1930 BST
PORTUGAL	Fri 25 June 1500 BST

Brasilia

Zone	South America
Population	199m
Language	Portuguese
Top league	Serie A
Playing season	May - December

Major clubs and capacities
Flamengo (95,402), Internacional (56,000), Sao Paulo (80,312), Corinthians (38,800)

Where probable squad players play:

Premier League	-	Ligue 1	-
Serie A	10	Eredivisie	-
La Liga	5	Other Europe	3
Bundesliga	1	Outside Europe	4

Number of Brazilian players playing:

Premier League	14	Bundesliga	26
Serie A	37	Ligue 1	23
La Liga	23	Eredivisie	14

World Cup record   * best performance

1930 - Round 1	1974 -	4th place
1934 - Round 1	1978 -	3rd place
1938 - 3rd place	1982 -	Round 2
1950 - Runners up	1986 -	Quarter finals
1954 - Quarter finals	1990 -	Last 16
1958 - * Champions	1994 -	* Champions
1962 - * Champions	1998 -	Runners up
1966 - Round 1	2002 -	* Champions
1970 - * Champions	2006 -	Quarter finals

THE SQUAD

Goalkeepers	Club side	Age	QG
Julio Cesar	Inter Milan	30	18
Doni	Roma	30	0
Defenders			
Daniel Alves	Barcelona	27	9
Andre Santos	Fenerbahce	27	3
Adriano	Sevilla	25	3
Gilberto	Cruzeiro	34	8
Kleber	Internacional	30	6
Miranda	Sao Paulo	25	4
Maicon	Inter Milan	28	15
Lucio	Inter Milan	32	14
Luisao	Benfica	29	8
Juan	Roma	31	10
Midfielders			
Josue	Wolfsburg	30	10
Gilberto Silva	Panathinaikos	33	14
Julio Baptista	Roma	28	7
Elano	Galatasaray	28	14
Mineiro	Schalke	34	6
Ronaldinho	AC Milan	30	8
Diego	Juventus	25	5
Kaka	Real Madrid	28	11
Felipe Melo	Juventus	26	6
Ramires	Benfica	23	5
Forwards			
Robinho	Man City/Santos	26	15
Luis Fabiano	Sevilla	29	11
Nilmar	Villarreal	25	5
Alexandre Pato	AC Milan	20	3

■ Probable ■ Possible **QG** Qualification Games

KEY PLAYER

KAKA REAL MADRID

A supremely talented player, Kaka is often described as an attacking midfield player, but scores so many goals that he could just as easily be seen as a support striker.

Naturally gifted, Kaka's game is more than fancy tricks, it's his clever runs, decent pace and a great eye for a pass that set him apart as one of the world's best. He plays as one of a trio of attacking players behind Fabiano in Brazil's formation in World Cup qualifying, Kaka is all-but guaranteed a starting place if fit, with the likes of Robinho, Ronaldinho and Nilmar competing to play alongside him. A threat when given space to shoot from distance, Kaka's link-up play with Fabiano will be the key to any success.

Kaka is a Top 12 midfielder.

AGE 28   **MIDFIELDER**   **DREAM TEAM RANKING** 6

KEY GOALKEEPERS

JULIO CESAR
INTER MILAN

Cesar is a Top 4 goalkeeper

AGE 30	DREAM TEAM	RANKING 2

DONI
ROMA

Playing record	12 months lge	wcq
Appearances:	17	0
Minutes played:	1530	0
Percentage played:	44.7%	0%
Goals conceded:	29	-
Clean sheets:	3	-
Cards:	Y2, R0	-
Minutes between goals:	53mins	-
Goalkeeper ranking:	33rd	-

AGE 30	DREAM TEAM	RANKING 1060

KEY DEFENDERS

MAICON
INTER MILAN

A superbly talented right-back, the true mark of Maicon's quality is that he has been considered Brazil's first-choice in that position over the last few years, despite competition from a player of the quality of Dani Alves.

Along with a dangerous attacking game, Maicon is reliable defensively, while his phenomenal work-rate and an aggressive streak mean that he is not a player that any opposing left-winger should take lightly.

Maicon is a Top 12 defender

JUAN
ROMA

A hugely experienced centre-back, Juan has become a mainstay of the Brazil team. Unspectacular yet effective in defence, Juan impressed in a five-year spell at Bayer Leverkusen, before furthering his reputation at AS Roma.

Juan's partnership with Lucio at the back is likely to be key if Brazil claim another World title.

Playing record	12 months lge	wcq
Appearances:	22	10
Minutes played:	1805	830
Percentage played:	48.9%	51.2%
Goals conceded:	19	5
Clean sheets:	11	6
Cards:	Y1, R0	Y2, R0
Defensive rating:	95mins	166mins
Defender ranking:	42nd	42nd

AGE 31	DREAM TEAM	RANKING 360

THE MANAGER

A former World Cup-winning Brazil captain, Dunga was appointed manager of Brazil in 2006, despite having no previous coaching experience.

A defensive midfielder in a playing career that spanned 20 years, Dunga was capped 91 times by Brazil, leading the Canarinho to World Cup glory in 1994 and again to the final at France '98.

A surprise choice to replace Carlos Alberto

LUCIO
INTER MILAN

Instantly recognisable with his upright running style and aggressive approach to the game, Lucio was the obvious candidate to take over the Brazilian captaincy when Dunga was appointed head coach in 2006 due to his vocal on-field presence and all-action qualities.

A towering presence in the air, the centre-back is as dangerous in the opposition box as he is commanding in his own, which he highlighted with a headed winner in the 2009 Confederations Cup Final against the United States. Nine years in the Bundesliga – with Bayer Leverkusen and Bayern Munich – saw Lucio cement his reputation as one of the leading defenders in world football and a move to Jose Mourinho's Inter Milan in the summer of 2009 saw him finally test himself in one of the 'Big Three' European leagues. South Africa will be the defender's third World Cup, after he played every single minute en-route to the 2002 title and also set a record in 2006 for the most minutes without conceding a foul at a World Cup – 386. His partnership with Juan in the centre of defence has impressed over recent years and his vocal presence in the box ensures that he also works well with goalkeeper Julio Cesar. A key component of this Brazil side, Lucio's form and fitness will be vital to the Samba Kings hopes of lifting a sixth World Cup. Although he can be sometimes exposed for a lack of pace, a new defensive formation with two holding midfielders should protect the skipper's weaknesses.

Lucio is a Top 12 defender

AGE 32	DREAM TEAM	RANKING 5

Parreira as head coach of the national side after the last World Cup, Dunga's tenure got off to a shaky start, with his negative tactics – mixed with poor results – leading to widespread media criticism...and even from the president of Brazil.

However, success in the 2007 Copa America and a comfortable World Cup qualification campaign saw Dunga's defensive mindset help add uncharacteristic steel to this Brazilian side. His decision to mix domestic talent with the big names from Europe has given the squad both balance and unity.

His decision to move to a more balanced 4-2-3-1 formation – with an out-and-out front man and two defensive midfielders, allowing the creative players freedom to express themselves – has made Brazil a more consistent side, making them one of the clear favourites to become the world champions in South Africa.

DANI ALVES
BARCELONA

The most expensive right-back in the history of the game, Dani Alves still can't tie down a regular starting place in the Brazil side, with manager Dunga preferring Inter Milan's Maicon.

Hugely attacking, Alves made a name for himself with two-time UEFA Cup champions Sevilla, before sealing a move to Spanish giants Barcelona. It was feared that a partnership with Lionel Messi down the right might be exposed defensively, but Alves proved his critics wrong, playing a key role in Barcelona's all-conquering 2008-09 campaign, winning the Champions League and a Spanish league and cup double in his first season, before adding the Spanish and UEFA Supercups and the FIFA World Club Cup at the end of 2009. Alves offers natural width down the right, and with a terrific set-piece delivery and a wicked shot, he is an extremely dangerous player to bring off the bench in tight matches. It could be that Dunga opts to use Alves on the left of defence to find a place for such quality in the starting line-up.

Alves is a Top 12 defender.

AGE 27 | **DREAM TEAM** **RANKING** 33

KEY PLAYER

LUIS FABIANO SEVILLA

Luis Fabiano is a clinical finisher, with an aggressive streak and the ability to hold the ball up.

The striker provides the perfect foil to allow the more typically 'Brazilian' talents of the likes of Kaka, Robinho, Ronaldinho and Nilmar the space to play in and around opposition defences. Fabiano made not a single appearance for the national side in three years, before finally being recalled by Dunga in 2007. The move to bring a genuine target man into the side proved vital in changing Brazil's fortunes, as the new manager turned the team from occasionally magical to consistently efficient. Expect Fabiano to find the back of the net with alarming regularity in South Africa.

Fabiano is a Top 12 striker.

AGE 29 | **STRIKER** | **DREAM TEAM** **RANKING** 58

KEY MIDFIELDERS

GILBERTO SILVA
PANATHINAIKOS

A veteran in this Brazil side, defensive midfielder Gilberto Silva has defied his declining club form to remain a key part of the national set-up.

Benefitting from manager Dunga's use of two holding midfielders in a defensive formation, Gilberto's partnership with Felipe Melo shields a central defensive partnership that has plenty of quality but lacks pace. He has his fair share of critics and playing his club football in the Greek league with Panathinaikos does little to suggest that his career is not one on the wane. However, he still has terrific ability in the air and the sort of leadership skills that a team needs.

Playing record	12 months lge	wcq
Appearances:	-	14
Minutes played:	-	1260
Percentage played:	-	77.8%
Goals scored:	-	0
Clean sheets:	-	7
Cards:	-	Y2, R0
Strike rate:	-	-
Midfielder ranking:	-	-

AGE 33	DREAM TEAM RANKING 557

FELIPE MELO
JUVENTUS

Dunga's preference for two defensive midfield players has seen Felipe Melo tie down a regular starting spot in the Brazil side since his debut in February 2009.

The manager's tactics may have attracted many critics in Brazil, but Melo's partnership with Gilberto Silva in the middle of the park has been the cornerstone of Brazil's transformation into a side who are as strong at the back as they are going forward. More than comfortable on the ball, Melo's pace and eye for a pass perfectly off-sets veteran Gilberto's more physical approach to the game. A starting player in all five games as the South Americans won the Confederations Cup last summer, the midfielder's impressive displays allowed Brazil's creative midfielders a platform to attack. His displays at the tournament saw him attract attention from some of the biggest clubs in European football – and the fact that Arsene Wenger was publically interested in taking the midfielder to north London should indicate what a natural footballer Melo is. Instead he opted to remain in Italy and move from Fiorentina to Juventus, where he struggled to settle into the team in his debut season. His defensive skills will be tested by the talented Ivory Coast and Portugal and he will play an important role if Brazil are going to lift the title.

Melo is a Top 12 midfielder.

AGE 26	DREAM TEAM RANKING 21

ELANO BLUMER
GALATASARAY

Elano's versatility makes him the perfect squad member for a Brazil side who have high hopes of going all the way in South Africa.

Decent on the ball with an eye for a pass and a terrific long-distance shot, the former Manchester City man can play anywhere across the midfield. A reliable penalty taker, Elano will be a useful asset if Brazil progress.

Playing record	12 months lge	wcq
Appearances:	-	14
Minutes played:	-	594
Percentage played:	-	36.7%
Goals scored:	-	1
Clean sheets:	-	8
Cards:	-	Y1, R0
Strike rate:	-	594mins
Midfielder ranking:	-	-

AGE 28	DREAM TEAM RANKING 216

KEY STRIKERS

ROBINHO
MAN CITY

The World Cup comes at the perfect time for Robinho to restart a career that appears to have reached a crossroads.

Signed by Manchester City from Real Madrid in the summer of 2008, the attacking midfielder failed to impress in the Premier League and returned on loan to the club with whom he started his career – Santos – in January 2010. A typical Brazilian flair player, with sumptuous ability on the ball and an eye for goal. However, with the likes of Ronaldinho, Kaka and Nilmar all competing for a place in midfield in support of lone striker Fabiano, his place in the Brazil starting line-up is far from assured. A player of Robinho's talent with a point to prove is a dangerous combination and if Dunga does find a place for him in the side then Portugal, Ivory Coast and North Korea should be beware.

Playing record	12 months lge	wcq
Appearances:	25	15
Minutes played:	1796	1201
Percentage played:	49.9%	74.1%
Goals scored:	3	4
Percentage share:	4.84%	12.12%
Cards:	Y1, R0	Y0, R0
Strike rate:	599mins	300mins
Strike rate ranking:	120th	60th

AGE 26	DREAM TEAM RANKING 100

ALEXANDRE PATO
AC MILAN

A talented young striker, Alexandre Pato has had limited playing time for Brazil so far in his career, but is likely to feature in the tournament, either as a replacement for Fabiano up front, or as a partner for the front man.

Decent pace, lightning reactions and predatory instinct in the box have seen Pato become a regular for club side AC Milan, and the influence of legendary finisher Filippo Inzaghi is clear to see in the youngster's evolving style. The 20-year-old has more ability on the ball than the Italian veteran, but is similarly effective in and around the penalty box.

Playing record	12 months lge	wcq
Appearances:	35	3
Minutes played:	2650	66
Percentage played:	73.6%	4.1%
Goals scored:	16	0
Percentage share:	21.92%	0.00%
Cards:	Y1, R0	Y0, R0
Strike rate:	166mins	-
Strike rate ranking:	-	32nd

AGE 20   **DREAM TEAM RANKING 121**

ONE TO WATCH

NILMAR VILLARREAL

Nilmar was recalled to the national set-up by Dunga in 2008, four years after his previous cap.

Still just 25, the talented attacker can be used either as a striker or one of the three support players in Brazil's 4-2-3-1 formation, and his club performances over the last year have seen him emerge as a genuine contender for a starting place.

Playing record	12 months lge	wcq
Appearances:	13	5
Minutes played:	781	358
Percentage played:	22.3%	22.1%
Goals scored:	4	5
Percentage share:	6.67%	15.15%
Cards:	Y0, R0	Y0, R0
Strike rate:	-	-
Strike rate ranking:	-	-

AGE 25   **STRIKER**   **DREAM TEAM RANKING 1177**

ROUTE TO THE FINALS

The most highly-fancied African side at the World Cup, Ivory Coast cruised through qualification, topping their groups in both stages of CAF qualifying.

The Elephants eased through round two with three wins at home and three draws on the road enough to see off Mozambique, Botswana and Madagascar. A 4-0 win versus Botswana was a highlight, as even defensive midfielder Didier Zokora got his name on the score-sheet – his first goal for his country and only the fourth in his entire professional career. The second and final group stage saw Ivory Coast really turn on the style, with Didier Drogba bagging six of his side's 19 goals in just half a dozen games. A 5-0 hammering of Burkina Faso was a highlight, and qualification was confirmed with a 1-1 draw away in Malawi.

However, the campaign was overshadowed by a crowd crush in March 2009, thousands of extra fans crammed into the stadium to watch them hammer Malawi 5-0 in their opening game. The incident left at least 22 dead and hundreds injured.

FINAL QUALIFYING TABLE
AFRICA ROUND 3 GROUP E

	P	W	D	L	F	A	Pts
Ivory Coast	6	5	1	0	19	4	16
Burkina Faso	6	4	0	2	10	11	12
Malawi	6	1	1	4	4	11	4
Guinea	6	1	0	5	7	14	3

#	Date	Venue	Opponent	Avge FIFA ranking	Result	Score	Scorers
1	01 Jun 08	Home	Mozambique	91	W	1 0	Cisse 75
2	08 Jun 08	Away	Madagascar	136	D	0 0	
3	14 Jun 08	Away	Botswana	120	D	1 1	Meite 65
4	22 Jun 08	Home	Botswana	120	W	4 0	Sanogo 16, Zokora 22, Cisse 46, 70
5	07 Sep 08	Away	Mozambique	91	D	1 1	B.Kone 48
6	11 Oct 08	Home	Madagascar	136	W	3 0	Sanogo 41, 55, S.Kalou 65
7	29 Mar 09	Home	Malawi	109	W	5 0	Romaric 1, Drogba 6pen, 27, S.Kalou 59, B.Kone 70
8	07 Jun 09	Away	Guinea	47	W	1 2	
9	20 Jun 09	Away	Burkina Faso	64	W	2 3	Yaya.Toure 14, M.Tall 54og, Drogba 70
10	05 Sep 09	Home	Burkina Faso	64	W	5 0	Panandetiguiri 12og, Drogba 48, 65, Yaya.Toure 55, K.Keita 68
11	10 Oct 09	Away	Malawi	109	D	1 1	Drogba 67
12	14 Nov 09	Home	Guinea	47	W	3 0	Gervinho 16, 31, Cisse 67

Average FIFA ranking of opposition	94

MAIN PLAYER PERFORMANCES IN QUALIFICATION

Match	1 2 3 4 5 6 7 8 9 10 11 12	Appearances	Started	Subbed on	Subbed off	Mins played	% played	Goals	Yellow	Red
Venue	H A A H A H H A A H A H									
Result	W D D W D W W W W W D W									
Goalkeepers										
Boubacar Barry		11	11	0	0	990	91.7	0	1	0
Aristide Zogbo		1	1	0	0	90	8.3	0	0	0
Defenders										
Benjamin Angoua		2	1	1	0	95	8.8	0	0	0
Souleymane Bamba		5	3	2	0	285	26.4	0	1	0
Arthur Boka		8	8	0	0	720	66.7	0	0	0
Guy Demel		7	7	0	2	588	54.4	0	1	0
Emmanuel Eboue		12	11	1	0	1004	93.0	0	1	0
Igor Lolo		3	2	1	0	225	20.8	0	0	0
Abdoulaye Meite		6	6	0	3	482	44.6	1	0	0
Siaka Tiene		10	8	2	2	741	68.6	0	2	0
Habib Kolo Toure		7	7	0	1	610	56.5	0	0	0
Marco Zoro		3	1	2	0	117	10.8	0	2	0
Midfielders										
Kanga Akale		6	4	2	3	333	30.8	0	0	0
Emerse Fae		6	3	3	2	246	22.8	0	1	0
Jean-Jacques Gosso		2	1	1	0	111	10.3	0	0	0
Emmanuel Kone		7	4	3	1	391	36.2	0	1	0
Yaya Toure		7	6	1	2	542	50.2	2	1	0
Didier Zokora		12	12	0	0	1080	100	1	1	0
Forwards										
Sekou Cisse		7	3	4	3	271	25.1	4	1	0
Aruna Dindane		1	1	0	1	81	7.5	0	0	0
Didier Drogba		5	4	1	2	366	33.9	6	0	0
Salomon Kalou		8	7	1	4	626	58.0	2	1	0
Abdul Kader Keita		3	2	1	2	182	16.9	1	0	0
Bakary Kone		5	5	0	3	418	38.7	2	1	0
Gervais Yao Kouassi		3	1	2	0	112	10.4	2	0	0
Boubacar Sanogo		8	6	2	1	554	51.3	3	0	0
Kandia Traore		5	3	2	1	261	24.2	0	0	0

FINAL PROSPECTS

Ivory Coast are rightly seen as the pick of a strong African contingent at the World Cup, despite once again being drawn in the 'Group of Death'.

The Elephants qualified for their first Finals in 2006, where they were handed a tough draw against Argentina, Netherlands and a highly-rated Serbia and Montenegro side.

Yet nearly qualified after narrowly losing out 2-1 in the first two games, despite terrific performances, before beating the Serbians in the final match of the group.

The core of the talented 2006 squad remains intact four years on, and with experienced players across the park there is a nice balance to the side.

Progress to the latter stages is likely to depend on the form and fitness of the hugely influential Didier Drogba, but Aruna Dindane and the Kone brothers – Arouna and Bakari – offer decent support in attack, while Salomon Kalou and the lively Abdul-Kader Keita are useful options up-front and out wide if the team need goals.

Manager Vahid Halihodzic's preference for Emmanuel Eboue on the right of midfield gives the team solidity down that flank, while Kalou offers a more direct threat on the left.

Many pundits had picked this group of players as possible dark horses for the title prior to the draw, but ...

One of the strengths of the Ivory Coast side is their experienced and talented central defensive midfield partnership of Didier Zokora and Yaya Toure, with the former's presence in front of the back-four allowing the more naturally gifted Barcelona man the freedom to support the attacking players.

Adboulaye Meite and Kolo Toure offer Premier League experience in the centre of a reliable defensive quartet that gives the team a solid base, and the Ivorians will feel they have the talent at the back to cope with the better teams in South Africa on their day.

Many pundits had picked this group of players as possible dark horses for the title prior to the draw, but a place in Group G alongside Brazil and Portugal could see one of the most talented African teams ever seen at a World Cup struggle to even make the knockout stages.

That said, as long as at least some of their star men perform, Ivory Coast are more than capable of beating their European foes and could even spring a surprise against Brazil.

DREAM TEAM	**TOP 15 RANKING**	11

GROUP FIXTURES

PORTUGAL	Tue 15 June 1500 BST
BRAZIL	Sun 20 June 1930 BST
NORTH KOREA	Fri 25 June 1500 BST

Yamoussoukro

Zone	Africa
Population	17.5m
Language	French
Top league	Cote d'Ivoire Premier Division
Playing season	February - November

Major clubs and capacities
ASEC Mimosas (35,491), Africa Sports National (20,000), Stella Club d'Adjame (20,842)

Where probable squad players play:

Premier League	4	Ligue 1	7
Serie A	-	Eredivisie	1
La Liga	2	Other Europe	7
Bundesliga	2	Outside Europe	-

Number of Ivorian players playing:

Premier League	6	Bundesliga	4
Serie A	-	Ligue 1	10
La Liga	4	Eredivisie	3

World Cup record   * best performance

1930 - Did not enter	1974 - Did not qualify
1934 - Did not enter	1978 - Did not qualify
1938 - Did not enter	1982 - Did not enter
1950 - Did not enter	1986 - Did not qualify
1954 - Did not enter	1990 - Did not qualify
1958 - Did not enter	1994 - Did not qualify
1962 - Did not enter	1998 - Did not qualify
1966 - Did not enter	2002 - Did not qualify
1970 - Did not enter	2006 - * Round 1

THE SQUAD

Goalkeepers	Club side	Age	QG
Boubacar Barry	Beveren	30	10
Aristide Zogbo	Maccabi Netanya	28	1
Defenders			
Benjamin Angoua	Budapest Honved	23	2
Souleymane Bamba	Hibernian	25	5
Arthur Boka	Stuttgart	27	7
Guy Demel	Hamburg	28	7
Emmanuel Eboue	Arsenal	27	11
Igor Lolo	AS Monaco	27	2
Abdoulaye Meite	West Brom	29	5
Siaka Tiene	Valenciennes	28	9
Habib Kolo Toure	Man City	29	6
Marco Zoro	Setubal	26	3
Midfielders			
Kanga Akale	Lens	29	5
Emerse Fae	Nice	26	5
Jean-Jacques Gosso	AS Monaco	27	2
Emmanuel Kone	International Curtea	23	6
Yaya Toure	Barcelona	27	7
Didier Zokora	Sevilla	29	11
Forwards			
Sekou Cisse	Feyenoord	25	6
Didier Drogba	Chelsea	32	5
Salomon Kalou	Chelsea	24	8
Abdul Kader Keita	Galatasaray	28	3
Bakary Kone	Marseille	28	5
Gervais Yao Kouassi	Lille	23	3
Boubacar Sanogo	St Etienne	27	7
Kandia Traore	Caen	29	4

■ Probable ■ Possible **QG** Qualification Games

KEY PLAYER

DIDIER DROGBA CHELSEA

One of, if not the best striker in world football, Didier Drogba is the spearhead of an impressive Ivory Coast side.

The most highly-rated African side at the tournament have quality throughout their ranks, but it is the presence of such a talented front man that means that the Ivorians are even some people's dark horses for the title. A major player at Chelsea since his move from Marseille in 2004, the striker's only negative quality is a perceived attitude problem, which has seen him lacking drive at some points in his career. Drogba's combination of pace, power and finishing ability make him extremely difficult to play against. Drogba will be key for Ivory Coast.

Drogba is a Top 12 Striker

AGE 32   **STRIKER**   **DREAM TEAM** **RANKING** 23

KEY GOALKEEPER

BOUBACAR BARRY
LOKEREN

The Ivory Coast goalkeeper will know that he's likely to be in for a tough time in Group G.

Protected by a solid defence and a decent midfield, Boubacar Barry – who goes by the name of Copa in club football – will need to be at his shot-stopping best in South Africa. It's fair to say that Barry may be the Ivorians' main weakness, but the Belgium-based stopper has an opportunity to prove his critics wrong and earn a move to one of the major European leagues if he excels at the World Cup.

Playing record	12 months lge	wcq
Appearances:	-	11
Minutes played:	-	990
Percentage played:	-	91.7%
Goals conceded:	-	3
Clean sheets:	-	6
Cards:	-	Y1, R0
Minutes between goals:	-	330mins
Goalkeeper ranking:	-	2nd

AGE 30 | **DREAM TEAM** | **RANKING 1027**

KEY DEFENDERS

EMMANUEL EBOUE
ARSENAL

Emmanuel Eboue may not be the most glamorous option on the right, but the Arsenal man is extremely effective at back or half-back.

Playing record	12 months lge	wcq
Appearances:	26	12
Minutes played:	1198	1004
Percentage played:	33.3%	93%
Goals conceded:	11	6
Clean sheets:	18	8
Cards:	Y4, R1	Y1, R0
Minutes between goals:	190mins	167mins
Defender ranking:	2nd	43rd

AGE 27 | **DREAM TEAM** | **RANKING 589**

HABIB KOLO TOURE
MAN CITY

The older of the Toure brothers, Kolo Toure brings proven quality to the Ivory Coast defence. The Manchester City skipper will need to be in good form if The Elephants are to withstand the inevitable assault on their defence from Brazil and Portugal.

Playing record	12 months lge	wcq
Appearances:	33	7
Minutes played:	2879	610
Percentage played:	80.0%	56.5%
Goals conceded:	37	2
Clean sheets:	15	5
Cards:	Y1, R0	Y0, R0
Minutes between goals:	78mins	305mins
Defender ranking:	92nd	13th

AGE 29 | **DREAM TEAM** | **RANKING 75**

KEY MIDFIELDERS

DIDIER ZOKORA
SEVILLA

A defensive midfielder, Didier Zokora is one of the most experienced members of the Ivory Coast squad.

His partnership with Yaya Toure in the centre of midfield is one of the strengths of the side, with his work-rate and energy allowing the more naturally gifted Toure the opportunity to get forward more than he does at club level. Zokora's performances in the 2006 World Cup saw him attract attention from some of Europe's biggest clubs and opted for a move to Tottenham Hotspur.

Playing record	12 months lge	wcq
Appearances:	25	12
Minutes played:	1760	1008
Percentage played:	50.1%	100%
Goals scored:	0	1
Clean sheets:	10	8
Cards:	Y8, R0	Y1, R0
Strike rate:	-	1008mins
Midfielder ranking:	158th	-

AGE 29 | **DREAM TEAM** | **RANKING 408**

GUY DEMEL
HAMBURG

Playing record	12 months lge	wcq
Appearances:	27	7
Minutes played:	1983	588
Percentage played:	64.8%	54.4%
Goals scored:	1	0
Clean sheets:	8	4
Cards:	Y6, R0	Y1, R0
Strike rate:	983mins	-
Midfielder ranking:	151st	118th

AGE 28 | **DREAM TEAM** | **RANKING 383**

THE MANAGER

Fearsome man-manager Vahid Halihodzic was brought in as Ivory Coast head coach in 2008 with the aim of uniting a talented squad of players and ensuring they fulfil their huge collective potential in South Africa.

A talented striker back in his playing career, winning the Ligue 1 title in his first season with Nantes and twice finishing top-scorer of the French league. He also achieved fame as a coach in France with Rennes and Lille, helping the former avoid relegation and leading the latter into the Champions League. An undefeated record in World Cup qualifying saw Halihodzic's choice of a 4-4-2 formation turn Ivory Coast into a more solid side defensively. The manager often uses Emmanuel Eboue on the right of midfield, despite the availability of more creative options, meaning that a quality midfield four of Eboue, Yaya Toure, Didier Zokora and Salomon Kalou give Didier Drogba and his usual strike partner Bakary Kone a solid platform.

KEY STRIKER

SALOMON KALOU
CHELSEA

Salomon Kalou brings yet more big game experience to an Ivory Coast side packed full of players who have competed at the top level of European football.

The Chelsea man is often deployed as a left winger for his country, making up an impressive first-choice midfield four with Yaya Toure, Didier Zokora and Emmanuel Eboue. With Didier Drogba occupying defenders up top, Kalou has more time to make runs from deep, take on the full-back and cut inside to support the front players. Still only 24, Kalou doesn't score enough goals, but has a habit of finding the back of the net in important games for his club.

Playing record	12 months lge	wcq
Appearances:	24	8
Minutes played:	1351	626
Percentage played:	38.5%	58.0%
Goals scored:	4	2
Percentage share:	5.48%	7.69%
Cards:	Y1, R0	Y1, R0
Strike rate:	338mins	313mins
Strike rate ranking:	101st	61st

AGE 24   **DREAM TEAM**   **RANKING 492**

ONE TO WATCH

YAYA TOURE BARCELONA

Central midfielder Yaya Toure joins Didier Drogba as one of the Ivory Coast's world-class players.

A terrific box-to-box midfielder with an eye for a pass, decent strength, and good defensive awareness, the midfielder has often been used as a holding midfielder for Barcelona, but has much more to his game than just defending.

Playing record	12 months lge	wcq
Appearances:	21	7
Minutes played:	1552	542
Percentage played:	44.2%	50.2%
Goals scored:	2	2
Clean sheets:	12	5
Cards:	Y2, R0	Y1, R0
Strike rate:	776mins	271mins
Midfielder ranking:	134th	22nd

AGE 27   **MIDFIELDER**   **DREAM TEAM**   **RANKING 206**

ROUTE TO THE FINALS

North Korea qualified for only their second World Cup thanks to a point away in Saudi Arabia in the final game of a marathon Asian qualifying campaign.

A staggering 9-2 aggregate win over Mongolia back in 2007 earned the nation a place in the opening group stage of the Asian qualifying process, where they were drawn alongside neighbours South Korea, Jordan and Turkmenistan.

Despite scoring just four goals in the six games, they went through the group unbeaten, winning three games and amassing twelve points, mainly thanks to a faultless defensive record, qualifying in second place behind group favourites South Korea. After a tricky draw for the fourth and final round of qualifying – including being paired with their neighbours once again – North Korea started with a 2-1 win over the United Arab Emirates. Their impressive defensive record continued as they lost just two of their next six games, leaving them in the second automatic qualifying place in Group B with one game remaining, just ahead of their final opponents, Saudi Arabia, on goal difference. The team were at their defensive best again in the winner-takes-all clash, never giving the home side a sniff as they secured the 0-0 draw that the nation needed to make it to the World Cup for the first time in over 40 years.

For final qualification table see Korea Republic.

Avge FIFA ranking

1	06 Feb 08	Away	Jordan	120	W	**0 1**	Hong 44
2	26 Mar 08	Home	Korea Republic	48	D	**0 0**	
3	02 Jun 08	Away	Turkmenistan	152	D	**0 0**	
4	07 Jun 08	Home	Turkmenistan	152	W	**1 0**	KC.Choe 72
5	14 Jun 08	Home	Jordan	120	W	**2 0**	Hong 44, 72
6	22 Jun 08	Away	Korea Republic	48	D	**0 0**	
7	06 Sep 08	Away	United Arab Emirates	113	W	**1 2**	KC.Choe 72, CH.An 80
8	10 Sep 08	Home	Korea Republic	48	D	**1 1**	Hong 64 pen
9	15 Oct 08	Away	Iran	50	L	**2 1**	Jong 72
10	11 Feb 09	Home	Saudi Arabia	55	W	**1 0**	
11	28 Mar 09	Home	United Arab Emirates	113	W	**2 0**	NC.Pak 51, Mun 90
12	01 Apr 09	Away	Korea Republic	48	L	**1 0**	
13	06 Jun 09	Home	Iran	50	D	**0 0**	
14	17 Jun 09	Away	Saudi Arabia	55	D	**0 0**	

Average FIFA ranking of opposition	84

MAIN PLAYER PERFORMANCES IN QUALIFICATION

Match	1 2 3 4 5 6 7 8 9 10 11 12 13 14	Appearances	Started	Subbed on	Subbed off	Mins played	% played	Goals	Yellow	Red
Venue	A H A H H A A H A H H H A H									
Result	W D D W W D W D L W W L D D									
Goalkeepers										
Myong Guk Ri		14	14	0	0	1260	100.0	0	2	0
Defenders										
Chol Hyok An		3	0	3	1	111	8.8	1	1	0
Jong Hyok Cha		14	12	2	1	1141	90.6	0	0	0
Yun Nam Ji		5	5	0	1	439	34.8	0	0	0
Song Chol Nam		10	9	1	0	821	65.2	0	2	0
Chol Jin Pak		12	12	0	2	986	78.3	0	0	0
Jun Il Ri		14	14	0	0	1260	100.0	0	0	0
Kwang Chon Ri		13	13	0	0	1170	92.9	0	1	0
Midfielders										
Yong Hak An		13	13	0	2	1115	88.5	0	2	0
Song Chol Han		5	3	2	1	303	24.0	0	1	0
Tae Se Jong		12	12	0	2	1077	85.5	1	4	0
Yong Jun Kim		11	8	3	7	514	40.8	0	0	1
In Guk Mun		14	14	0	3	1239	98.3	1	1	0
Nam Choi Pak Jr		6	2	4	1	324	25.7	0	0	0
Nam Choi Pak Snr		6	5	1	0	451	35.8	1	0	0
Song Chol Pak		1	1	0	0	90	7.1	0	0	0
Kwang Hyok Ri		1	1	0	0	90	7.1	0	0	0
Yong Gi Ryang		1	0	1	1	50	4.0	0	0	0
Forwards										
Kum Chol Choe		8	2	6	2	334	26.5	2	0	0
Yong Jo Hong		14	14	0	5	1121	89.0	4	1	0
Kum Il Kim		3	0	3	0	128	10.2	0	0	0
Myong Won Kim		3	0	3	0	95	7.5	0	0	0

FINAL PROSPECTS

North Korea face the toughest of tasks to make it out of qualifying after being drawn alongside Brazil, Portugal and Ivory Coast.

South Africa will be the nation's second taste of World Cup football, after they shocked the world in 1966, beating Italy to become the first ever Asian team to make it out of the first round.

However, a 5-3 defeat to Portugal in the quarter-finals – with the tournament's top-scorer Eusebio bagging four – put paid to a glamour semi-final clash with hosts England. North Korea's squad is relatively unknown, with most players yet to ply their trade outside of their home nation. Much will rely on the fitness of star man and captain in qualifying Hong Yong-Jo – who plays for Russian Premier League side FC Rostov – while young striker Jong Tae-se has a formidable striking record for both club – Japan's Kawasaki Frontale – and country and could be a threat on the counter-attack. Qualification from Group G is unlikely for a side who will need to recreate their superb defensive form from qualifying to stand any chance of picking up points against some of the best players in world football.

DREAM TEAM	TOP 15 RANKING	32

THE MANAGER

North Korea manager Kim Jong-Hun is an unknown quantity, much like his team, but has put together an efficient defensive unit who qualified with a phenomenal record of nine goals conceded in 16 matches.

Secrecy surrounding the squad – with key players rested and friendly fixtures cancelled – suggests that Jong-Hun may have a surprise or two up his sleeve for the Finals. But he will need luck on his side to even get a positive result against three strong sides in Group G. Whatever happens in South Africa, Jong-Hun will be remebered for gettng North Korea to their first finals since 1966.

GROUP FIXTURES

BRAZIL	Tue 15 June 1930 BST
PORTUGAL	Mon 21 June 1230 BST
IVORY COAST	Fri 25 June 1500 BST

Pyongyang

Zone	Asia
Population	23.5m
Language	Korean
Top league	DPR Korea League
Playing season	February - June

Major clubs and capacities
Locomotive LS (17,50), Ch'ongjin Chandongcha (15,000), Nampo April (30,000)

Where probable squad players play:

Premier League	-	Ligue 1	-
Serie A	-	Eredivisie	-
La Liga	-	Other Europe	1
Bundesliga	-	Outside Europe	22

Number of North Korean players playing:

Premier League	-	Bundesliga	-
Serie A	-	Ligue 1	-
La Liga	-	Eredivisie	1

World Cup record   * *best performance*

1930 - Did not enter	1974 - Did not qualify
1934 - Did not enter	1978 - Withdrew
1938 - Did not enter	1982 - Did not qualify
1950 - Did not enter	1986 - Did not qualify
1954 - Did not enter	1990 - Did not qualify
1958 - Did not enter	1994 - Did not qualify
1962 - Did not enter	1998 - Did not enter
1966 - * Quarter finals	2002 - Did not enter
1970 - Withdrew	2006 - Did not qualify

THE SQUAD

Goalkeepers	Club side	Age	QG
Myong Guk Ri	Pyongyang City	23	14
Kim Myong-Gil	Amrokgang	26	0
Defenders			
Chol Hyok An	Rimyongsu	24	3
Jong Hyok Cha	Amrokgang	24	14
Yun Nam Ji	April 25	24	5
Song Chol Nam	April 25	28	10
Chol Jin Pak	Amrokgang	24	12
Jun Il Ri	Sobaeksu	22	14
Kwang Chon Ri	April 25	24	13
Pak Chol-Min	Rimyongsu	21	0
Midfielders			
Yong Hak An	Suwon Bluewings	31	13
Song Chol Han	April 25	27	5
Tae Se Jong	Kawasaki Frontale	26	12
Yong Jun Kim	Chengdu Blades	26	11
In Guk Mun	April 25	31	14
Nam Choi Pak Jr	Amrokgang	21	6
Nam Choi Pak Snr	April 25	24	6
Song Chol Pak	Rimyongsu	22	1
Kwang Hyok Ri	Kyonggongop	22	1
Yong Gi Ryang	Vegalta Sendai	28	1
Kim Kuk-Jin	FC Wil 1900	21	0
Forwards			
Kum Chol Choe	Floating	23	8
Yong Jo Hong	FC Rostov	28	14
Kum Il Kim	April 25	22	3
Myong Won Kim	Amrokgang	26	3
Jong Chol-Min	Rimyongsu	21	0

■ Probable ■ Possible **QG** Qualification Games

KEY PLAYER

YONG JO HONG FC ROSTOV

Being the only man in the North Korea squad to play his football in Europe, Yong-Jo Hong is likely to come under the spotlight this summer as he tries to engineer his country's path to the knockout stages.

Captain of his country, Hong was highly instrumental in North Korea's stunning qualification for South Africa.

Playing record 12 months	lge	wcq
Appearances:	-	14
Minutes played:	-	1121
Percentage played:	-	89.0%
Goals scored:	-	4
Percentage share:	-	36.3%
Cards:	-	Y1, R0
Strike rate:	-	302mins
Strike rate ranking:	-	61st

AGE 28   **STRIKER**   **DREAM TEAM** **RANKING** 3100

ROUTE TO THE FINALS

Portugal made hard work of qualifying, scraping a play-off spot with a second-place finish in Group One, before beating Bosnia and Herzogivina 1-0 home and away to reach their third consecutive World Cup.

A routine 4-0 win away in the opening game against Malta was quickly forgotten, as a shock 3-2 defeat to Denmark in Lisbon – which saw four goals scored in the last eight minutes – set the tone for a dismal campaign by Portugal's recent high standards. Nani's first-half strike looked to have won the game for the home side, only for Nicklas Bendtner to level in the 82nd minute. A Deco penalty restored Portugal's advantage, but heartbreakingly late

goals from Christian Poulsen and Daniel Jensen consigned the group favourites to a defeat that left them facing an uphill struggle. Three straight 0-0 draws left Carlos Queiroz's side on just six points at the half-way stage of the group, trailing eventual group winners Denmark, as well as Sweden and Hungary. An injury-time winner by Bruno Alves away in Albania and a late equaliser by debutant Liedson in Denmark gave Portugal the momentum they needed to mount a late challenge for second place ahead of Sweden, before three wins in their last three games ensured Portugal entered the play-offs, where Bosnia and Herzegovina were brushed aside 2-0 on aggregate.

For final qualification table see Denmark.

Avge FIFA ranking

#	Date	Venue	Opponent	Rank	Res	Score	Scorers
1	06 Sep 08	Away	Malta	144	W	0 4	Said 24og, Hugo Almeida 61, Fonseca Sabrosa 71, Nani 78
2	10 Sep 08	Home	Denmark	30	L	2 3	Nani 42, de Souza 86pen
3	11 Oct 08	Away	Sweden	32	D	0 0	
4	15 Oct 08	Home	Albania	89	D	0 0	
5	28 Mar 09	Home	Sweden	32	D	0 0	
6	06 Jun 09	Away	Albania	89	W	1 2	Pereira de Almeida 27, Regufe Alves 90
7	05 Sep 09	Away	Denmark	30	D	1 1	da Silva Muniz 86
8	09 Sep 09	Away	Hungary	49	W	0 1	Lima Ferreira 9
9	10 Oct 09	Home	Hungary	49	W	3 0	Simao 18, 79, Liedson 73
10	14 Oct 09	Home	Malta	144	W	4 0	Nani 14, Simao 45, Miguel 52, Edinho 90
11	14 Nov 09	Home	Bosnia	57	W	1 0	Bruno Alves 31
12	18 Nov 09	Away	Bosnia	57	W	0 1	Meireles 56

Average FIFA ranking of opposition	67

MAIN PLAYER PERFORMANCES IN QUALIFICATION

Match	1 2 3 4 5 6 7 8 9 10 11 12	Appearances	Started	Subbed on	Subbed off	Mins played	% played	Goals	Yellow	Red
Venue	A H A H H A A A H H H A									
Result	W L D D D W D W W W W W									
Goalkeepers										
Eduardo		8	8	0	0	720	66.7	0	0	0
Quim		4	4	0	0	360	33.3	0	0	0
Defenders										
Jose Bosingwa		9	9	0	1	764	70.7	0	1	0
Fernando Meira		1	1	0	0	90	8.3	0	0	0
Miguel		3	2	1	1	175	16.2	1	0	0
Pepe		11	11	0	0	990	91.7	1	3	0
Vitorino Antunes		1	1	0	0	90	8.3	0	0	0
Rolando		2	0	2	0	47	4.4	0	0	0
Paulo Ferreira		5	5	0	0	450	41.7	0	0	0
Bruno Alves		9	9	0	0	810	75.0	2	0	0
Ricardo Carvalho		10	10	0	1	885	81.9	0	0	0
Midfielders										
Danny		4	2	2	2	143	13.2	0	1	0
Duda		7	7	0	0	630	58.3	0	1	0
Tiago		5	4	1	3	292	27.0	0	0	0
Pedro Mendes		2	2	0	0	180	16.7	0	0	0
Deco		10	8	2	2	710	65.7	1	1	0
Simao Sabrosa		10	8	2	6	729	67.5	4	1	0
Joao Moutinho		5	2	3	1	181	16.8	0	0	0
Carlos Martins		2	2	0	1	152	14.1	0	0	0
Manuel Fernandes		1	1	0	0	90	8.3	0	0	0
Raul Meireles		12	12	0	2	1042	96.5	1	1	0
Forwards										
Nani		11	6	5	5	618	57.2	3	1	0
Liedson		6	5	1	4	449	41.6	2	1	0
Cristiano Ronaldo		7	7	0	1	565	52.3	0	0	0
Hugo Almeida		7	5	2	4	388	35.9	2	0	0
Ricardo Quaresma		2	0	2	0	62	5.7	0	1	0
Nuno Gomes		5	0	5	0	76	7.0	0	0	0

FINAL PROSPECTS

Despite a dismal qualification campaign, Portugal are likely to be one of the teams to avoid in the knock out stages... as long they make it out of a particularly tough group.

Semi-finalists in 2006, Portugal have been a force to be reckoned with on the international stage over the last decade, which makes the fact that South Africa will be just their fifth taste of World Cup football even more surprising.

An appearance back in 1966 saw the legendary Eusebio finish top-scorer with nine goals as he led Portugal to the semi-finals, but the nation had to wait another 20 years before they qualified again.

Back-to-back World Cup appearances in 2002 and 2006, as well as decent displays in recent European Championships, mean that this talented group of players shouldn't be discounted as title outsiders.

How to fit so many top-drawer creative players in one team is a problem that most would struggle to solve.

Cristiano Ronaldo is the star man, supported by a talented crop of attacking players including vice-captain Simao Sabrosa, Deco and Nani.

Tiago, Miguel Veloso, Raul Meireles and Joao Moutinho offer creative options in the centre of midfield, while a decent group of defenders – Ricardo Carvalho, Bruno Alves, Jose Bosingwa and Pepe – are at the core of a quality unit that kept five successive clean sheets at the end of qualifying.

With so many Portuguese players excelling at club level across Europe, the poor performance of the national side in qualifying has been partly blamed on manager Carlos Queiroz, whose tactics and selections have been confusing at times.

How to fit so many top-drawer creative players in one team is a problem that most would struggle to solve.

An opening game against Ivory Coast will be crucial to Portugal's hopes of making the knock out stages. Anything other than a win over North Korea would be a huge disappointment. Queiroz will want to have qualification sewn up before the final group game against Brazil, but the possibility of a head-to-head qualification match-up between the two is one of the most exciting clashes in the whole of the tournament's group stage.

DREAM TEAM	TOP 15 RANKING	9

GROUP FIXTURES

IVORY COAST	Tue 15 June 1500 BST
NORTH KOREA	Mon 21 June 1230 BST
BRAZIL	Fri 25 June 1500 BST

●Lisbon

Zone	Europe
Population	10.6m
Language	Portuguese
Top league	Portuguese Liga Sagres
Playing season	August - May

Major clubs and capacities
FC Porto (52,000), Sporting Lisbon (52,000), Benfica (65,000)

Where probable squad players play:

Premier League	5	Ligue 1	-
Serie A	-	Eredivisie	-
La Liga	6	Other Europe	11
Bundesliga	1	Outside Europe	-

Number of Portuguese players playing:

Premier League	7	Bundesliga	4
Serie A	5	Ligue 1	3
La Liga	13	Eredivisie	1

World Cup record   *** best performance**

1930 - Did not qualify	1974 -	Did not qualify
1934 - Did not qualify	1978 -	Did not qualify
1938 - Did not qualify	1982 -	Did not qualify
1950 - Did not qualify	1986 -	Round 1
1954 - Did not qualify	1990 -	Did not qualify
1958 - Did not qualify	1994 -	Did not qualify
1962 - Did not qualify	1998 -	Did not qualify
1966 - 3rd place	2002 -	Round 1
1970 - Did not qualify	2006 -	* Semi finals

THE SQUAD

	Club side	Age	QG
Goalkeepers			
Eduardo	Braga	27	8
Quim	Benfica	34	4
Defenders			
Jose Bosingwa	Chelsea	27	9
Fernando Meira	Zenit St Petersburg	32	1
Miguel	Valencia	30	3
Pepe	Real Madrid	27	11
Vitorino Antunes	Leixoes	23	1
Rolando	Porto	24	2
Paulo Ferreira	Chelsea	31	5
Bruno Alves	Porto	28	9
Ricardo Carvalho	Chelsea	32	10
Midfielders			
Danny	Zenit St Petersburg	26	4
Duda	Malaga	29	7
Tiago	Atl Madrid	29	5
Pedro Mendes	Rangers	31	2
Deco	Chelsea	32	10
Simao Sabrosa	Atl Madrid	30	10
Joao Moutinho	Sp Lisbon	23	5
Carlos Martins	Benfica	28	2
Raul Meireles	Porto	27	12
Forwards			
Nani	Man Utd	23	11
Liedson	Sp Lisbon	32	6
Cristiano Ronaldo	Real Madrid	25	7
Hugo Almeida	W Bremen	26	7
Ricardo Quaresma	Inter Milan	26	2
Nuno Gomes	Benfica	33	5

■ Probable ■ Possible **QG** Qualification Games

KEY PLAYER

RICARDO CARVALHO CHELSEA

Perhaps one of the most underrated defenders in world football, Ricardo Carvalho is the bedrock on which Portugal lay their foundations.

The centre-back's career exploded in 2004 when he was named UEFA Defender of the Year as Porto won the Champions League. He's guided Chelsea to domestic success and will be vital for Portugal.

Playing record	12 months lge	wcq
Appearances:	19	10
Minutes played:	1654	885
Percentage played:	47.1%	81.9%
Goals conceded:	20	5
Clean sheets:	9	7
Cards:	Y5, R0	Y0, R0
Minutes between goals:	83mins	177mins
Defender ranking:	69th	39th

AGE 32   **DEFENDER**   **DREAM TEAM RANKING** 395

KEY GOALKEEPERS

EDUARDO
BRAGA

Playing record	12 months lge	wcq
Appearances:	-	8
Minutes played:	-	720
Percentage played:	-	66.7%
Goals conceded:	-	2
Clean sheets:	-	6
Cards:	-	Y0, R0
Minutes between goals:	-	360mins
Goalkeeper ranking:	-	1st

AGE 27	DREAM TEAM	RANKING 310

QUIM
BENFICA

Playing record	12 months lge	wcq
Appearances:	-	4
Minutes played:	-	360
Percentage played:	-	33.3%
Goals conceded:	-	3
Clean sheets:	-	3
Cards:	-	Y0, R0
Minutes between goals:	-	120mins
Goalkeeper ranking:	-	17th

AGE 34	DREAM TEAM	RANKING 380

KEY DEFENDERS

PEPE
REAL MADRID

One of the most expensive defenders in history, Pepe is set to test his reputation at the world's greatest football tournament for the first time. Real Madrid splashed out €30 million to acquire the centre back from Porto in 2007.

Playing record	12 months lge	wcq
Appearances:	25	11
Minutes played:	2189	990
Percentage played:	62.4%	91.7%
Goals conceded:	15	5
Clean sheets:	16	8
Cards:	Y5, R1	Y3, R0
Minutes between goals:	146mins	198mins
Defender ranking:	6th	29th

JOSE BOSINGWA
CHELSEA

A pacey, skilful Brazilian-style full back who never misses an opportunity to hare down the right flank, Jose Bosingwa has come into his own over the last two years. Making his international debut in 2007, and joining Chelsea a year later, Bosingwa's performances have seen him emerge as one of the best right-backs in the world.

Playing record	12 months lge	wcq
Appearances:	22	9
Minutes played:	1819	764
Percentage played:	51.8%	70.7%
Goals conceded:	17	5
Clean sheets:	10	6
Cards:	Y3, R0	Y1, R0
Minutes between goals:	107mins	153mins
Defender ranking:	20th	48th

AGE 27	DREAM TEAM	RANKING 280

KEY MIDFIELDERS

DECO
CHELSEA

The focal point around which Portugal's attacking exploits have centered since Luis Figo's retirement, Deco is perhaps the ultimate luxury player.

The Brazilian-born midfielder is never happier than when sitting behind strikers and threading passes through defences. His first call up to the national team was controversial but a debut goal, ironically against Brazil, helped win over the Portugal supporters. Match-winning displays at Euro 2004 followed, a red card against Holland at the 2006 World Cup stained his reputation. At club level he has enjoyed tremendous success, winning the Champions League with Porto and Barcelona. One criticism aimed at Deco is his poor goalscoring record – he averages a goal every 14 games.

Playing record	12 months lge	wcq
Appearances:	18	10
Minutes played:	891	710
Percentage played:	25.4%	65.7%
Goals scored:	2	1
Clean sheets:	11	7
Cards:	Y1, R0	Y1, R0
Strike rate:	445mins	710mins
Midfielder ranking:	82nd	65th

RAUL MEIRELES
PORTO

Playing record	12 months lge	wcq
Appearances:	-	12
Minutes played:	-	1042
Percentage played:	-	96.5%
Goals scored:	-	1
Clean sheets:	-	9
Cards:	-	Y1, R0
Strike rate:	-	1042mins
Midfielder ranking:	-	-

AGE 27	DREAM TEAM	RANKING 497

THE MANAGER

Question marks remain over Carlos Queiroz's leadership skills and tactical nous after a disappointing qualification campaign.

After never really making it as a player, Queiroz turned to coaching, nurturing the Portuguese 'golden generation' as under-20 coach and leading South Africa to the 2002 World Cup.

A disappointing spell in charge of Real Madrid was a low point, but Queiroz's subsequent return to Manchester United saw him achieve further success at Old Trafford as assistant to Sir Alex Ferguson.

His preference for a 4-5-1 formation seems to fit the players at his disposal, but Portugal have struggled for fluency since Queiroz's appointment as national team manager in July 2008.

Portugal will have to put in a performance in South Africa to prove that they are still the top class side they were a few years ago, and Queiroz will have his work cut out.

KEY STRIKER

NANI
MAN UTD

A raw, lightning-quick two-footed winger in the Cristiano Ronaldo mould, Nani could finally be ready to step out of his team-mate's shadow.

He has been forced to play second fiddle at both club and international level for the last three years to Cristiano Ronaldo, with whom he has so much in common. Immaturity has been holding Nani back but recent performances for Manchester United have suggested he has blossomed into a potentially world-beating footballer. Nani moved from Sporting Lisbon to United in 2007 and immediately impressed with his fleet-footed dribbling and long-range shooting. Nani came to the fore in World Cup 2010 qualification, making 11 appearances.

Playing record	12 months lge	wcq
Appearances:	14	11
Minutes played:	788	618
Percentage played:	21.4%	57.2%
Goals scored:	1	3
Percentage share:	-	-
Cards:	Y0, R0	Y1, R0
Strike rate:	-	206mins
Strike rate ranking:	226th	12th

AGE 23   **DREAM TEAM** **RANKING 1347**

ONE TO WATCH

CRISTIANO RONALDO REAL MADRID

Often regarded as the finest footballer on the planet, expectations surrounding Cristiano Ronaldo at this summer's World Cup are inevitably sky high.

However the man who has every possible attacking attribute contained within his armoury, and who enthralls and delights millions of football fans around the world week in week out, would surely have it no other way. Able to play on either flank or up front, Ronaldo's exceptional pace, dribbling ability and goalscoring exploits led Manchester United to two successive Champions League finals. Ronaldo has changed many a game in one fell swoop and his list of individual and club honours is endless. Ronaldo has the world at his feet.

Ronaldo is a Top 12 Striker

AGE 25   **STRIKER**   **DREAM TEAM** **RANKING 4**

Position	1st	2nd	3rd	4th	5th	6th	7th	8th
Group	E	D	B	H	A	G	F	C
Total FIFA ranking	88	89	98	104	130	147	160	161

HONDURAS V CHILE
Nelspruit, Wednesday 16 June 1230 BST

Two vastly underrated sides, Honduras and Chile will both have high hopes of making it out of the group, but are likely to need to win this game to do so. The nation celebrated when Honduras qualified for only their second World Cup, but the team have enough proven quality to cause the South Americans problems. Chile swept through qualification on a fantastic run of form, playing some scintillating attacking football and will be disappointed if they don't make the last 16. But probably lack the quality to go much further than that. Humberto Suazo spearheads an attack who will fancy their chances against the Honduras defence.

SPAIN V SWITZERLAND
Durban, Wednesday 16 June 1500 BST

One of the less glamorous sides at the tournament, Switzerland are consistent overachievers. An organised defence has been the bedrock of the team's success over recent years, but they will struggle to contain a Spain side that is magical going forward. The Euro 2008 Champions have got their last two tournaments off to explosive starts. They will expect to do the same against Switzerland, with Fernando Torres and David Villa both aiming to get on the scoreboard early in the tournament. The underdogs will look to hit Spain on the break when possible, but aren't likely to see a great deal of the ball.

Chile's Humberto Suazo

CHILE V SWITZERLAND
Bloemfontein, Monday 21 June 1500 BST

With Spain expected to win the group at a canter, the fight to join them in the last 16 is impossible to call. Chile play some fluid football and score plenty of goals – 32 in qualifying, as many as Brazil – and have a real threat up front in Humberto Suazo. But they won't have it all their own way as Switzerland are tough to break down and offer plenty going forward, particularly if Alexander Frei is fit and in form.

SPAIN V HONDURAS
Durban, Monday 21 June 1930 BST

Wilson Palacios has earned a terrific reputation during his time in the Premier League, but will need to be at his very best at the heart of the Honduras midfield if they are to get anything out of a game against one of the tournament favourites. Xavi and Andres Iniesta run rings around the best, and it will be tough enough for the Hondurans to even get the ball up the other end of the pitch.

CHILE V SPAIN
Pretoria, Friday 25 June 1930 BST

Spain will fully expect to have already bagged a place in the second round by the time they face Chile, but if their fate still hangs in the balance then they could be in for a shock against a side who play some great football and score goals freely. The Spanish defence rarely gets fully tested, but the joint top goal-scorers in South American qualifying have enough going forward to give Iker Casillas a testing afternoon between the sticks. Chile's passing game may play straight into the hands of their European opponents, but if Spain have already qualified and give some of their squad players a run-out then there is real potential for an upset here. Marcelo Bielsa's side will be up against it if they need a win to qualify.

SWITZERLAND V HONDURAS
Bloemfontein , Friday 25 June 1930 BST

If either of these teams still have a chance of qualification for the last 16 then this should be hugely entertaining game. With the two attractive teams in the group battling it out in the other game, this match is an opportunity for one of these teams to stamp their mark on the tournament. Even if qualification is out of the question for Switzerland or Honduras, expect them to put in a good showing to end their tournament on a high.

VIEW FROM THE EXPERTS

SPAIN: A superb team that could easily win the trophy. They have a fantastic squad with great midfielders and a world-class striker in the shape of Torres. The Spaniards will not disappoint as they have done at previous World Cups and will be a real threat to England's chances.
HARRY'S VERDICT: Semi finals.
SWITZERLAND: A good side but I can't see them having enough firepower or defensive strength to hold back Spain and the other rivals. Only lasted the minimum three matches at Euro 2008 and nothing has radically changed in the Swiss camp since then.
HARRY'S VERDICT: Group stage only.
HONDURAS: I'd love to see them make it through the group even if only for Wilson Palacios, my midfielder at Tottenham who has endured terrible sadness with the kidnap and murder of his brother. Wigan defender Figueroa is another familiar name to English fans but I feel they'll be heading home after three matches.
HARRY'S VERDICT: Group stage only.
CHILE: A bit of a resurgence going on in Chilean football with several players out to make a name for themselves in front of a world audience in South Africa. I can see them snatching second place behind Spain and enjoying a bit of a run.
HARRY'S VERDICT: Last 16.

SPAIN: The Spaniards will be looking to add the World Cup to the European Championship they won two years ago, and you have to say they have every chance of accomplishing that. They have so many talented players, such as Fabregas, Iniesta, Xavi and Torres that, just like Brazil, it is impossible to back against them.
TEL'S VERDICT: Going all the way.
SWITZERLAND: The Swiss impressed at the last World Cup. But Ottmar Hitzfeld's team are blighted by inconsistency, as their qualifying campaign showed when they suffered a shock defeat to Luxembourg before embarking on an eight-match unbeaten run.
TEL'S VERDICT: Too unpredictable to call.
HONDURAS: Qualified for the finals against the backdrop of a military coup in their country, so we can't say their players lack focus on the job in hand. What they do lack, however, is experience with this being only the second finals they have reached. The previous one was in 1982.
TEL'S VERDICT: Group stage only.

CHILE: Reckoned to be the most attractive team in South America at the moment, even more than Brazil, their first appearance at the finals since 1998 is bound to be entertaining, certainly if their qualification is anything to go by as they conceded 22 goals.

TEL'S VERDICT: Face a battle with Swiss to get out of group.

SPAIN: They used to be the team that always choked at major tournaments, but not any more. Their success at Euro 2008 has given the Spaniards a level of belief to match their undoubted talent. Expect Torres, Fabregas, Xavi, Iniesta and co. to have a major say and prove why they are my joint-favourites with Brazil.

WRIGHTY'S VERDICT: Viva Espana. Spain to cruise on and upwards.

SWITZERLAND: The Swiss impressed at the last World Cup, where they did not concede a single goal prior to a second-round penalty shoot-out loss against Ukraine, and the experience that will come from co-hosting Euro 2008 should put them in good shape for South Africa.

WRIGHTY'S VERDICT: Lack of quality could cost them.

HONDURAS: Reaching the finals was a major achievement for a country that has Wilson Palacios and Wigan duo Hendry Thomas and Maynor Figueroa in their ranks. Getting past the group stage would be an even bigger feat.

WRIGHTY'S VERDICT: Potential to cause an upset.

CHILE: One of the youngest squads at the finals with an average age of 23. But with players like Matias Fernandez and Jorge Valdivia and the goal-scoring prowess of strikers Alexis Sanchez and Humberto Suazo. Chile could well be one to keep an eye on and could well upset a few sides.

WRIGHTY'S VERDICT: Keep an eye on them.

"They have so many talented players, such as Fabregas, Iniesta, Xavi and Torres it is impossible to back against them"

THE LIKELY ROUTES FOR THE TOP TWO TEAMS FROM THE GROUP

For the full draw please see page 80

GROUP STAGE

FIRST GROUP H

SPAIN

SECOND GROUP H

CHILE

LAST SIXTEEN

v SECOND GROUP G

SPAIN v PORTUGAL

v FIRST GROUP G

CHILE v BRAZIL

QUARTER-FINALS

v FIRST GROUP F or SECOND GROUP E

SPAIN v ITALY

v FIRST GROUP E or SECOND GROUP F

BRAZIL v NETHERLANDS

GROUP H
SPAIN, SWITZERLAND, HONDURAS, CHILE

GROUP G
BRAZIL, NORTH KOREA (KOREA DPR), IVORY COAST, PORTUGAL

GROUP E
NETHERLANDS, DENMARK, JAPAN, CAMEROON

GROUP F
ITALY, PARAGUAY, NEW ZEALAND, SLOVAKIA

ROUTE TO THE FINALS

Fresh from their triumph in the 2008 European Championships, Spain waltzed through qualifying with the best record of any European team to reach the World Cup finals.

Their 100% record was constructed over two more games than the Dutch and only England averaged more goals in qualifying.

A 5-0 win over Belgium was the highlight, with Valencia duo David Villa and David Silva both scoring twice. Striker Villa was in prolific form throughout qualifying, continuing his terrific scoring record for the national team with seven goals.

With the squad seemingly even stronger than in 2008, Spain's performances in qualifying simply confirmed their status as the team to beat in South Africa.

FINAL QUALIFYING TABLE
EUROPE GROUP 5

	P	W	D	L	F	A	Pts
Spain	10	10	0	0	28	5	30
Bosnia-Herz	10	6	1	3	25	13	19
Turkey	10	4	3	3	13	10	15
Belgium	10	3	1	6	13	20	10
Estonia	10	2	2	6	9	24	8
Armenia	10	1	1	8	6	22	4

					FIFA ranking		Result		
1	06 Sep 08	Home	Bosnia	57	W	1	0	Villa Sanchez 58
2	10 Sep 08	Home	Armenia	110	W	4	0	Capdevila 7, Villa Sanchez 16, 79, Senna 83
3	11 Oct 08	Away	Estonia	119	W	0	3	Moreno 34, Villa Sanchez 38pen, Puyol Saforcada 69
4	15 Oct 08	Away	Belgium	56	W	1	2	Iniesta Lujan 36, Villa Sanchez 88
5	28 Mar 09	Home	Turkey	17	W	1	0	Pique 60
6	01 Apr 09	Away	Turkey	17	W	1	2	Alonso 63pen, Riera 90
7	05 Sep 09	Home	Belgium	56	W	5	0	Jimenez Silva 40, 67, Villa Sanchez 46, 84, Pique 60
8	09 Sep 09	Home	Estonia	119	W	3	0	Fabregas 32, Cazorla Gonzalez 81, Mata 90
9	10 Oct 09	Away	Armenia	110	W	1	2	Fabregas 32, Mata 63pen
10	14 Oct 09	Away	Bosnia	57	W	2	5	Pique 13, Silva 14, Negredo 50, 55, Mata 89

Average FIFA ranking of opposition	72

MAIN PLAYER PERFORMANCES IN QUALIFICATION

Key: ■ played 90 mins ◄◄ subbed off ►► subbed on ▨ on bench

Match	1 2 3 4 5 6 7 8 9 10	Appearances	Started	Subbed on	Subbed off	Mins played	% played	Goals	Yellow	Red
Venue	H H A A H H H H A A									
Result	W W W W W W W W W W									
Goalkeepers										
Iker Casillas		9	9	0	0	810	90.0	0	0	0
Jose Reina		1	1	0	0	90	10.0	0	0	0
Defenders										
Raul Albiol		6	5	1	0	459	51.0	0	0	0
Alvaro Arbeloa		1	1	0	1	81	9.0	0	0	0
Joan Capdevila		9	9	0	0	810	90.0	1	0	0
Andoni Iraola		2	1	1	0	127	14.1	0	1	0
Carlos Marchena		3	3	0	1	225	25.0	0	1	0
Nacho Monreal		1	1	0	0	90	10.0	0	0	0
Juanito		2	2	0	0	180	20.0	1	0	0
Gerard Pique		6	5	1	1	481	53.4	3	0	0
Carles Puyol		6	6	0	0	540	60.0	1	4	0
Sergio Ramos		8	7	1	1	607	67.4	0	1	0
Midfielders										
Xabi Alonso		8	5	3	0	537	59.7	1	0	0
Sergi Busquets		3	2	1	0	196	21.8	0	1	0
Diego Capel		1	1	0	1	71	7.9	0	0	0
Santiago Cazorla		8	5	3	3	453	50.3	1	0	0
Francesc Fabregas		7	3	4	1	378	42.0	2	1	0
Xavi		9	9	0	2	771	85.7	0	1	0
Andres Iniesta		6	5	1	3	433	48.1	1	2	0
David Silva		5	4	1	3	336	37.3	3	0	0
Juan Mata		4	1	3	1	114	12.7	3	0	0
Albert Riera Ortega		4	2	2	0	217	24.1	1	0	0
Marcos Senna		8	7	1	1	630	70.0	1	0	0
Forwards										
Daniel Guiza		5	1	4	1	107	11.9	0	0	0
Bojan		1	0	1	0	26	2.9	0	0	0
Fernando Llorente		1	0	1	0	3	0.3	0	0	0
Alvaro Negredo		2	1	1	0	127	14.1	2	0	0
Fernando Torres		7	7	0	6	451	50.1	0	0	0
David Villa		7	7	0	4	550	61.1	7	0	0

FINAL PROSPECTS

Spain are ranked as a favourite to lift the trophy in South Africa, along with five-time champions Brazil.

This will be Spain's 12th visit to a World Cup finals, but they have yet to even make it to a final – a terrible record for a country that has consistently been one of the most talented in the world.

Victory in Euro 2008 was only their second major title, but was achieved in style, and the core of that side remain in place going into South Africa.

A strike partnership of Fernando Torres and David Villa is the best in the world by some distance, and, as ever, Spain have an abundance of quality in midfield. Barcelona duo Xavi and Andres Iniesta pull the strings, ably supported by the talented David Silva – who has fought off quality opposition to tie down a spot on the left of midfield. Much of the praise for Spain's improvement in 2008 was directed towards defensive midfielder Marcos Senna, but he is far from guaranteed a place in the first XI in South Africa, with Sergio Busquets of Barcelona and Real Madrid's Xabi Alonso in the squad as more youthful and creative alternatives.

Spain have an abundance of quality in midfield

The fact that Cesc Fabregas hasn't even been mentioned yet is an indication of just how strong the Spanish midfield is. In tough games it isn't out of the question that Villa's place might be sacrificed to allow a second deeper-lying midfielder to come in and protect the back line.

If Spain have a weakness then it is their defence, although opponents may not see enough of the ball to really test the back-four. Joan Capdevila and Sergio Ramos are decent full-backs, although Ramos' attacking instincts may see him leave the central defenders exposed, particularly with no out-and-out right midfielder to track back. Carles Puyol and Gerard Pique offer a combination of physical presence and a more cultured approach in an all-Barca centre-back partnership, with Alvaro Arbeloa a versatile replacement for all positions.

Goalkeeper Iker Casillas is one of the best around, but will need to keep his concentration in games when the ball is likely to spend most of the time at the other end of the pitch. Group H should be straightforward for a team as talented as Spain, and if they are knocked out early on then it will be a major shock.

DREAM TEAM TOP 15 RANKING 1

GROUP FIXTURES

SWITZERLAND	Wed 16 June 1500 BST
HONDURAS	Mon 21 June 1930 BST
CHILE	Fri 25 June 1930 BST

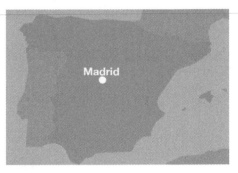

Madrid

Zone	Europe
Population	40.5m
Language	Spanish
Top league	La Liga
Playing season	September - June

Major clubs and capacities
Real Madrid (80,440), Barcelona (98,772), Valencia (55,848)

Where probable squad players play:

Premier League	4	Ligue 1	-
Serie A	-	Eredivisie	-
La Liga	18	Other Europe	1
Bundesliga	-	Outside Europe	-

Number of Spanish players playing:

Premier League	14	Bundesliga	-
Serie A	3	Ligue 1	1
La Liga	361	Eredivisie	4

World Cup record   ** best performance*

1930 - Did not enter	1974 -	Did not qualify
1934 - Quarter finals	1978 -	Round 1
1938 - Banned	1982 -	Round 2
1950 - * 4th place	1986 -	Quarter finals
1954 - Did not qualify	1990 -	Last 16
1958 - Did not qualify	1994 -	Quarter finals
1962 - Round 1	1998 -	Round 1
1966 - Round 1	2002 -	Quarter finals
1970 - Did not qualify	2006 -	Last 16

KEY PLAYER

FERNANDO TORRES LIVERPOOL

One of the deadliest strikers in world football, Fernando Torres has been a big contributing factor to Spain's recent success - they are ranked the best in the world and one of the firm favourites for the tournament.

Tall and powerful, he is as strong as he is skilful and while he may not have scored as many goals for country as he has for Liverpool in the last couple of years, his pace and physical presence are a key part of Spain's plans in attack. When he does score, though, it is often in the big games as he proved in the final of Euro 2008 when his first half goal sealed Spain's win over Germany and earned him the man-of-the-match award.

Torres is a Top 12 Striker

AGE 26   STRIKER   DREAM TEAM   RANKING 13

THE SQUAD

Goalkeepers	Club side	Age	QG
Iker Casillas	Real Madrid	29	9
Jose Reina	Liverpool	27	1
Defenders			
Raul Albiol	Real Madrid	24	6
Alvaro Arbeloa	Real Madrid	27	1
Joan Capdevila	Villarreal	32	9
Andoni Iraola	Athl Bilbao	27	2
Carlos Marchena	Valencia	30	3
Nacho Monreal	Osasuna	24	1
Juanito	Atl Madrid	33	2
Gerard Pique	Barcelona	23	6
Carles Puyol	Barcelona	32	6
Sergio Ramos	Real Madrid	24	8
Midfielders			
Xabi Alonso	Real Madrid	28	8
Sergi Busquets	Barcelona	21	3
Santiago Cazorla	Villarreal	25	8
Francesc Fabregas	Arsenal	23	7
Xavi	Barcelona	30	9
Andres Iniesta	Barcelona	26	6
David Silva	Valencia	24	5
Juan Mata	Valencia	22	4
Albert Riera	Liverpool	28	4
Marcos Senna	Villarreal	33	8
Forwards			
Daniel Gonzalez Guiza	Fenerbahce	29	5
Alvaro Negredo	Sevilla	24	2
Fernando Torres	Liverpool	26	7
David Villa	Valencia	28	7

■ Probable ■ Possible **QG** Qualification Games

KEY GOALKEEPERS

IKER CASILLAS
REAL MADRID

All set to become the most capped Spain international of all time, Iker Casillas will surely go down as one of the best ever Spanish keepers.

After breaking into the Galactico filled Madrid side of the late 90's, the teenager was often required to be a one man defence with the ultra attacking Zidane and Co. giving him little cover.

Casillas is a Top 4 goalkeeper.

JOSE REINA
LIVERPOOL

Playing record	12 months lge	wcq
Appearances:	38	1
Minutes played:	3420	90
Percentage played:	97.4%	10.0%
Goals conceded:	39	1
Clean sheets:	16	0
Cards:	Y1, R0	Y0, R0
Minutes between goals:	88mins	-
Goalkeeper ranking:	-	11th

AGE 27	DREAM TEAM RANKING 28

KEY DEFENDERS

GERARD PIQUE
BARCELONA

A big physical centre back, still maturing as a player, Gerard Pique will only be 24 at the World Cup and has made a big impact in a short space of time for Spain.

In competition with Carlos Marchena to partner Pique's club captain at Barcelona, Carles Puyol, he scored three goals in six games in qualifying and will be a big part of Spain's tournament.

Pique is a Top 12 defender.

JOAN CAPDEVILA
VILLARREAL

An ultra attacking left-back, Joan Capdevila is crucial to the makeup of the Spain side and as such, no player played more minutes in qualifying.

Having sealed his place in the squad during Euro 2008 when he played all but one game, he will be one of the most experienced heads in the side in South Africa.

Playing record	12 months lge	wcq
Appearances:	36	9
Minutes played:	3203	810
Percentage played:	93.7%	90.0%
Goals conceded:	50	5
Clean sheets:	7	6
Cards:	Y7, R0	Y0, R0
Minutes between goals:	64mins	162mins
Defender ranking:	135th	44th

AGE 32	DREAM TEAM RANKING 73

SERGIO RAMOS
REAL MADRID

When he moved to Real Madrid from Seville in 2005, 19-year old Sergio Ramos became the most expensive player to move within La Liga and the second most expensive teenager in history with Madrid paying a reported 27 million euros.

It is testament to the youngster's talent and maturity that, despite the enormous pressure that came with the move, he has been a big hit at Madrid and translated this onto the international stage.

Comfortable playing fullback, centre-back or even as a defensive midfielder, Ramos usually plays right-back for club and country and was a regular there for Spain during qualifying in what has become a well established back four.

A gifted natural all-round footballer with great delivery from the flanks plus impressive passing, pace and a decent shot, Ramos is also pretty handy in the air. He was an ever present throughout the victorious Euro 2008 finals, where his presence on the right side of a solid defensive unit was a key part of Spain's success.

Playing record	12 months lge	wcq
Appearances:	33	8
Minutes played:	2869	607
Percentage played:	81.7%	67.4%
Goals conceded:	31	5
Clean sheets:	18	4
Cards:	Y14, R1	Y1, R0
Minutes between goals:	93mins	121mins
Defender ranking:	-	48th

AGE 24	DREAM TEAM RANKING 43

THE MANAGER

Vincente del Bosque took over as Spain boss after their Euro 2008 triumph. A former defensive midfielder, Del Bosque made over 300 appearances for Real Madrid and was a popular choice when appointed manager of the club in 1999.

In charge during the first 'Galacticos' era, he led Real to their most consistent run of success in the modern era, winning two Champions Leagues and two La Liga titles between 2000 and 2003. Let go by Real in favour of Carlos Queiroz, he failed to impress in his next job – at Besiktas – lasting less than a season in Turkey.

Manager of the current Spanish national team is not a tough job, with a host of the world's top players at his disposal and confidence on a high after Euro 2008, but he did lead the side through qualifying with a 100% record.

Injury to Andres Iniesta ensured he avoided the headache of how to set up the Spain midfield, but he has shown a willingness to bring fresh faces into an established squad – with Barcelona's Sergi Busquets a good example.

Yet to be truly tested, Del Bosque will need to show he has tactical nous and the ability to make the right substitutions at the right times if Spain are to win their first ever World Cup in South Africa.

CARLES PUYOL
BARCELONA

Every side needs at least one player like Carles Puyol and his heart-on-sleeve, no nonsense and physical style make him a perfect centre-half.

He is the long term captain at Barcelona - where he has won trophy after trophy - and the inspiration he provides and dogged approach are the perfect foil to some of his more silky skilled team-mates. Having started his career as a marauding right back, he matured superbly into a place in the centre and has been a mainstay of Spain's side for the best part of a decade. If Spain manage to make a serious impact in South Africa, Puyol will be key.

Playing record	12 months lge	wcq
Appearances:	27	6
Minutes played:	2354	540
Percentage played:	67.1%	60.0%
Goals conceded:	25	2
Clean sheets:	12	4
Cards:	Y6, R0	Y4, R0
Minutes between goals:	94mins	270mins
Defender ranking:	-	45th

AGE 32 **DREAM TEAM** **RANKING** 50

KEY PLAYER

XAVI BARCELONA

One of the most effective central midfield playmakers in world football, Xavi is an extremely intelligent footballer and uses his immaculate technique and speed of thought to run rings around most teams.

Never hurried in possession and with superb distribution, the lifelong Barcelona fan and player graces the middle of the park at the Nou Camp and also for Spain with fellow Barca stalwart, Andres Iniesta. Player of the tournament at Euro 2008, he scored in the semi-final and provided the assist for Fernando Torres to score the winning goal in the final. A player who makes this game look so simple, Xavi might be the most crucial of all Spain's great assets.

Xavi is a Top 12 midfielder.

AGE 30 **MIDFIELDER** **DREAM TEAM** **RANKING** 1

KEY MIDFIELDERS

FRANCESC FABREGAS
ARSENAL

One of the finest midfield playmakers in modern football, Cesc Fabregas is mature beyond his 23-years and the current captain of Arsenal.

A prodigious talent from a young age, Fabregas rose through the youth ranks at Barcelona before joining Arsenal and becoming the youngest player to play, and score a goal for, the club at just 16. He was a first team regular by 18 and was the man pulling the strings for Arsene Wenger's fiercely talented side, playing a brand of football that was leaving the pundits struggling for superlatives. Simply put, Fabregas understands football and has the innate ability to put the ball where he wants to, picking passes that few others would be able to see, let alone execute. If he gets his chance in South Africa, he will not disappoint.

Playing record	12 months lge	wcq
Appearances:	23	7
Minutes played:	1846	378
Percentage played:	51.3%	42.0%
Goals scored:	11	2
Clean sheets:	9	6
Cards:	Y4, R0	Y1, R0
Strike rate:	168mins	189mins
Midfielder ranking:	14th	10th

AGE 23	DREAM TEAM	RANKING 161

MARCOS SENNA
VILLARREAL

A composed, skilful central midfielder with a thunderbolt of a shot, Marcos Senna was born in Brazil but has represented Spain since he became eligible to do so in 2006.

Something of a late starter, Senna was on the books at a number of Brazilian clubs – including Corinthians – but made very few appearances before moving to Spain, joining Villarreal in 2002 at the age of 26. He spent two seasons on the periphery before bursting into life as a starter and then being installed captain as the Yellow Submarines got to the semi-finals of the Champions League in 2006. Having been granted Spanish citizenship, he was called up to the side by Luis Aragones and went to the 2006 World Cup. A good passer and tenacious in the tackle, he plays a holding role for Spain, allowing Xavi and Andres Iniesta to roam.

Playing record	12 months lge	wcq
Appearances:	24	8
Minutes played:	1948	630
Percentage played:	55.5%	70.0%
Goals scored:	0	1
Clean sheets:	9	4
Cards:	Y7, R0	Y0, R0
Strike rate:	630mins	-
Midfielder ranking:	172nd	59th

AGE 33	DREAM TEAM	RANKING 404

XABI ALONSO
REAL MADRID

One of the best passers in world football, Xabi Alonso always has time on the ball and will be a vital part of Spain's bid to add to their Euro 2008 triumph.

Having made his mark with Real Sociedad, Alonso secured a £10m move to Liverpool and became part of the side that tasted Champions League victory in 2005, and FA Cup win in 2006. During his time at Liverpool he became the creative hub in midfield and built up a superb understanding with Steven Gerrard, often providing the ammunition for the Liverpool captain. His form and ability persuaded Real Madrid to part with £30m in the summer of 2009 and Alonso became one of the newly established Galacticos. At 28, he is entering his prime and is one of the most experienced players in Spain's squad. He might not start every game but he will make an impact when he plays.

Alonso is a Top 12 midfielder.

AGE 28	DREAM TEAM	RANKING 8

ANDRES INIESTA
BARCELONA

One of the best midfield practitioners in world football, Andres Iniesta is also one of the most understated and his modest demeanour makes him popular with Spain fans of all domestic club persuasions.

A selfless servant to Barcelona, Iniesta has spent his entire career at Camp Nou where he has played in every position across the middle of the park since his debut at 18, becoming a regular starter by the time he had hit 20. A technically gifted player, comfortable runner with the ball and with a great range of passing, Iniesta was often deployed on the wing early in his career. He has developed and adapted as the needs of his team have changed and he now forms one half of the most creative midfield partnerships in football, alongside Xavi, for both club and country. Iniesta was one of Spain's best players at Euro 2008, and will be looking to add a world crown to his trophy cabinet.

Iniesta is a Top 12 midfielder.

AGE 26	DREAM TEAM	RANKING 36

KEY STRIKER

DAVID VILLA
VALENCIA

One of the most feared strikers in world football, David Villa's partnership with Fernando Torres is far and away the best strike pairing of any team at the tournament.

Villa's phenomenal form for Valencia saw him finally – and deservedly – oust Raul from the national side. The all-action front-man has gone on to fully justify his place in the side with an exceptional goals to game ratio, which comfortably betters that of both Raul and Torres. Villa was top-scorer as Spain won Euro 2008 – despite the fact that he only played in four games – and would be expecting to also challenge for the 'Golden Boot' in South Africa. His constant harrying of defenders, lightning pace, razor-sharp reactions and natural finishing ability make him the perfect foil to the Liverpool forward, although, with Spain so strong in midfield, it is Villa who misses out if the manager opts for a 4-5-1 formation. There isn't a single club in Europe who wouldn't be interested in signing Villa.

Villa is a Top 12 striker.

AGE 28	DREAM TEAM	RANKING 35

ONE TO WATCH

DAVID SILVA VALENCIA

A diminutive attacking midfielder, David Silva is quick, direct, can play on either flank, or in the middle, and offers a very potent attacking threat to Vincente del Bosque's side.

Linked with a move to some of the biggest clubs in Europe over the past year, the Valencia winger is extremely skilful and started all but one of Spain's qualifying games.

Playing record 12 months lge		wcq
Appearances:	28	5
Minutes played:	2267	336
Percentage played:	66.2%	37.3%
Goals scored:	5	3
Percentage share:	8.1%	11.1%
Cards:	Y6, R1	Y0, R0
Strike rate:	453mins	112mins
Strike rate ranking:	-	15th

AGE 24	MIDFIELDER	DREAM TEAM	RANKING 341

ROUTE TO THE FINALS

Four matches into qualifying Chile were hammered at home by Paraguay in a result that suggested they were going to struggle to get anywhere near the top four.

Nine games later and they were visiting Asuncion on 20 points, just four behind group leaders Paraguay. Sporting Lisbon's Matias Fernandez scored from the edge of the area and first choice striker Humberto Suazo headed the second to move Chile on point behind in third place.

Chile had momentum and they finished strongly, winning six and drawing two of their last nine games, with Nilmar's hat-trick condemning them to a solitary defeat in Brazil.

Marcelo Biesla's side played some scintillating football at times and scored 32 goals in the campaign, a tally that only Brazil could better.

For final qualification table see Paraguay.

Avge FIFA ranking

#	Date	Venue	Opposition	Rank	Res	Score	Scorers
1	13 Oct 07	Away	Argentina	6	L	2 0	
2	17 Oct 07	Home	Peru	76	W	2 0	Suazo 11, Fernandez 51
3	18 Nov 07	Away	Uruguay	22	D	2 2	Salas 59pen, 69pen
4	22 Nov 07	Home	Paraguay	20	L	0 3	
5	16 Jun 08	Away	Bolivia	66	W	0 2	Medel 29, 76
6	20 Jun 08	Away	Venezuela	60	W	2 3	Suazo 54pen, 90, Jara 72
7	08 Sep 08	Home	Brazil	4	L	0 3	
8	10 Sep 08	Home	Colombia	38	W	4 0	Jara 26, Suazo 38, I.Fuentes 48, Fernandez 70
9	12 Oct 08	Away	Ecuador	44	L	1 0	
10	16 Oct 08	Home	Argentina	6	W	1 0	Orellana 35
11	30 Mar 09	Away	Peru	76	W	1 3	Sanchez 2, Suazo 32pen, Fernandez 70
12	01 Apr 09	Home	Uruguay	22	D	0 0	
13	06 Jun 09	Away	Paraguay	20	W	0 2	Fernandez 13, Suazo 51
14	11 Jun 09	Home	Bolivia	66	W	4 0	Beausejour 44, Estrada 74, Sanchez 77, 89
15	06 Sep 09	Home	Venezuela	60	D	2 2	Vidal 10, Millar 52
16	10 Sep 09	Away	Brazil	4	L	4 2	Suazo 45pen, 52
17	10 Oct 09	Away	Colombia	38	W	2 4	W.Ponce 35, Suazo 36, Valdivia 72, Orellana 79
18	14 Oct 09	Home	Ecuador	44	W	1 0	Suazo 53
	Average FIFA ranking of opposition	37					

MAIN PLAYER PERFORMANCES IN QUALIFICATION

Match	Appearances	Started	Subbed on	Subbed off	Mins played	% played	Goals	Yellow	Red
Venue A H A H A A H H A H A H A H A H A H									
Result L W D L W W L W L W W D W W D L W W									
Goalkeepers									
Claudio Bravo	18	18	0	0	1620	100.0	0	1	0
Defenders									
Cristian Alvarez	3	3	0	1	201	12.4	0	1	1
Jean Beausejour	12	11	1	5	812	50.1	1	1	0
Roberto Cereceda	10	7	3	4	631	39.0	0	3	0
Pablo Contreras	5	2	3	0	289	17.8	0	1	0
Marco Estrada	9	6	3	0	639	39.4	1	3	0
Ismael Fuentes	7	4	3	0	369	22.8	1	1	1
Gonzalo Jara	13	12	1	0	1097	67.7	2	3	1
Gary Medel	12	12	0	1	1076	66.4	2	2	0
Waldo Ponce	13	12	1	1	1116	68.9	1	1	0
Miguel Augusto Riffo	4	4	0	0	360	22.2	0	1	0
Arturo Vidal	11	10	1	3	788	48.6	1	2	0
Midfielders									
Carlos Carmona	11	11	0	2	929	57.3	0	6	0
Hugo Droguett	6	4	2	1	434	26.8	0	1	0
Matias Fernandez	15	15	0	5	1150	71.0	4	2	0
Gonzalo Fierro	4	2	2	2	161	9.9	0	2	0
Mark Gonzalez	13	11	2	4	868	53.6	0	1	0
Mauricio Anabal Isla	5	3	2	1	214	13.2	0	1	1
Manuel Iturra	5	4	1	3	294	18.1	0	2	0
Claudio Maldonado	2	1	1	0	119	7.3	0	0	0
Rodrigo Millar	6	4	2	2	420	25.9	1	0	0
Pedro Morales	4	2	2	2	153	9.4	0	0	0
Esteban Paredes	1	0	1	0	59	3.6	0	0	0
Jorge Valdivia	6	1	5	0	247	15.2	1	1	1
Carlos Villanueva	3	0	3	0	126	7.8	0	1	0
Forwards									
Fabian Orellana	5	2	3	0	258	15.9	2	1	1
Eduardo Rubio	4	3	1	3	142	8.8	0	0	0
Marcelo Salas	4	3	1	1	312	19.3	2	0	0
Alexis Sanchez	12	12	0	2	1052	64.9	3	4	1
Humberto Suazo	18	18	0	8	1475	91.0	10	1	0

FINAL PROSPECTS

Arguably the form team of South America, Chile have risen almost 50 places in the world rankings in just four years, firmly establishing themselves in Fifa's top 20.

2010 will be Chile's eighth visit to a World Cup, but just the national team's third since 1974. A third place finish as hosts back in 1962 was their best showing, losing 4-2 to eventual winners Brazil in the semi-final, and while there is little chance of them bettering that in South Africa, a last-eight spot isn't out of the question.

Vastly underrated going into the tournament, Chile are a talented side who play decent football and score plenty of goals. They concede a fair few too, which will make their group match against Spain a bit interesting, but the South Americans are definitely a good team for the neutrals. Strikers Humberto Suazo and Alexis Sanchez are two of a number of players in the squad who play for top European sides. The 21-year-old Udinese forward Sanchez has the ability to become a real star.

Spain are clear favourites to top Group H, but Chile have a real chance to go through.

DREAM TEAM   TOP 15 RANKING   23

THE MANAGER

An innovative manager, Argentinean Marcelo Bielsa has turned around the fortunes of the Chile national side.

He dropped veteran Marcelo Salas soon after his appointment and has since put the emphasis on a promising crop of young players.

Bielsa's policy with Chile is to keep the ball on the floor and attack in numbers, which has seen them become one of the most entertaining teams in world football.

The manager is a firm favourite of the press, with post-match press conferences known to last for up to four hours, as he insists on answering every question.

GROUP FIXTURES

HONDURAS	Thur 16 June 1230 BST
SWITZERLAND	Tue 21 June 1500 BST
SPAIN	Sat 25 June 1930 BST

Santiago ●

Zone	South America
Population	16.5m
Language	Spanish
Top league	Primera Division del Futbol Prof Chileno
Playing season	January - June

Major clubs and capacities
Unión Española (22,041), Colo-Colo (49,953),
Universidad de Chile (65,127)

Where probable squad players play:

Premier League	-	Ligue 1	-
Serie A	3	Eredivisie	-
La Liga	2	Other Europe	7
Bundesliga	1	Outside Europe	10

Number of Chilean players playing:

Premier League	1	Bundesliga	1
Serie A	5	Ligue 1	-
La Liga	2	Eredivisie	-

World Cup record   * best performance

1930 - Round 1	1974 -	Round 1
1934 - Withdrew	1978 -	Did not qualify
1938 - Withdrew	1982 -	Round 1
1950 - Round 1	1986 -	Did not qualify
1954 - Did not qualify	1990 -	Disqualified
1958 - Did not qualify	1994 -	Banned
1962 - * 3rd place	1998 -	Round 2
1966 - Round 1	2002 -	Did not qualify
1970 - Did not qualify	2006 -	Did not qualify

KEY PLAYER

ALEXIS SANCHEZ UDINESE

A talented winger turned striker, Alexis Sanchez was snapped up by Udinese in 2007, aged just 17.

Initially loaned back to South America to continue his development, the youngster is now a first-team option in Serie A and has shown enough in the Italian championship to suggest that he could be a star of the tournament.

Playing record	12 months lge	wcq
Appearances:	30	12
Minutes played:	1656	1052
Percentage played:	46.0%	64.9%
Goals scored:	1	3
Percentage share:	1.79	9.38
Cards:	Y6, R1	Y4, R1
Strike rate:	656mins	351mins
Strike rate ranking:	123rd	66th

AGE 21   **STRIKER**   **DREAM TEAM**   **RANKING** 773

THE SQUAD

Goalkeepers	Club side	Age	QG
Claudio Bravo	Real Sociedad	27	18
Defenders			
Jean Beausejour	Club America	26	12
Roberto Cereceda	Colo Colo	25	10
Pablo Contreras	PAOK Salonika	31	5
Marco Estrada	Universidad de Chile	27	9
Ismael Fuentes	Universidad Catolica	28	7
Gonzalo Jara	West Brom	24	13
Gary Medel	Boca Juniors	22	12
Waldo Ponce	Velez Sarsfield	27	13
Miguel Augusto Riffo	Colo Colo	29	4
Arturo Vidal	B Leverkusen	23	11
Midfielders			
Carlos Carmona	Reggina	23	11
Hugo Droguett	Monarcas Morelia	27	6
Matias Fernandez	Sp Lisbon	24	15
Mark Gonzalez	CSKA Moscow	25	13
Mauricio Anabal Isla	Udinese	21	5
Manuel Iturra	Universidad de Chile	25	5
Luis Jimenez	West Ham	25	2
Rodrigo Millar	Colo Colo	28	6
Pedro Morales	Dinamo Zagreb	25	4
Jorge Valdivia	Al Ain	26	6
Carlos Villanueva	Audax Italiano	24	3
Forwards			
Fabian Orellana	Deportivo Xerez	24	5
Eduardo Rubio	Union Espanola	26	4
Alexis Sanchez	Udinese	21	12
Humberto Suazo	Real Zaragoza	20	18

■ Probable ■ Possible **QG** Qualification Games

ROUTE TO THE FINALS

Honduras qualified for only their second World Cup thanks to 1-0 win in El Salvador in the final game of their CONCACAF qualifying campaign.

The three points brought Reinaldo Rueda's side level on points with Costa Rica – who drew their final game against the United States – with a superior goal difference securing the third automatic qualification spot behind United States and Mexico.

A 1-0 win over Mexico back in November 2008 had almost forced Sven Goran Eriksson's side out of qualifying in the initial group stage, and a 3-1 win in the fourth and final stage cost the Swede his job. Carlos Pavon bagged seven goals in qualifying, but it was the team's defence that saw them through, with no other side conceding fewer goals in the CONCACAF group.

FINAL QUALIFYING TABLE NORTH, CENTRAL AMERICA & CARIBBEAN

	P	W	D	L	F	A	Pts
USA	10	6	2	2	19	13	20
Mexico	10	6	1	3	18	12	19
Honduras	10	5	1	4	17	11	16
Costa Rica	10	5	1	4	15	15	16
El Salvador	10	2	2	6	9	15	8
Trinidad & Tobago	10	1	3	6	10	22	6

#	Date	Venue	Opponent	Avge FIFA ranking	Result	Score	Scorers
1	04 Jun 08	Home	Puerto Rico	150	W	4 0	De Leon 25, W.Palacios 51, D.Suazo 52, 90
2	14 Jun 08	Away	Puerto Rico	150	D	2 2	D.Suazo 22, W.Palacios 52
3	21 Aug 08	Away	Mexico	24	L	2 1	De Leon 35
4	07 Sep 08	Away	Canada	79	W	1 2	R.Nunez 47, 56
5	11 Sep 08	Home	Jamaica	81	W	2 0	R.Nunez 65, Guevara 73pen
6	12 Oct 08	Home	Canada	79	W	3 1	W.Martinez 8, Costly 60, Thomas 90
7	16 Oct 08	Away	Jamaica	81	L	1 0	
8	20 Nov 08	Home	Mexico	24	W	1 0	Osorio 51og
9	12 Feb 09	Away	Costa Rica	53	L	2 0	
10	28 Mar 09	Away	Trinidad & Tobago	79	D	1 1	C.Pavon 50
11	02 Apr 09	Home	Mexico	24	W	3 1	Costly 17, 79, C.Pavon 43
12	07 Jun 09	Away	United States	8	L	2 1	Costly 4
13	11 Jun 09	Home	El Salvador	107	W	1 0	C.Pavon 15
14	13 Aug 09	Home	Costa Rica	53	W	4 0	Costly 30, 90, C.Pavon 50, Valladares 90
15	06 Sep 09	Home	Trinidad & Tobago	79	W	4 1	C.Pavon 20, 28, Guevara 62, D.Suazo 83
16	10 Sep 09	Away	Mexico	24	L	1 0	
17	11 Oct 09	Home	United States	8	L	2 3	De Leon 46, 77
18	15 Oct 09	Away	El Salvador	107	W	0 1	C.Pavon 64
	Average FIFA ranking of opposition			67			

MAIN PLAYER PERFORMANCES IN QUALIFICATION

Match	1 2 3 4 5 6 7 8 9 10 11 12 13 14 15 16 17 18	Appearances	Started	Subbed on	Subbed off	Mins played	% played	Goals	Yellow	Red
Venue	H A A A H H A H A H A A H A H H H A H A									
Result	W D L W W W L W L D W L W W W L L W									
Goalkeepers										
Noel Valladares		18	18	0	0	1620	100.0	1	1	0
Defenders										
Mario Beata		2	2	0	0	180	11.1	0	1	0
Victor Bernardez		10	9	1	0	811	50.1	0	1	0
Jorge Samuel Caballero		1	1	0	0	90	5.6	0	0	0
Osman Chavez		11	11	0	1	978	60.4	0	4	0
Maynor Figueroa		16	16	0	1	1406	86.8	0	3	1
Junior Izaquirre		11	10	1	0	991	61.2	0	0	0
Sergio Mendoza		8	8	0	1	713	44.0	0	1	0
Erick Norales		2	2	0	0	180	11.1	0	1	0
Mauricio Sabillon		8	8	0	1	675	41.7	0	0	0
Danilo Turcios		12	6	6	4	673	41.5	0	3	0
Midfielders										
Edgar Alvarez		4	3	1	3	223	13.8	0	0	0
Julio Cesar De Leon		10	8	2	5	735	45.4	4	3	0
Oscar Garcia		5	2	3	0	242	14.9	0	1	0
Ivan Guerrero		5	2	3	0	233	14.4	0	0	0
Amado Guevara		17	17	0	4	1486	91.7	2	2	0
Emil Jose Martinez		2	2	0	1	160	9.9	0	0	0
Ramon Nunez		14	10	4	8	824	50.9	3	1	0
Milton Palacios		1	1	0	0	90	5.6	0	0	0
Wilson Palacios		15	15	0	1	1325	81.8	2	5	0
Hendry Thomas		15	10	5	2	868	53.6	1	2	0
Forwards										
Carlo Costly		16	12	4	5	1062	65.6	6	5	0
Walter Martinez		8	2	6	2	240	14.8	1	0	0
Jerry Palacios		2	2	0	1	148	9.1	0	0	0
Carlos Alberto Pavon		9	9	0	4	741	45.7	7	1	0
David Suazo		11	9	2	3	807	49.8	4	1	0

FINAL PROSPECTS

One of the tournament's lesser rated sides, Honduras have enough quality in their squad to surprise a few teams, and even make it out of their group.

A reasonably kind draw has given Reinaldo Rueda's side a chance of reaching the last 16, with games against Switzerland and Chile definitely winnable, but they will do well to match the 1-1 draw with Spain from the country's last and only other World Cup appearance – back in 1982.

Midfielder Wilson Palacios is the team's stand out player, but there is plenty of quality elsewhere in the side. Inter Milan's David Suazo and the prolific Carlos Pavon are a dangerous partnership up front and have the potential to disrupt any defence, while Hendry Thomas and the captain Amado Guevara complement Palacios well in midfield. Maynor Figueroa brings more proven quality, but there isn't a great deal of strength in depth, with over half the squad still playing in the domestic league.

Honduras are a better side than many pundits have given them credit for, but if they do make it into the last 16 then that is likely to be as far as they will go due to strong potential opponents.

DREAM TEAM TOP 15 RANKING 25

THE MANAGER

A highly respected manager, Reinaldo Rueda has had a short but successful career to date.

Making a name for himself with the Colombia national side – Rueda was brought in to take charge of an underperforming Honduras side in 2007. Helped by an unprecedentedly talented crop of players, he led the country to their second World Cup in some style, beating Central American giants Mexico three times along the way. He has built his side around a solid defence and hard-working midfield, but likes to play with width to make chances for an experienced front two.

GROUP FIXTURES

CHILE	Thur 16 June 1230 BST
SPAIN	Tue 21 June 1930 BST
SWITZERLAND	Sat 25 June 1930 BST

Tegucigalpa

Zone	Central America
Population	7.6m
Language	Spanish
Top league	Liga Nacional de Futbol de Honduras
Playing season	July - November

Major clubs and capacities
CD Olimpia (32,863), CD Marathon (45,881), CD Motagua (34,985)

Where probable squad players play:

Premier League	4	Ligue 1	-
Serie A	3	Eredivisie	-
La Liga	-	Other Europe	5
Bundesliga	-	Outside Europe	11

Number of Honduran players playing:

Premier League	4	Bundesliga	-
Serie A	3	Ligue 1	-
La Liga	-	Eredivisie	-

World Cup record   *best performance*

1930 - Did not qualify	1974 - Did not qualify
1934 - Did not qualify	1978 - Did not qualify
1938 - Did not qualify	1982 - *Round 1
1950 - Did not qualify	1986 - Did not qualify
1954 - Did not qualify	1990 - Did not qualify
1958 - Did not qualify	1994 - Did not qualify
1962 - Did not qualify	1998 - Did not qualify
1966 - Did not qualify	2002 - Did not qualify
1970 - Did not qualify	2006 - Did not qualify

THE SQUAD

Goalkeepers	Club side	Age	QG
Noel Valladares	Olimpia	33	18
Defenders			
Mario Beata	Marathon	35	2
Victor Bernardez	Anderlecht	28	10
Osman Chavez	Platense	25	11
Maynor Figueroa	Wigan	27	16
Junior Izaquirre	Victoria	30	11
Sergio Mendoza	Motagua	29	8
Erick Norales	Marathon	25	2
Mauricio Sabillon	Hangzhou	31	8
Danilo Turcios	Olimpia	32	12
Midfielders			
Edgar Alvarez	Bari	30	4
Miguel Castillo	Motagua	23	2
Marvin Chavez	FC Dallas	26	3
Julio Cesar De Leon	Torino	30	10
Oscar Garcia	Wigan	25	5
Ivan Guerrero	Motagua	32	5
Amado Guevara	Motagua	34	17
Emil Jose Martinez	Indios	27	2
Ramon Nunez	Floating	24	14
Wilson Palacios	Tottenham	25	15
Hendry Thomas	Wigan	25	15
Forwards			
Carlo Costly	GKS Belchatow	27	16
Walter Martinez	Marathon	28	8
Jerry Palacios	Marathon	28	2
Carlos Alberto Pavon	Floating	36	9
David Suazo	Genoa	30	11

■ Probable ■ Possible **QG** Qualification Games

KEY PLAYER

WILSON PALACIOS TOTTENHAM

A talented central midfielder, Wilson Palacios is crucial to the fortunes of Honduras in South Africa.

Defensively strong, the Tottenham Hotspur man is comfortable on the ball and a driving influence in the middle of the park. He'll need to be at his tough-tackling best against Spain, but will have an opportunity to shine in the other two group games.

Playing record 12 months lge		wcq
Appearances:	34	15
Minutes played:	2821	1325
Percentage played:	80.4%	81.8%
Goals scored:	1	2
Clean sheets:	14	6
Cards:	Y9, R1	Y5, R0
Strike rate:	821mins	662mins
Midfielder ranking:	140th	60th

AGE 25   **MIDFIELDER**   **DREAM TEAM RANKING** 272

ROUTE TO THE FINALS

Just one defeat in ten games ensured Switzerland topped their European qualifying group to reach South Africa.

A draw away in Israel in their opening game was a followed by a humiliating 2-1 loss at home to usual whipping-boys Luxembourg – the minnows' first win in World Cup qualifying since 1972.

Despite such an atrocious start, Ottmar Hitzfeld's side recovered in style, winning six of their next seven games, and avoiding any further defeats in the whole of the campaign.

2-1 wins at home to Latvia and away in Greece put the Swiss back in contention to qualify automatically from one of the easier groups, before they avoided another slip-up with consecutive wins over Moldova.

Centre-back Phillipe Senderos scored twice in a 3-0 revenge win over Luxembourg in the penultimate game and a draw at home to Israel was enough to seal top spot, just a point ahead of Greece.

Five clean-sheets and just eight goals conceded was the basis of Switzerland's success, and while they failed to find the back of the net in only one game, they were frighteningly consistent in front of goal, scoring twice in seven of the ten matches and only bagging more on one occasion.

If they keep their discipline at the back then Switzerland will be very tricky opponents for any team in Group H, but don't expect too many fireworks. They will once again rely heavily on the contribution of legendary striker Alexander Frei.

For final qualification table see Greece.

Avge FIFA ranking

#	Date	Venue	Opponent	Rank	Result	Score	Scorers
1	06 Sep 08	Away	Israel	21	D	2 2	H.Yakin 45, N'Kufo 56
2	10 Sep 08	Home	Luxembourg	131	L	1 2	N'Kufo 43
3	11 Oct 08	Home	Latvia	63	W	2 1	Frei 63, N'Kufo 72
4	15 Oct 08	Away	Greece	15	W	1 2	Frei 42pen, N'Kufo 77
5	28 Mar 09	Away	Moldova	78	W	0 2	Frei 32, Fernandes 90
6	01 Apr 09	Home	Moldova	78	W	2 0	Nkufo 20, Frei 53
7	05 Sep 09	Home	Greece	15	W	2 0	Grichting 84, Padalino 88
8	09 Sep 09	Away	Latvia	63	D	2 2	Frei 43, Derdiyok 80
9	10 Oct 09	Away	Luxembourg	131	W	0 3	Senderos 6, 8, Huggel 22
10	14 Oct 09	Home	Israel	21	D	0 0	

Average FIFA ranking of opposition	62

MAIN PLAYER PERFORMANCES IN QUALIFICATION

	Match Venue Result	1 2 3 4 5 6 7 8 9 10 A H H A A H H A A H D L W W W W W D W D	Appearances	Started	Subbed on	Subbed off	Mins played	% played	Goals	Yellow	Red
Goalkeepers											
Diego Benaglio			9	9	0	0	810	90.0	0	0	0
Marco Wolfi			1	1	0	0	90	10.0	0	0	0
Defenders											
Johan Djourou			4	3	1	1	226	25.1	0	0	0
Mario Eggimann			2	1	1	0	135	15.0	0	0	0
Stephane Grichting			9	9	0	0	810	90.0	1	1	0
Stephan Lichtsteiner			8	8	0	0	720	80.0	0	3	0
Ludovic Magnin			5	5	0	0	450	50.0	0	1	0
Alain Nef			2	2	0	2	131	14.6	0	0	0
Philippe Senderos			4	4	0	0	360	40.0	2	0	0
Christoph Spycher			6	5	1	0	453	50.3	0	0	0
Steve von Bergen			3	3	0	0	270	30.0	0	1	0
Reto Ziegler			1	0	1	0	9	1.0	0	0	0
Midfielders											
Almen Abdi			3	0	3	0	46	5.1	0	0	0
Tranquillo Barnetta			10	10	0	6	792	88.0	0	1	0
Valon Behrami			3	3	0	1	267	29.7	0	0	0
Blerim Dzemaili			1	0	1	0	19	2.1	0	0	0
Gelson Fernandes			6	3	3	2	310	34.4	1	2	0
Benjamin Huggel			8	8	0	1	701	77.9	1	1	0
Gokhan Inler			8	8	0	0	720	80.0	0	1	0
Marco Padalino			5	5	0	3	419	46.6	1	1	0
Valentin Stocker			1	1	0	0	90	10.0	0	0	0
Hakan Yakin			7	2	5	2	228	25.3	1	1	0
Forwards											
Eren Derdiyok			7	1	6	1	160	17.8	1	0	0
Alexander Frei			9	8	1	4	662	73.6	5	0	0
Mauro Lustrinelli			1	0	1	0	26	2.9	0	1	0
Blaise Nkufo			10	10	0	4	868	96.4	5	0	0
Johan Vonlanthen			5	1	4	1	128	14.2	0	1	0

FINAL PROSPECTS

Switzerland have achieved great success with limited resources over recent years, qualifying for the last four major tournaments.

Knocked out on penalties by Ukraine in the second round of the last World Cup, the Swiss did themselves proud, not conceding a single goal in any of their four games at the tournament.

The side's defensive solidity remains their great strength, with a settled back-line ably assisted by a hard-working midfield. Phillipe Senderos is the most high-profile name amongst those defensive ranks, but Stephan Lichsteiner, Cristoph Spycher and Stephane Gichting all proved themselves to be reliable during qualifying.

Gokhan Inler and Valon Behrami bring genuine class to a team that lacks spark, particularly in the absence of Hakan Yakin, who was ignored by manager Ottmar Hitzfeld for much of qualifying.

As ever, much depends on the form and fitness of star striker Alexander Frei. Switzerland's all-time record goal-scorer was a pivotal figure again in qualifying, top-scoring with five, and his clinical finishing will be vital again in South Africa.

DREAM TEAM TOP 15 RANKING 14

THE MANAGER

Legendary coach Ottmar Hitzfeld was a popular choice when he took over as coach of the Switzerland side in 2008.

A handy striker in a playing career that saw him win two Swiss League titles with FC Basle, Hitzfeld has eclipsed his on-field success in the last 20 years of management.

A two-time World Coach of the Year, the 60-year-old has won the Champions League with both Borussia Dortmund and Bayern Munich and has seven Bundesliga titles to his name.

Tactically astute, Hitzfeld got the most out of an average Switzerland squad to lead them to South Africa.

GROUP FIXTURES

SPAIN	Wed 16 June 1500 BST
CHILE	Mon 21 June 1500 BST
HONDURAS	Fri 25 June 1930 BST

KEY PLAYER

ALEXANDER FREI BASEL

A classic centre-forward, Alexander Frei leads the line expertly for Switzerland.

Frei is the country's all-time goal-scorer, with a record of better than a goal every other game, he is the first name on Ottmar Hitzfeld's team-sheet if fit. A clinical finisher, Frei will need to be on form if the Swiss side are to make it beyond the group stage and he will carry the nation on his shoulders.

Playing record	12 months	lge	wcq
Appearances:		-	9
Minutes played:		-	662
Percentage played:		-	73,6%
Goals scored:		-	5
Percentage share:		-	27.7%
Cards:		-	Y0, R0
Strike rate:		-	132mins
Strike rate ranking:		-	18th

AGE 30 **STRIKER** **DREAM TEAM** **RANKING** 816

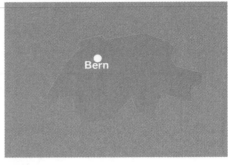
Bern

Zone	Europe
Population	7.5m
Language	German, French, Italian
Top league	Swiss Super League
Playing season	July - May

Major clubs and capacities
FC Zürich (26,682), Grasshopper-Club Zürich (24,012), FC Basel (42,903)

Where probable squad players play:

Premier League	3	Ligue 1	3
Serie A	3	Eredivisie	1
La Liga	-	Other Europe	7
Bundesliga	6	Outside Europe	-

Number of Swiss players playing:

Premier League	6	Bundesliga	12
Serie A	5	Ligue 1	3
La Liga	3	Eredivisie	1

World Cup record   * *best performance*

1930 - Did not enter		1974 -	Did not qualify
1934 - * Quarter finals		1978 -	Did not qualify
1938 - * Quarter finals		1982 -	Did not qualify
1950 - Round 1		1986 -	Did not qualify
1954 - * Quarter finals		1990 -	Did not qualify
1958 - Did not qualify		1994 -	Round 2
1962 - Round 1		1998 -	Did not qualify
1966 - Round 1		2002 -	Did not qualify
1970 - Did not qualify		2006 -	Round 2

THE SQUAD

Goalkeepers	Club side	Age	QG
Diego Benaglio	Wolfsburg	26	9
Marco Wolfi	Young Boys	27	1
Defenders			
Johan Djourou	Arsenal	23	4
Mario Eggimann	Hannover 96	29	2
Stephane Grichting	Auxerre	31	9
Stephan Lichtsteiner	Lazio	26	8
Ludovic Magnin	FC Zurich	31	5
Alain Nef	Triestina	28	2
Philippe Senderos	Arsenal	25	4
Christoph Spycher	Eintr Frankfurt	32	6
Steve von Bergen	Hertha Berlin	27	3
Midfielders			
Almen Abdi	Le Mans	23	3
Tranquillo Barnetta	B Leverkusen	25	10
Valon Behrami	West Ham	25	3
Blerim Dzemaili	Parma	24	1
Gelson Fernandes	St Etienne	23	6
Benjamin Huggel	Basel	32	8
Gokhan Inler	Udinese	25	8
Marco Padalino	Sampdoria	26	5
Valentin Stocker	Basel	21	1
Hakan Yakin	Lucerne	33	7
Forwards			
Eren Derdiyok	B Leverkusen	21	7
Alexander Frei	Basel	30	9
Mauro Lustrinelli	AC Bellinzona	34	1
Blaise Nkufo	Twente	35	10
Johan Vonlanthen	Zurich	24	5

■ Probable ■ Possible **QG** Qualification Games

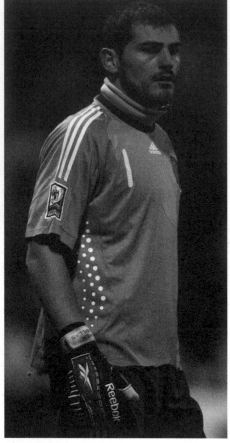

4th

GIANLUIGI BUFFON
ITALY & JUVENTUS

One of the standout keepers of the modern era, Gianluigi Buffon is no stranger to World Cup finals and set a remarkable record as Italy triumphed at Germany 2006, keeping five clean sheets and conceding only two goals in the entire tournament.

With peerless reflexes and anticipation, Buffon is the bedrock of Italy's defence and his talent and experience will be invaluable for the Azzurri in South Africa as the reigning champions seek to defend their title. He comes into the tournament in good form and will be vital.

Playing record	12 mths lge	wcq
Appearances:	35	7
Minutes played:	3150	630
Percentage played:	89.7%	70.0%
Goals conceded:	42	4
Clean sheets:	11	4
Cards:	Y0, R0	Y0, R0
Concede rate:	75mins	157mins
Concede rate ranking:	22nd	13th

AGE 32 | **DREAM TEAM** **RANKING 20**

3rd

TIM HOWARD
UNITED STATES & EVERTON

A player who has continued to improve throughout his career, Tim Howard is an extremely athletic, well-rounded keeper and is widely regarded as one of the best in the English Premier League after an unsettled start to his career in England with Manchester United.

Now number one for Everton – where he set a new clean sheet club record in 2008/09 – Howard has also cemented his place as first-choice for the US and will play a big part if they are to reach the last 16.

Playing record	12 mths lge	wcq
Appearances:	37	13
Minutes played:	3330	1170
Percentage played:	97.4%	72.2%
Goals conceded:	44	12
Clean sheets:	13	6
Cards:	Y1, R0	Y2, R0
Concede rate:	76mins	97mins
Concede rate ranking:	19th	24th

AGE 31 | **DREAM TEAM** **RANKING 17**

2nd

IKER CASILLAS
SPAIN & REAL MADRID

A quite simply brilliant goalkeeper, Iker Casillas has been a big part of Spain's success over the last few years and, as the current captain, will be a key figure in South Africa.

Already a Spain and Real Madrid legend, people sometimes forget that, at 29, Iker Casillas is still some years away from what traditionally is seen as a goalkeeper's prime. Destined to go down as one of the players of his generation, he often singlehandedly keeps an attacking Real side in games.

Playing record	12 mths lge	wcq
Appearances:	38	9
Minutes played:	3420	810
Percentage played:	100%	90.0%
Goals conceded:	39	4
Clean sheets:	20	6
Cards:	Y0, R0	Y0, R0
Concede rate:	88mins	202mins
Concede rate ranking:	12th	9th

AGE 29 | **DREAM TEAM** **RANKING 12**

THE TOP GOALKEEPER

BRAZIL **JULIO CESAR**

A prodigiously gifted keeper with a big personality, Julio Cesar has matured into one of the best in the world and it is not hard to see why.

A phenomenal shot-stopper, he is also a vocal and dominant figure in the defensive unit and – crucially in the modern game – is very comfortable under the high ball. He has been in cracking form for Inter.

Playing record	12 mths lge	wcq
Appearances:	37	18
Minutes played:	3299	1620
Percentage played:	94.0%	100%
Goals conceded:	31	11
Clean sheets:	16	10
Cards:	Y1, R0	Y1, R0
Concede rate:	106mins	147mins
Concede rate ranking:	6th	15th

AGE 30 **INTER MILAN** **DREAM TEAM** **RANKING 2**

1st

THE TEAMS

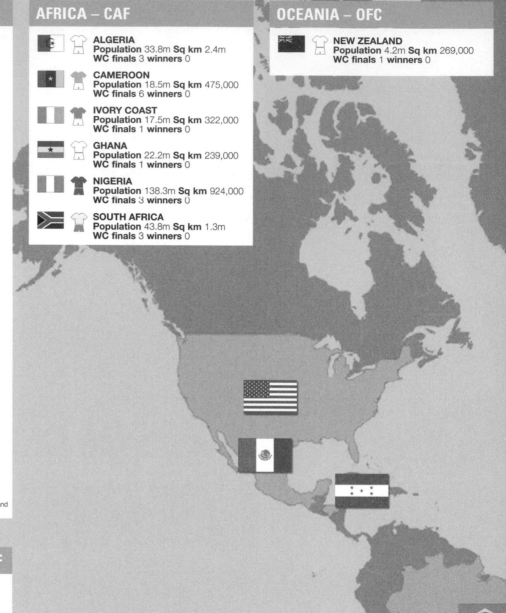

EUROPE – UEFA

DENMARK
Population 5.5m **Sq km** 43,000
WC finals 3 **winners** 0

ENGLAND
Population 51m **Sq km** 130,000
WC finals 12 **winners** 1

FRANCE
Population 62.1m **Sq km** 547,000
WC finals 12 **winners** 1

GERMANY*
Population 82.3m **Sq km** 357,000
WC finals 16 **winners** 3

GREECE
Population 10.7m **Sq km** 132,000
WC finals 1 **winners** 0

ITALY
Population 58.1m **Sq km** 301,000
WC finals 16 **winners** 4

NETHERLANDS
Population 16.4m **Sq km** 42,000
WC finals 9 **winners** 0

PORTUGAL
Population 10.6m **Sq km** 92,000
WC finals 5 **winners** 0

SERBIA*
Population 10.1m **Sq km** 102,000
WC finals 11 **winners** 0

SLOVAKIA
Population 5.5m **Sq km** 48,000
WC finals 1 **winners** 0

SLOVENIA
Population 2m **Sq km** 20,000
WC finals 2 **winners** 0

SPAIN
Population 40.5m **Sq km** 505,000
WC finals 9 **winners** 0

SWITZERLAND
Population 7.5m **Sq km** 41,000
WC finals 8 **winners** 0

* includes records for countries of West Germany and Yugoslavia

NORTH AMERICA – CONCACAF

HONDURAS
Population 7.6m **Sq km** 112,000
WC finals 2 **winners** 0

MEXICO
Population 109m **Sq km** 2m
WC finals 13 **winners** 0

UNITED STATES
Population 303m **Sq km** 9.6m
WC finals 8 **winners** 0

SOUTH AMERICA – CONMEBOL

ARGENTINA
Population 39.8m **Sq km** 2.8m
WC finals 14 **winners** 2

BRAZIL
Population 187m **Sq km** 8.5m
WC finals 18 **winners** 5

CHILE
Population 16.5m **Sq km** 760,000
WC finals 8 **winners** 0

PARAGUAY
Population 6.4m **Sq km** 407,000
WC finals 8 **winners** 0

URUGUAY
Population 3.5m **Sq km** 170,000
WC finals 10 **winners** 2

AFRICA – CAF

ALGERIA
Population 33.8m **Sq km** 2.4m
WC finals 3 **winners** 0

CAMEROON
Population 18.5m **Sq km** 475,000
WC finals 6 **winners** 0

IVORY COAST
Population 17.5m **Sq km** 322,000
WC finals 1 **winners** 0

GHANA
Population 22.2m **Sq km** 239,000
WC finals 1 **winners** 0

NIGERIA
Population 138.3m **Sq km** 924,000
WC finals 3 **winners** 0

SOUTH AFRICA
Population 43.8m **Sq km** 1.3m
WC finals 3 **winners** 0

ASIA – AFC

AUSTRALIA
Population 20.1m **Sq km** 7.7m
WC finals 2 **winners** 0

JAPAN
Population 127m **Sq km** 378,000
WC finals 4 **winners** 0

KOREA DPR
Population 23.5m **Sq km** 121,000
WC finals 2 **winners** 0

KOREA REPUBLIC
Population 48.8m **Sq km** 98,000
WC finals 7 **winners** 0

OCEANIA – OFC

NEW ZEALAND
Population 4.2m **Sq km** 269,000
WC finals 1 **winners** 0

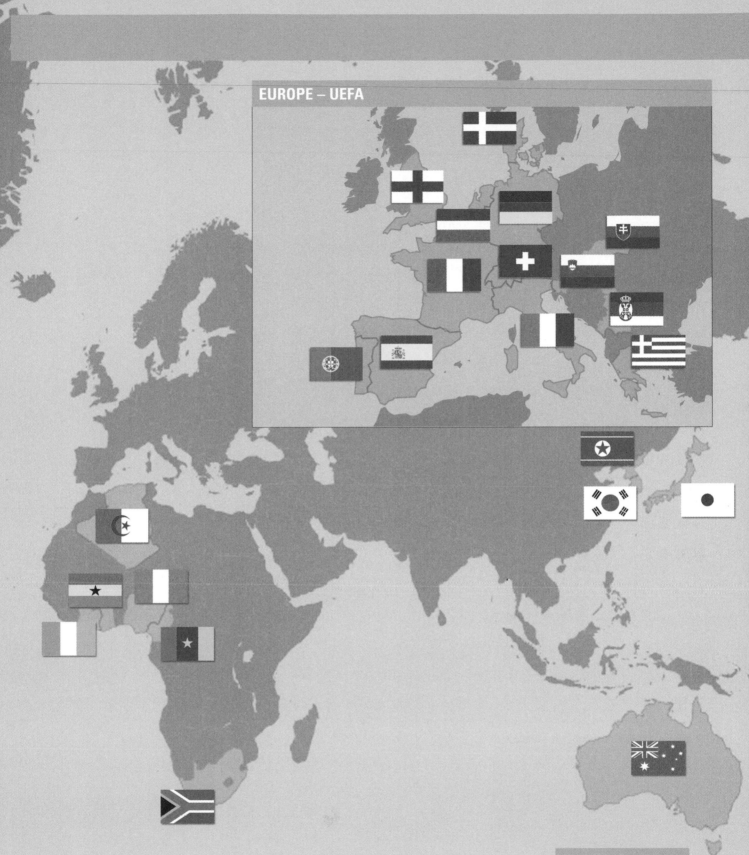

EUROPE – UEFA

OCEANIA – OFC

PREVIOUS WINNERS & HOSTS

Year	Winners	Host	Year	Winners	Host
1930	Uruguay	Uruguay (South America)	1974	Germany	Germany (Europe)
1934	Italy	Italy (Europe)	1978	Argentina	Argentina (South America)
1938	Italy	France (Europe)	1982	Italy	Spain (Europe)
1950	Uruguay	Brazil (South America)	1986	Argentina	Mexico (South America)
1954	Germany	Switzerland (Europe)	1990	Germany	Italy (Europe)
1958	Brazil	Sweden (Europe)	1994	Brazil	USA (South America)
1962	Brazil	Chile (South America)	1998	France	France (Europe)
1966	England	England (Europe)	2002	Brazil	Japan/S.Korea (Asia)
1970	Brazil	Mexico (North America)	2006	Italy	Germany (Europe)

STADIUMS

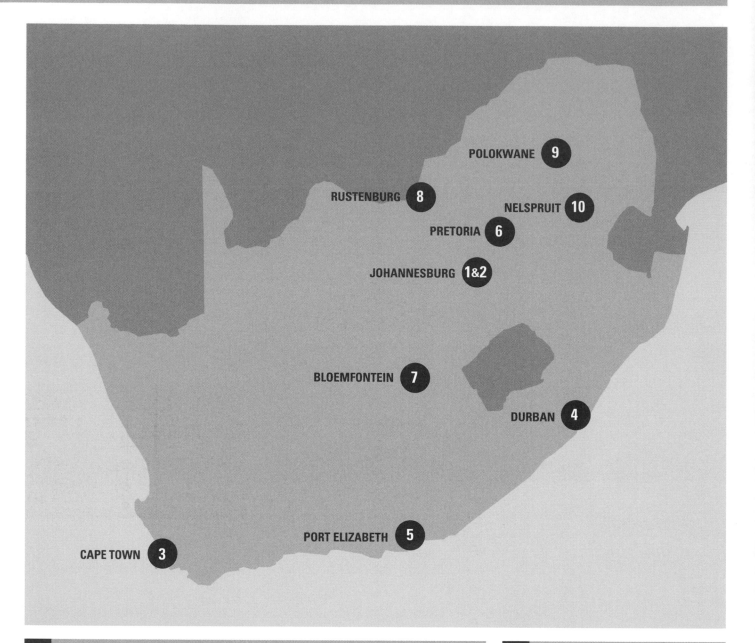

POLOKWANE	9	
RUSTENBURG	8	
	NELSPRUIT	10
PRETORIA	6	
JOHANNESBURG	1&2	
BLOEMFONTEIN	7	
	DURBAN	4
PORT ELIZABETH	5	
CAPE TOWN	3	

1 JOHANNESBURG

Stadium Soccer City
Built 1987 (upgrade 2009)
Capacity 94,700
City population 3.2 million
Altitude 1,753 metres
Matches
South Africa v Mexico (Opening match of tournament); Netherlands v Denmark; Argentina v South Korea; Brazil v Ivory Coast; Ghana v Germany; Round of 16; Quarter-final; Final

2 JOHANNESBURG

Stadium Ellis Park Stadium (Coca-Cola Park)
Built 1928 (upgrade 2009)
Capacity 61,000
City population 3.2 million
Altitude 1,753 metres
Matches
Argentina v Nigeria; Brazil v North Korea; Slovenia v USA; Spain v Honduras; Slovakia v Italy; Round of 16; Quarter-final

3 CAPE TOWN

Stadium	Green Point Stadium
Built	2009
Capacity	70,000
City population	3.0 million
Altitude	0 metres (sea level)
Matches	

Uruguay v France; Italy v Paraguay;
England v Algeria; Portugal v North Korea;
Cameroon v Netherlands; Round of 16;
Quarter-final; Semi-final

4 DURBAN

Stadium	Durban Stadium
Built	2009
Capacity	70,000
City population	3.1 million
Altitude	0 metres (sea level)
Matches	

Germany v Australia; Spain v Switzerland;
Netherlands v Japan; Nigeria v South Korea;
Portugal v Brazil; Round of 16; Semi-final

5 PORT ELIZABETH

Stadium	Nelson Mandela Bay Stadium
Built	2009
Capacity	48,000
City population	1.0 million
Altitude	0 metres (sea level)
Matches	

South Korea v Greece; Ivory Coast v Portugal;
Germany v Serbia; Chile v Switzerland;
Slovenia v England; Round of 16; Quarter-final;
Match for third place

6 PRETORIA

Stadium	Loftus Versfeld Stadium
Built	1906 (upgrade 2008)
Capacity	50,000
City population	2.2 million
Altitude	1,214 metres
Matches	

Serbia v Ghana; South Africa v Uruguay;
Cameroon v Denmark; USA v Algeria;
Chile v Spain; Round of 16

7 BLOEMFONTEIN

Stadium	Free State Stadium
Built	1952 (upgrade 2008)
Capacity	48,000
City population	369,500
Altitude	1,400 metres
Matches	

Japan v Cameroon; Greece v Nigeria;
Slovakia v Paraguay; France v South Africa;
Switzerland v Honduras; Round of 16

8 RUSTENBURG

Stadium	Royal Bafokeng Stadium
Built	1999 (upgrade 2010)
Capacity	42,000
City population	395,539
Altitude	15,000 metres
Matches	

England v USA; New Zealand v Slovakia;
Ghana v Australia; Mexico v Uruguay;
Denmark v Japan; Round of 16

9 POLOKWANE

Stadium	Peter Mokaba Stadium
Built	2010
Capacity	46,000
City population	508,272
Altitude	1,310 metres
Matches	

Algeria v Slovenia; France v Mexico;
Greece v Argentina; Paraguay v New Zealand

10 NELSPRUIT

Stadium	Mbombela Stadium
Built	2009
Capacity	46,000
City population	221,541
Altitude	660 metres
Matches	

Honduras v Chile; Italy v New Zealand;
Australia v Serbia; North Korea v Ivory Coast